All In

Written by three leading thinkers in the field of sustainability, *All In* defines the essential attributes of high-impact corporate sustainability leadership and describes how companies can combine and apply those characteristics for future success.

All In draws on research involving thousands of experts globally as collected via the GlobeScan-SustainAbility Leaders Survey over two decades. The book also reveals insights from dozens of interviews with Chairs, CEOs and Chief Sustainability Officers of pioneering companies, including 3M, BASF, BP, DuPont, Google, GE, Huawei, IKEA, Interface, Marks & Spencer, Natura, Nestlé, Nike, Novo Nordisk, Patagonia, Shell, Tata, Toyota, Unilever and Walmart, explaining how they have gained recognition, created value and boosted resiliency based on their sustainability leadership. *All In* also outlines what the private sector must do to lift sustainability performance, protect business's license to operate and help deliver the UN Sustainable Development Goals by 2030.

This unique book, rich with quantitative and qualitative insights, offers current and aspiring business leaders a succinct overview of the most important developments and trends in corporate sustainability leadership. *All In* will also appeal to others interested in why sustainability has become a critical mainstream business issue.

David Grayson is Emeritus Professor of Corporate Responsibility at the Cranfield School of Management. He is also chair of the charity Carers UK. He is a former Managing Director of Business in the Community.

Chris Coulter is CEO of GlobeScan, an insights and strategy consultancy focused on helping leadership organizations build trust with their stakeholders. He also serves on the boards of Good World Solutions and Canadian Business for Social Responsibility (CBSR).

Mark Lee is Executive Director of SustainAbility, a think tank and consultancy accelerating corporate sustainability leadership. He chairs the Advisory Board of Sustainable Brands and sits on the Senior Advisory Board of the Centre for Responsible Business in the Haas Business School at UC Berkeley.

"*All In* provides very useful insights for management thinking and helps define what a successful and purposeful business looks like in the future."
— **Dominic Barton**, *Global Managing Partner of McKinsey & Co*

"*All In* is required reading for leaders from all disciplines – business, non-profits, academia, government – to better understand the potential and necessity of an engaged and responsible private sector to create the future we want."
— **Rt. Hon. Joe Clark**, *former Prime Minister of Canada*

"*All In* does an outstanding job mapping best practice in corporate sustainability. While most past leadership examples feature European and North American companies, the lessons are universal, making the book a perfect primer for business leaders globally seeking to make sustainability core to how they manage their company in the future."
— **Clarissa Lins**, founder of Catavento *Consultoria, Brazil*

"*All In* provides a critical contribution to why and how business needs to commit to sustainability at pace and scale in the coming years; this should be required reading for the next generation of business leaders."
— **Liz Maw**, CEO, Net Impact, the global community of students and professionals who want to become the most effective change agents they can be

"*All In* is an accessible account of the landscape and the activities of vanguard companies and individuals seeking to embed strategic sustainability in their organisations. I'd like to think it is not a coincidence that many of them have participated in a CISL Sustainability Leadership programme over the past three decades!"
— **Dame Polly Courtice DBE, LVO**, *Director of the University of Cambridge Institute for Sustainability Leadership (CISL)*

"At Unipart Group, we aim to keep abreast of the very latest in management thinking and practice. *All In* offers a fascinating perspective for any business that wants to prosper in the future."
— **Dr John M. Neill CBE**, Executive Chairman, *Unipart Group of Companies*

"The Asian Institute of Management is committed to helping build Enterprises for Society. *All In* shows businesses just how to be an enterprise for society and more. The book illustrates global good practices with rigour. It hits the management sweet-spot!"
— **Dr Jikyeong Kang**, President and Dean, *Asian Institute of Management, Manila*

"I am going 'All In' after reading Coulter, Lee & Grayson's fresh angle on the challenges of business leadership, seen through a sustainability lens. What was once an optional corporate endeavour is now core to business strategy and will define company legacy and impact."

– **Tensie Whelan,** Clinical Professor of Business and Society, Director, *Center for Sustainable Business, Stern School of Business, New York University*

"My experience in the Asian Forum for Enterprise in Society and involvement on a number of corporate boards has shown that many businesses – large and small, public and private – want to understand and manage the risks and opportunities of their Social, Environmental and Economic impacts. *All In* is packed full with insights, examples and tips for how to do so. I also look forward to a future edition where I am confident there will be even more Asian examples quoted!"

– **Dato Timothy Ong,** Chairman, *Asia Inc Forum, Brunei*

All In
The Future of Business Leadership

David Grayson, Chris Coulter
and Mark Lee

Routledge
Taylor & Francis Group

LONDON AND NEW YORK

First published 2018
by Routledge
2 Park Square, Milton Park, Abingdon, Oxon OX14 4RN

and by Routledge
711 Third Avenue, New York, NY 10017

Routledge is an imprint of the Taylor & Francis Group, an informa business

British Library Cataloguing-in-Publication Data
A catalogue record for this book is available from the British Library

Library of Congress Cataloging-in-Publication Data
Names: Grayson, David, author. | Coulter, Chris, 1968– author. |
   Lee, Mark, 1969– author.
Title: All in : the future of business leadership / David Grayson,
   Chris Coulter, and Mark Lee.
Description: Abingdon, Oxon ; New York, NY : Routledge, 2018. |
   Includes index.
Identifiers: LCCN 2018009403 | ISBN 9781138549234 (hbk) |
   ISBN 9781138549227 (pbk)
Subjects: LCSH: Management—Environmental aspects. | Sustainable
   development. | Leadership.
Classification: LCC HD30.255 .G7295 2018 | DDC 658.4/092—dc23
LC record available at https://lccn.loc.gov/2018009403

ISBN: 978-1-138-54923-4 (hbk)
ISBN: 978-1-138-54922-7 (pbk)
ISBN: 978-1-351-00120-5 (ebk)

Typeset in Sabon
by Apex CoVantage, LLC
Printed and bound by CPI Group (UK) Ltd, Croydon, CR0 4YY

Contents

Figures

Appendix

Acknowledgements

Our thanks to Dan Hendrix for his Foreword and Paul Polman for his Afterword and to both for their many insights during the writing of this book and for being such exemplary *All In* leadership role models.

We thank Dan, Paul and all the business leaders who generously gave us their time and insights in interviews for the book, and for responding patiently to our follow-up queries. Thank you: Mike Barry, Kate Brandt, Paul Bulcke, Ian Cheshire, Michelle Edkins, Joao Paulo-Ferreira, Erik Fyrwald, Helen Hai, Dan Hendrix, Stephan Herbst, Chad Holliday, Steve Howard, Jeff Immelt, Amy Jadesimi, Hannah Jones, Lise Kingo, Gail Klintworth, Johnny Kwan, Colin le Duc, Ursula Mathar, Kathleen McLaughlin, Erin Meezan, Mark Moody-Stuart, Cherie Nursalim, Paul Polman, Mukund Rajan, David Rice, Rick Ridgeway, Jean Sweeney, Chris Tuppen, Jessica Uhl, Dirk Voeste, David Wheeler, and Victor Zhang.

An extra thank-you to Steve Howard: although we had already discussed *All In* as a potential book title, discovering Steve's TED Talk "All In" gave us added confidence in our own use of the term.

We are enormously grateful to friends and colleagues across the world that read and gave us feedback on drafts of *All In*. Thank you: Talia Aharoni, David Alcock, Dominic Barton, David Bent, Edward Bickham, Saulius Buivys, Greig Clark, Joe Clark, Stefan Crets, John Davies, Sabine Denis, John Elkington, Rob Frederick and his team at Brown-Forman, John Green, Chris Guenther, Adrian Hodges, Lavinia Rocha Hollanda, Peter Hunt, Jon Khoo, Clarissa Lins, Gerrit Loots, Momo Mahadav, James Melville-Ross, Thomas Osburg, Miguel Pestana, Bill Ratcliffe, Elaine Rodger, Michael Sadowski, Stefan Schepers, Steve Schilizi, Tomás Sercovich, KoAnn Skrzyniarz, Mike Tuffrey, Gerry Wade, Richard Weaver, Olaf Weber, Tensie Whelan, John Williams, and Charles Wookey.

At Cranfield School of Management: Rosina Watson; Visiting fellows: Ron Ainsbury, Kenneth Amaeshi, Mandy Cormack and Heiko Spitzeck.

At GlobeScan: Alvaro Almeida, Perrine Bouhana, Femke de Man, Corinne Fontaine, Anneke Greyling, Christophe Guibeleguie, Caroline Holme, Rob Kerr, Eugene Kritski, Wander Meijer, Doug Miller, James Morris and Eric Whan.

At SustainAbility: Rob Cameron, Denise Delaney, Matt Loose, Geoff Lye and John Schaetzl.

We are particularly grateful to our work colleagues Vanesa Berenstein, Abbie Curtis, Juanita Dewet, Jonathan Freeman, Melissa Hines, Terri Newman, Lynne Lewis, Robin Miller, Stacy Rowland and Shannon Stevenson for their practical help with project management, transcriptions, graphic design and clearances/permissions. And to John Stuart who, with zero notice, played a crucial role as our development editor as we finalized the manuscript.

Our thanks also to Rebecca Marsh, Judith Lorton and colleagues at Routledge/Taylor and Francis for their belief in *All In*, and for their commitment to bringing the book to publication in a timely fashion.

A very special thank you to the several thousand sustainability experts around the world inside companies, NGOs, academia, regulators, media and government who have freely shared their perceptions of sustainability leadership through the GlobeScan-SustainAbility Leaders Survey over the past twenty years – and we hope for many more years to come.

Finally, each of us wants to give heartfelt thanks and appreciation to family and friends, particularly Clare, Cormac, Eamon, Jane, Maggie, Norah, Sue and Valerie for their love and support – and to apologize for our absences – especially over Christmas 2017 and New Year 2018 as *All In* took shape. All three of us promise not to commit to such crazy book deadlines again! Fingers crossed!

The authors

DAVID GRAYSON, CBE

David is an independent commentator on sustainable business. He is Emeritus Professor of Corporate Responsibility in the Cranfield School of Management at Cranfield University. He is also chair of the charity Carers UK, a member of the faculty at The Forward Institute, and part of the Circle of Advisers for Business Fights Poverty. He is a former Managing Director of the corporate responsibility coalition Business in the Community, and has advised numerous other coalitions. He has chaired or been a board member of several UK government agencies. Much of his recent work has focused on how to shift corporate responsibility (CR) from being a bolt-on to business operations to being built into business purpose and strategy and how to make CR a source of innovation and new business, as well as societal good. He is the author of several books including *Everybody's Business* (2001) and *Corporate Social Opportunity* (2004), co-authored with Adrian Hodges; *Corporate Responsibility Coalitions: The Past, Present and Future of Alliances for Sustainable Capitalism* (2013) co-authored with Jane Nelson; *Social Intrapreneurism and All That Jazz* (2014) co-authored with Melody McLaren and Heiko Spitzeck; and *Take Care: How to Be a Great Employer for Working Carers* (2017).

He was educated at the universities of Cambridge, Brussels and Newcastle, has an honorary doctorate from London South Bank University and has been a visiting fellow of several international business schools. David has also been a Senior Fellow of the Corporate Responsibility Initiative at the Kennedy School of Government, Harvard.

CHRIS COULTER

Chris is co-CEO at GlobeScan, an insights and strategy consultancy focused on helping companies, NGOs and governmental organizations build trusting relationships with their stakeholders.

Chris works with executives in leadership organizations to help them better understand and respond to shifting stakeholder and societal expectations, build trust with key constituencies and exert greater influence in shaping the future. Chris has nearly two decades of experience in providing evidence-based counsel in the areas of reputation, sustainability and purpose.

Chris is a specialist in international relations, holding an MA in international affairs and has substantive global experience having lived and worked in North America, Europe and Asia. He advises clients across the world. Chris has been with GlobeScan since 1998 and is a member of the company's Board of Directors and Management Team. He is also a member of SustainAbility's Council and is a Board Member of CBSR and Good World Solutions.

MARK LEE

Mark Lee is SustainAbility's Executive Director. He is based in the San Francisco Bay Area and his work helps companies make more and faster progress on sustainable development.

Mark oversees SustainAbility's think tank as well as SustainAbility's consultancy in the Americas. With more than two decades of experience in key leadership positions in the sustainability field, he possesses expertise in sustainability strategy and implementation as well as the systems, governance, public policy, accountability and stakeholder engagement aspects of this agenda. Mark also has extensive knowledge of climate change, economic development, value chains and the linkages between sustainability and branding.

Mark's past and present portfolio of clients includes: Bayer, Brown Forman, BT, Cisco, Darden, Disney, Facebook, Ford, Fibria, Gap, Natura, Nestlé, Nike, Novo Nordisk, PG&E, Shell, Starbucks and TIAA. An exceptional consensus builder, Mark has led facilitation for numerous high-level, multi-sector stakeholder engagements. Mark is a valued partner to various public and non-profit organizations, a compelling presenter, and a regular contributor to media. Presently, Mark is the Chair of the Sustainable Brands Advisory Board and a member of the Senior Advisory Board at the Center for Responsible Business at Berkeley-Haas as well as a Lecturer at the Haas School of Business at UC Berkeley.

Mark was previously Vice President at Business for Social Responsibility in San Francisco and Manager, CSR at Vancity Savings in Vancouver.

Foreword

For nearly 25 years, I've been fortunate to be a part of an amazing sustainability journey that has forever changed industry for the better, demonstrating how doing well and doing good create value for today and tomorrow. For the past 20 years, the GlobeScan-SustainAbility Leaders Survey has recognized my company, Interface, as one of the global leaders of the sustainability movement. *All In* captures some of the lessons learned on our journey.

Imagine being the Chief Financial Officer of Interface in 1994 when Ray Anderson, our founder, decided we needed to save the world from industry because of the way that it was plundering our natural resources. It was exciting and daunting – the investment community considered Ray a "tree hugger," which was not a compliment. We had no road map, no company purpose around sustainability, no knowledge or plan and we didn't have a culture to support such a radical change. We did, however, have a charismatic and entrepreneurial founder who had a visionary knack.

Ray got serious about connecting us to the leading thinkers on the environment, who were amazing collaborators. And I got serious about building the business case for sustainability. Our purpose began to take shape. We expressed this as: *We will create a business that has no negative impact on the environment and through our actions we will have restorative influence.* That led us to create a seven-front plan: zero waste, benign emissions, renewable energy, resource-efficient transportation, closing the loop, sensitizing stakeholders and redesigning commerce. Ray called this climbing Mount Sustainability.

It was pretty clear it all had to change – not just how we designed, sourced, manufactured and distributed our carpet tile product, but also what happened at the end of its useful life. Along the way, we experimented with using landfill gas to fire factory boilers, and we designed a carpet product that mimicked how nature designed a forest floor. We invented technology to separate carpet fiber from backing, and another that would grind up backing to be used again. One of our major suppliers just couldn't "get it" – while another invented a process to recycle nylon yarn, our biggest input.

Interface was always entrepreneurial, but this was the next level, and the real accelerator was the culture that emerged. We weren't just creating a nice green product – we were reimagining everything, and we were doing it with a higher purpose in mind. We were saving the world. We became a culture of dreamers and doers. An associate wrote a poem that captured the spirit of the journey, called "Tomorrow's Child." Our sales people began dedicating a day of service to a local community each year during sales meetings. Biologists, ecologists and environmental scientists came to work for us.

Along the way, the business case emerged too. As the CFO, I learned to approve projects that might not appear to have positive returns, at least not in traditional timeframes. And investors began to appreciate that Interface would sacrifice nothing on the path to having a footprint of zero. We were delivering superior products, designed with sustainability in mind; energizing the marketplace with our bold and authentic progress; dispelling myths about how "expensive" sustainability might be thanks to millions saved in waste avoidance; and creating a culture of courageous innovation.

In 2001, I became CEO of Interface, and Ray moved into the Chairman role. Six years into the journey, we put a stake in the ground: Mission Zero, creating an environmental footprint of zero by 2020.

We're approaching our Mission Zero milestone, and all the indications are that we'll claim victory on that goal, so in early 2016 we began to look for our next mission. With carbon levels rising faster and climate change becoming more real, we doubled down on carbon as both a threat and an opportunity and created Climate Take Back. We plan to demonstrate that industry can operate with negative carbon models and create a climate fit for all life.

Climate Take Back is in its early days, but we're using the lessons learned from the past 25 years. We are clear on our purpose. We have a four-pronged plan. We are engaging our culture and reaching out to collaborators around the world. We've begun an advocacy campaign to encourage others. And it's all fueled by our people – a new generation of dreamers and doers.

The Interface story is just one of many. Companies much bigger than us, like Unilever, and companies that were built with this ethos from the ground up, like Patagonia, are among other leaders we admire. *All In* provides a framework that is built from our collective experiences, with a common thread: Leaders with a visionary knack and a skill for creating value by doing well and doing good.

The best of luck on your journey.

Dan Hendrix,
Chairman, Interface

Introduction

We know it instinctively, feel it intuitively and see it empirically. The world is going through unprecedented change at extraordinary speed thanks to revolutions affecting markets, technology, demographics, development, and values. Any one such revolution would have major implications. Taken together, mutually reinforcing and interacting with other macro forces like biodiversity, the disruption they cause presents both escalating risks and amazing opportunities.

The scale and pace of these global forces of change creates what the US military calls a volatile, uncertain, complex, and ambiguous (VUCA) world. This VUCA world – our world – is characterized by systemic risks. Whether the net overall change in such a world is positive is unclear in the moment, unknowable until after the fact. Risks include potentially catastrophic global warming, greater political instability, growing dislocation and migration, escalating conflict and terror, and hyper inequality. Each risk is massive; together, they are immense and intimidating. It's little wonder that systems theorists label these kinds of problems "wicked."

When we began work on this book, we planned to reflect the challenges posed by the speed and scale of these changes by titling our book "What Now," but as we advanced we decided the best response to "What Now" was going *All In*. Overcoming global challenges requires that societal choices maintain and regenerate ecosystems; strengthen communities, nations, and the community of nations; and create a fair and sustainable economy that maximizes opportunity and inclusion by giving everyone a stake in the future.

Some choices are being made now to tackle macro risks in the systemic manner the situation demands. Model initiatives include the Task Force on Climate-related Financial Disclosures launched by Bank of England Governor Mark Carney to improve climate risk disclosure, and the Commission on Global Economic Transformation led by Nobel Laureates Joseph Stiglitz and Michael Spence to tackle global economic challenges, from stagnating growth and inequality to migration. The Paris Agreement on climate change and the UN Sustainable Development Goals (SDGs) illuminate pathways for action on the greatest environmental and developmental challenges faced globally. But despite the initiatives in play – and the collective efforts behind them – progress appears insufficient to ensure a future where opportunity will outweigh risk in the VUCA world.

All In

All In: The Future of Business Leadership looks at the scale and pace of change that economies, the environment, and society are experiencing through the lens of sustainability leadership, particularly the private sector's contribution to ameliorating the challenges facing the world today. By "sustainability," we mean how 9–10 billion people will live reasonably well within the constraints of one planet by mid-century.[1]

While seeing sustainable development as a universal challenge in which governments, civil society, and citizens all have roles, *All In* focuses on the role of the private sector and concludes that business leadership in sustainable development is central to developing and maintaining the kind of markets and economies that the environment and society need to thrive. Today's multinational businesses have unparalleled scale and reach, touching thousands of suppliers and billions of consumers across hundreds of countries. They are the most global set of actors in existence, with both the ability and responsibility to drive greater sustainability across markets and society.

This is not to pretend that business alone can or should solve the world's problems. Governments have to create the enabling environment, the rules and the policy frameworks in which businesses can operate. Civil society has a crucial role in holding both governments and businesses to account, speaking truth to power, challenging the comfortable, and comforting the challenged. At this point in human history, however, businesses, and especially international businesses, have a crucial role to play.

Our sense is that if more businesses do not take more responsibility for their impacts and innovate to become more sustainable voluntarily, then a growing wave of populism and social unrest may compel governments to force changes on the private sector – especially if businesses and society do not prepare effectively for the job losses coming from automation and the Fourth Industrial Revolution.[2]

Equally important is our firm belief that only companies that plan for the long-term will thrive, maintain a social license to operate, and support the conditions required for stability and prosperity (including social harmony, access to natural resources, and middle-class growth) in the coming decades. As Keith Weed, Unilever's Chief Marketing Officer, wryly commented, "People often say to me – what is the business case for sustainability? And I always answer, 'I'd love to see the business case for the alternative.'"[3]

All In does not aim at some indefinite future, but at how we address these problems from now through 2030. This timeframe aligns with major global environmental goals including the ambitions enshrined in the Paris Agreement to keeping a global temperature rise this century well below 2 °C above pre-industrial levels and to pursue efforts to limit the temperature increase even further to 1.5 °C.[4] It also parallels the wider aims for human and economic development and environmental protection outlined in the UN Sustainable Development Goals (SDGs).

The Paris Agreement and the SDGs both came into being in 2015, giving humanity fifteen years to make good on their intentions. A decade and a half is a dangerous length of time: long enough to procrastinate, while close enough for alarm. Success depends on broad participation, tremendous determination, and outstanding leadership. At a moment in history where society seems bent on fracture and dissent, governments are not doing enough. Civil society is aware and committed but lacks power. This leaves it to business to go *All In* and fully commit to participate, partner, and lead – which should be a natural and obvious choice given sustainability is increasingly imperative to commercial success.

Going *All In* makes a business more resilient to future shocks because it has a better grasp of the changing external environment. It makes a business better able to attract, retain, and get the best out of employees, business partners, and suppliers. It makes the business more attractive to patient, long-term investors. It provides the business more opportunity to shape the future thanks to better influence and access to governments and civil society. It creates more hunger for better platforms to innovate successfully. In short, going *All In* is not a guarantee that a business will continue into the indefinite future, but it creates the optimum conditions for doing so.

We know that some commentators forecast climate breakdown, cataclysmic events, "Great Disruptions" and more. We do not dismiss these. However, all three of us have been working with businesses for several decades and are incorrigible optimists. In imagining a better future, we agree that: "the task of imagination will be to do the work of the crisis, without the crisis."[5]

Collective wisdom

The authors of this book and the organizations we represent have decades of experience and knowledge relating to corporate sustainability. Our own perspectives, plus the insights of our colleagues, partners, and clients inform *All In*.

To an even greater degree, this book is inspired by the wisdom of an expert crowd, specifically the respondents to the GlobeScan-SustainAbility Leaders Survey, through which, since 1997, we have consulted thousands of sustainability experts globally.

Comprising views from business, civil society, media, academia, regulators, and government from more than eighty countries, the Leaders Survey has provided a unique, well-informed snapshot on best-in-class corporate sustainability leadership for the last twenty years, plus perspectives on the leadership traits that will characterize private sector sustainability champions of the future.

We suspect Jessica Uhl, Shell's Chief Financial Officer, speaks for many business leaders when she told us: "Sustainability can mean a lot of different things to different people. There is a need to be clear on the scope."[6]

Like the United Nations Global Compact, we see corporate sustainability as "a company's delivery of long-term value in financial, environmental, social and ethical terms."[7]

Uhl described what she feels it means for Shell: "The way we conduct our business, where we choose to operate, the sectors and places where we choose to operate, the way we manage our supply chain, [and] the way we manage our relationships with partners and with our customers, based on sustainability principles. It is both the what and how of the work we do."[8]

Perceptions as to which companies are the sustainability leaders – and, crucially, why – have evolved and matured over the last twenty years as experts have judged how companies have responded to disruptions and forces of change. The companies that respondents have identified as most successful in managing environmental, social, and economic impacts, aligned with their belief that the private sector is best positioned to lead on sustainable development in the future, form the deepest underpinning of this book.

We recognize that some of the companies ranked highly in the Leaders Survey have sometimes under-performed the market. Still, we are clear that long-term commercial success and resilience is inextricably linked with going *All In*, as recent academic studies[9] bear out.

We are indebted to every Leaders Survey respondent for sharing their views with us, as their insights now form an inimitable set of longitudinal data on the evolution of leadership in corporate sustainability – a field that is itself not much more than twenty years old. The GlobeScan-SustainAbility Leaders Survey is one of the oldest, continuously running surveys of its kind, even longer established than ratings like the Dow Jones Sustainability Index and other surveys like the Edelman Trust Barometer, and the same age as the *Fortune* "World's Most Admired Companies" ranking. We could not imagine a better base on which to construct a view of what comprises best-in-class corporate sustainability leadership today and how business will need to stretch its capacities to harmonize commercial success and sustainability performance in the future.

Regarding that harmonization: we find deep truth in what Peter Drucker declared shortly before he died, that "Every global problem and social issue is a business opportunity in disguise" and expect that the corporate sustainability leaders of 2030 will also prove to be the most successful enterprises of the future. Indeed, the Business and Sustainable Development Commission has calculated a $12 trillion opportunity for business in implementing the UN Sustainable Development Goals, while Generation Investment Management's 2017 Sustainability Trends Report identifies significant sustainable business opportunities particularly in five key sectors: Mobility, Energy, Built Environment, Food Systems, and Wellbeing.[10]

Sustainability is a problem in need of solutions. The rewards for those who find the right solutions could be massive, a concept enshrined in former GE CEO Jeff Immelt's "Green is green" adage, his shorthand for saying that solving environmental problems – in ways that benefit your customers and/or make you more efficient and innovative – makes money.

Three eras

In Chapter 1 of this book we use the lens of the Leaders Survey to show how tremendously corporate sustainability understanding and practice have developed over the last twenty years. Importantly, we also define three eras of corporate sustainability leadership 2007 – present as follows:

- **The Harm Reduction Era, 1997–2005,** during which period the fundamental approach was to reduce risk and negative impacts;
- **The Strategic Integration Era, 2006–2015,** when increasingly doing less harm wasn't nearly enough to satisfy stakeholders. In this era, enlightened businesses saw that a more comprehensive means of addressing sustainability was required. This meant making it part of business planning and product and service development as well as putting in place performance measurement and disclosure programs to assess commercial contribution as well as social and environmental impacts, and;
- **The Purpose-Driven Era, 2016–ongoing,** in which there is stronger impetus for companies to declare and lead with values, which Leaders Survey respondents now say is the most important reason they identify companies as leaders. While still emerging and fully defining itself, this era is characterized by purpose-driven performance. Today's best corporate leaders focus what they do, from supply chain management to manufacturing to marketing, through the lens of the purposeful and positive impact they aspire to have in the world through the success of their business.

Looking to the future, we see a fourth epoch of corporate sustainability leadership on the horizon, which we are labelling **The Regenerative Era.** We believe that as we get closer to 2025 there will be a critical mass of companies committing to a circular economy or closed-loop approach to business, as well as a redesign of business models to optimize the economic, environmental, and social positives of all they do.[11]

Recognized leaders – and future disrupters

The Leaders Survey highlights the achievements of some ten to fifteen corporate leaders annually. Just one company, Interface, has been recognized every year from 1997–2017, with Unilever the most highly marked leader ever recognized by the experts. Case studies on both of these companies form an important part of this book and can be found in Chapters 8 and 9.

Our optimism does not mean we are blind to the challenges ahead. We recognize that the companies that have been highly ranked in the Leaders Survey are all on journeys: they are works in progress on going *All In* and deeply embedding sustainability. In writing this book we reached out to all top ranked companies that have appeared in the Leaders Survey, focusing especially on companies that endured for multiple years. We were fortunate that the leaders of all 13 global companies featured in the top 15 of the global list for 10 or more years participated.

The Chief Executive Officers, Chief Sustainability Officers, other executives and board members we talked to were incredibly generous in granting us interviews, and in all we conducted more than forty interviews. Discussions were far ranging and we asked myriad questions, but we focused especially on these two:

- What was done to create and maintain the conditions for sustainability leadership inside your organization?
- How do you believe corporate sustainability leadership will evolve through 2030?

Their responses helped us understand and articulate how companies become sustainability leaders and the characteristics required to remain one over time.

The businesses we discuss in this book are mostly incumbent multinationals, as big, established businesses tend to be the ones known by more Leaders Survey panelists across the world. We know, however, that some of the most exciting examples of businesses going *All In* are entrepreneurial start-ups, purposeful smaller businesses, and multi-generation family businesses with a strong sense of stewardship. One of the significant developments we observe is the way that big companies are now seeking to learn from such smaller role models, as well as vice versa.

Three Ps

While in no way having followed the same path, interviewees collectively revealed several constants which, variously combined, pushed their organizations through what we refer to as the **sustainability leadership threshold**. For simplicity, we label these catalysts as the **Three Ps**: *Pressure, Perspective, and People.*

- **Pressure:** Pressure relates to the external conditions that drive companies to embrace sustainability, for example changing societal expectations expressed by new policies and regulations, activist campaigns, and/or shifting consumer demand.
- **Perspective:** Perspective comprises several things including: the ability to plan long-term, which is connected to the nature of business ownership; capital investments and the degree of short-term financial pressure faced; origin and heritage, where organization longevity can develop a worldview that lends itself to sustainability; and the ability to see the world as it is evolving, not how it has been. In addition, being evidence-led, non-ideological, and committed to the best available science were consistently cited by interviewees as critical for strong leadership.
- **People:** While plural, "People" often comes down to one or a few key leaders who have had significant impact during company transitions to sustainability leadership status. Generally, this kind of impact relates to the founder and/or CEO's vision or epiphany – think Ray Anderson of Interface after reading *The Ecology of Commerce* in the 1990s, or Lee Scott of Walmart after Hurricane Katrina in 2005 – but can also be a powerful CSO working with the right leadership team, such as Hannah Jones at Nike or Mike Barry at Marks & Spencer. We also find that catalytic roles can be played in some situations by external provocateurs.

We describe the 3Ps in more detail in Chapter 2, along with threshold case studies.

Five attributes

The top-ranked companies have more in common than the 3Ps that pushed them over their sustainability leadership thresholds. A set of leadership attributes – *Purpose, Plan, Culture, Collaboration, and Advocacy* – together underpin current best practice in leading companies and represent the essential qualities for corporate sustainability leadership now through 2030.

> PURPOSE: *Why we do what we do; the organizing idea for why the business exists*
> PLAN: *What we do and what we aspire to do as an organization*
> CULTURE: *How we do things around here*
> COLLABORATION: *Who we work with in other businesses and other sectors of society to be more effective*
> ADVOCACY: *Where we use the authority of the business to encourage others to act to advance sustainable development*

These attributes did not emerge at a single point in time over the last two decades. They first materialized individually, with companies discovering and experimenting with them à la carte. Only in hindsight did our analysis of leadership patterns over the past two decades – and our definition of the three distinct eras of corporate sustainability – reveal the full set.

While no guarantee, we believe these attributes – engaged with collectively, not selectively as in the past – give businesses the best chance of surviving and thriving long-term through the cultivation of the sustainability mindset critical both to future commercial success and the more inclusive and sustainable economy we believe is essential for society's collective future.

Purpose, Plan, Culture, Collaboration, and Advocacy are explained in detail and illustrated by Leaders Survey examples in Chapters 3–7. We also provide a Best Practice Checklist in Chapter 10 that lays out what today's leaders do so that others can use their example and experience as a foundation for improving their own performance.

Individual leadership roles

The greater part of *All In* explores institutional leadership on sustainable development, focusing on the role of the private sector. But all companies are communities of people whose success is determined not just by a shared workplace or a common cause, but also by skills and styles. We also asked the leaders we interviewed what individual characteristics have been and will be most critical to corporate sustainability leadership through 2030. We summarize the answers and our reflections in Chapter 11.

2030 leadership horizon

We are certain that the three eras and the five attributes we have identified are not the full story. Maintaining and improving business leadership on sustainability is certain to require the discovery and mastery of more attributes, and we already anticipate at least one more distinct era of leadership will establish itself between now and 2030. In Chapter 12, we discuss how present leadership attributes will be stretched and extended over the next few years and speculate about how the circular and net positive business models we anticipate in the Regenerative Era will be tested and become more robust – in good degree out of necessity.

The UN's SDGs run until 2030. The Paris Agreement requires that huge progress on climate needs to be locked in by that date if we are to avoid catastrophic global warming. The 8.5 billion people expected to be living on earth by then are consciously or unconsciously in need of corporate leadership to help governments and civil society create the fair and sustainable economy necessary to ensure equal opportunity to individuals and institutions worldwide, and to ensure inter-generational equity.

The transition from the present Purpose-Driven Era to the Regenerative Era anticipated in the next decade will help companies deliver the leadership required. But the revolutions and forces of change discussed earlier will intensify and evolve in the years ahead. Further pressure on incumbents will come from disruptive innovators, insurgents, and upstart market entrants, particularly from renascent China and other fast-growing economies. For these and other reasons, as we shift eras we expect that the leadership attributes required to succeed will evolve and extend, and we predict that there will be greater emphasis on Collaboration and Advocacy.

The scale and systemic nature of the sustainability challenges thrown up by the global forces of change de facto make individual approaches to problem solving obsolete. To address them, we have to go from the "tyranny of the 'or'" to "the genius of the 'and,'" drawing on the best business can offer in terms of coopetition: both competition *and* Collaboration.

Such Collaboration will work best when business operates not apart from society and nature but as an integral part of it. Business in 2030 will thrive when it is trusted; if an enabling environment for sustainable business success emerges, it will, in part, be based on Advocacy for policies that favor sustainability like carbon pricing and extended producer responsibility. Such Advocacy will be most effective if undertaken collectively – by groups of businesses in and across sectors, and by companies in partnership with civil society and policy-makers themselves.

Without trying to pick winners, in our 2030 chapter we speculate about the types of businesses that might rank highly in the Leaders Survey by the end of the next decade and where they might come from. We recognize that some of these future leaders may not even yet exist and that new, entrepreneurial businesses we can't imagine will eventually displace some of the best-established global firms in the rankings today.

The future of business leadership

We believe the very act of thinking about the future helps to shape it, but also that you cannot think your way into a new way of acting. Instead, people and institutions need to model the right behaviors – in the context of this book, the right behaviors for delivering commercial success and sustainable development. In this way, behaviors and actions underpin new ways of thinking.

The action required of business at this moment is to be *All In* on sustainability leadership – fully and unwaveringly committed to developing pathways that make the economy, environment and society more sustainable in 2030 and beyond than it is today; fully and unwaveringly committed to overcoming the systemic risks that characterize the VUCA world and which threaten business as much as any other actor.

This action will be rooted in Purpose and ultimately needs to be Regenerative. Business cannot do this alone, but business at its best, with its competitive and collaborative skills fully deployed behind business models designed to be profitable *and* solve society's problems, has a special opportunity to respond to the leadership demands placed on it and show what it is capable of when its Purpose aligns with society's needs.

Notes

1 Adapted from the World Business Council for Sustainable Development.
2 The First Industrial Revolution used water and steam power to mechanize production. The Second used electric power to create mass production. The Third used electronics and information technology to automate production. Now a Fourth Industrial Revolution is building on the Third, the digital revolution that has been occurring since the middle of the last century. It is characterized by a fusion of technologies that is blurring the lines between the physical, digital, and biological spheres. There are three reasons why today's transformations represent not merely a prolongation of the Third Industrial Revolution but rather the arrival of a Fourth and distinct one: velocity, scope, and systems impact. "The Fourth Industrial Revolution: what it means, how to respond: Klaus Schwab," World Economic Forum, Jan 16th 2016.
3 HBR, "Reinventing the Chief Marketing Officer: An Interview with Unilever CMO Keith Weed," *Gardiner Morse*, July 21, 2014, Leadership, https://hbr.org/2014/07/reinventing-the-chief-marketing-officer-an-interview-with-unilever-cmo-keith-weed
4 United Nations Paris Climate Agreement, 2015, http://unfccc.int/paris_agreement/items/9485.php accessed Feb 10 2018.
5 Roberto Mangaberia Unger quoted in Williams, L., *Disrupt: Think the Unthinkable to Spark Transformation in Your Business* (2015). Pearson Education.
6 Authors' interview, Oct 3rd 2017.
7 UN Global Compact, 2015, www.unglobalcompact.org/docs/publications/UN_Global_Compact_Guide_to_Corporate_Sustainability.pdf. We also like an expanded version of the definition found in *The Sustainability Yearbook 2008* (PWC-SAM), namely, "a business commitment to sustainable development, and an approach that creates long-term shareholder and societal value by embracing the opportunities and managing the risks associated with economic, environmental and social developments."
8 Authors' interview, Oct 3rd 2017.
9 Robert G. Eccles, Ioannis Ioannou, and George Serafeim compared a matched sample of 180 companies, 90 of which they classify as High Sustainability firms and 90 as Low Sustainability firms, in order to examine issues of governance, culture, and performance. Findings for an 18-year period show that High Sustainability firms dramatically outperformed the Low Sustainability ones in terms of both stock market and accounting measures. However, the results suggest that this outperformance occurs only in the long term.
See also "The Business Case for Purpose," Harvard Business Review Analytics and EY's Beacon institute which declares "a new leading edge: those companies able to harness the power of purpose to drive performance and profitability enjoy a distinct competitive advantage."
10 Generation Investment Management, Sustainability Trends, 2017, www.generationim.com/sustainability-trends/sustainability-trends/ accessed Jan 5 2018.
11 For a good introduction to circular economy and models and skills for this, see Rutqvist, J. and Lacy, P., *Waste to Wealth: The Circular Economy Advantage* (2015), Palgrave.

Part one
The evolution of corporate sustainability leadership

1 Twenty years of the GlobeScan-SustainAbility Leaders Survey

"Every body perseveres in its state of being at rest or of moving uniformly straight forward, except insofar as it is compelled to change its state by forces impressed."

Sir Isaac Newton

At the heart of this book is a belief that corporate leadership in sustainability isn't just a new management fad but the *only* way to be a successful business in the long-term. Companies can only aspire to survive into the indefinite future if they help society find solutions to the most acute environmental, social, and economic challenges we face. There is also a moral imperative for business leadership in sustainability.

Corporate sustainability leadership provides incredible business opportunities too: it reduces risks, it enhances brand equity, it increases attraction and retention of talent, and it provides a lens for innovation that meets customer needs. According to the Business and Sustainable Development Commission, there will be at least a $12 trillion opportunity available to companies delivering on the United Nations' 17 Sustainable Development Goals (SDGs) through 2030,[1] and the best evidence suggests that strong corporate sustainability performance drives better financial returns in the long run.[2]

Business also needs a social license to operate. Given the perniciously low trust in business across societies, corporate motives and actions are increasingly contested, often eroding the private sector's ability to lead. Rebuilding trust with society is a critical priority for many CEOs around the world. According to recent GlobeScan global public opinion research,[3] there remains low trust in global companies, but also in national governments and especially the press and media, making it harder to engage in broad societal debates on the role of institutions in society. This partly explains the "post-truth" context we are living in (see Figure 1.1). Further, there is a significant and growing gap between societal expectations for corporate responsibility and perceived corporate performance (see Figure 1.2). It is this gap that business leaders must address to create better conditions for trust and growth.

There are different ways to assess or measure corporate performance in sustainability, from established ratings such as the Dow Jones Sustainability

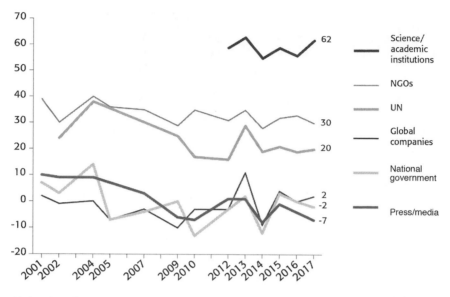

*"A lot of trust" and "Some trust" minus "Not much trust" and "No trust at all"

**Includes Canada, France, Germany, India, Indonesia, Mexico, Nigeria, Spain, Turkey, UK, and USA

Figure 1.1 Trust in Institutions

Net Trust,* General Public Opinion Across 11 Countries,** 2001–2017

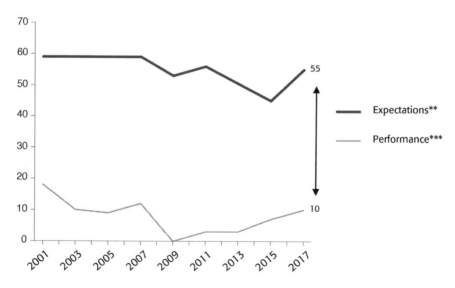

*Includes Brazil, Chile, Germany, Greece, India, Indonesia, Mexico, Nigeria, Russia, Spain, Turkey, UK, and USA

**Aggregate net expectations of up to ten responsibilities (not all responsibilities were asked in each country each year)

***Aggregate net performance ratings of ten industries (not all industries were asked in each country each year)

Figure 1.2 Expectations vs. Performance for Responsible Business (2001–2017)

General Public Opinion Across 13 Countries

Index (DJSI) or the FTSE4Good, to various NGO rankings such as Behind the Brands, the Access to Medicine Index, or the Guide to Greener Electronics. But another way to identify stellar performance is to have sustainability experts identify which companies are leaders and why.

Through the GlobeScan-SustainAbility Leaders Survey, we have engaged global experts in sustainability from business, NGOs, government, and academia to help us identify corporate leaders on an annual basis. The diverse nature of our stakeholder panel, combined with a simple quantitative approach, has been a powerful barometer of the state of sustainable leadership since 1997.

The findings of the Leaders Survey, comprised of the views of thousands of experts from over 100 countries across two decades, are rich and revealing:

- **51 companies** have been included in the top 15 over the twenty years
- **13 companies** have appeared in the top 15 ranking in ten or more years[4]
- **6 companies** have held the top leadership position
- **20 sectors** have been represented
- **11 home countries** have been represented.[5]

The wisdom of the crowd provides a unique lens to explore corporate sustainability leadership. The Leaders Survey has been asking experts not only to identify leading companies in sustainability, but also why they believe these companies are leaders, how they see the sustainable development agenda evolving, and what the priorities are going forward.

Since the launch of our first Leaders Survey report in 1997, we have seen our respondent pool grow to become a global cohort representing experienced sustainable development experts from all continents. From a small, finely targeted survey on what at the time was a niche topic, the Leaders Survey has become one of the most respected global studies tracking perceptions of organizational performance in areas related to the environment, society, and the economy.

The core question we have been analyzing is: "What specific companies do you think are leaders in integrating sustainability into their business strategy?" We ask experts to name up to three companies that fit this profile, why they believe the companies are leaders, and then aggregate the results. We look at the results across time, by stakeholder audience and geography, and draw conclusions on what this means for the evolving state of corporate sustainability leadership. In this book, we share publicly for the first time all of the tracking data we have accumulated over the past 20 years.

What good looks like

Our 2017 Leaders Survey results, based on responses from over 1,000 experts in 79 countries, showcase a set of companies that are demonstrating corporate leadership across environmental, social, and economic dimensions. (Please see Figure 1.3 for a breakdown of the sample from the 2017 study.)

Experience		Geography		Sectors	
Respondents have the following experience working on sustainability issues:		Experts surveyed span 74 countries in the following regions:		Respondents were drawn from the following sectors:	
More than 10 years	67%	Europe	40%	Corporate	29%
5 to 10 years	8%	North America	28%	Service/Media	26%
3 to 4 years	25%	Latin America	12%	Academic/Research	21%
		Asia	8%	NGO	12%
		Africa	8%	Other	7%
		Oceania	4%	Government	5%

Figure 1.3 GlobeScan-SustainAbility Leaders Survey: Methodology 2017
1,035 Qualified Sustainability Experts Completed the Survey, 2017

For the seventh year in a row, Unilever is ranked as the premier global sustainability leader, receiving nearly half the total mentions (45%) by global experts. Patagonia and Interface occupy the second and third positions (23% and 11%, respectively), with IKEA (8%), Natura (7%), M&S (7%), Tesla (7%), Nestlé (6%), Nike (3%), GE (3%), and BASF (3%) rounding out the top mentioned companies.[6]

The Leaders Survey rankings differ somewhat by region. The European and North American ratings are largely similar to those of the global findings, with the exception that Novo Nordisk, Coca-Cola, Siemens, and Triodos Bank get mentions in Europe, and Starbucks breaks into the top cadre in North America.

Unilever and Patagonia are perceived as leaders in most parts of the world. Latin America is the only region to have a home-grown company, Natura, the Brazilian cosmetics company committed to sustainable sourcing from the Amazon, ranked as the top sustainability leader. ARCOR, the Argentine food company, is also recognized as a leading company among Latin American stakeholders.

Woolworth's, the South African retailer with historic ties to M&S, breaks into the top three among African respondents. Nestlé has its strongest leadership positioning in Africa, perhaps a testament to the company's significant *Creating Shared Value* investments in smallholder farmers across the region.

In Asia, experts recognize Unilever, Patagonia, Nestlé, IKEA, Natura, BASF, and M&S as top leaders. The only Asia-based company to break through there is the Tata Group. Procter & Gamble (P&G) also uniquely gets mentioned as a leader in this region.[7]

In Australia and New Zealand, Unilever, Patagonia, and Interface occupy the top three leadership positions, consistent with the global sample. But experts in Oceania differ from other regions in mentioning Siemens with greater frequency. They also uniquely mention BMW, Dow, Puma, and Westpac – the only other bank apart from Triodos in Europe mentioned anywhere – as leading companies in sustainability.

Views of corporate leadership vary slightly by stakeholder audience. Experts from the NGO sector, for instance, while pointing to Unilever and Patagonia as the top two leaders, are more likely to mention Tesla as a leading company than other stakeholder audiences. Government stakeholders, in contrast, give slightly lower ratings to Unilever and distribute second place between Patagonia, IKEA, and Walmart. Academics are unique in mentioning BASF and Siemens, while corporate stakeholders stand out in giving the highest ratings to Unilever.

Three dominant leaders today

Overall, the survey has shown that values, committed executive leadership, and making sustainability part of their core operations is what has earned corporate leaders' admiration from experts to date. But drivers of recognized leadership vary and tend to be quite specific. A review of the three companies that currently dominate positive perceptions of corporate sustainability leadership – Unilever, Patagonia, and Interface – provides more insight into the drivers of leadership.

Unilever, the large Anglo-Dutch consumer goods company founded in 1872, is the most commanding corporate leader in the Leaders Survey's history, with its margin of victory in the survey increasing each year since it first took pole position in 2011. There are a number of factors that are driving this: the company's purposeful approach to business, a corporate culture conducive to sustainability, the company's ambitious Sustainable Living Plan, involvement in a significant number of partnerships and collaborations, and the role of Paul Polman, Unilever's CEO, as a tireless advocate for the full sustainability agenda, working not only to drive his company's business model toward a sustainable footing, but also to change the systemic conditions needed for the transition.

When asked why they believe Unilever is a leader, experts from the Leaders Survey cite a range of reasons:

- Unilever has "integrated sustainability practices – both social and environmental – throughout their operations,"
- The company's "sourcing practices for ingredients with attention to the triple bottom line: economic benefit for smallholders, social benefits, environmental considerations,"
- Unilever "has demonstrated that sustainability is driving its business growth and that its brands are benefiting from having a sustainable purpose as well as a societal benefit," and
- The CEO has "visionary leadership that takes a long view."[8]

Patagonia, the American outdoor clothing company founded by Yves Chouinard in 1973, has also risen through the leadership ranks over the past decade. It was first identified by stakeholders as a leader in 2007 and has steadily improved its standing since. Patagonia is now considered among the most sustainable companies by one in four experts surveyed.

Stakeholders cite Patagonia as a leader because:

- It believes that "sustainability isn't a business effort, it's a mission statement that permeates all departments,"
- "Its strategic goal is to contribute to sustainable development and this goal cannot be overwritten by market or financial goals,"
- The company's leadership stems from its "change in the business model in order to minimize demand for natural resources and to induce products to be used up to the end of life,"
- The fact that Patagonia is "an activist company [that] uses public and private partnerships to improve the supply chain and life cycle of the fashion, garment and outdoor retailing industry," and
- "Sustainability is core to their business goals. They seem to be as integrated a company as any I can think of."

Interface, the largest commercial carpet company in the world, founded in 1973 by Ray Anderson, placed in the top cohort of leadership yet again in 2017, something it has achieved every year since the survey's inception. Interface is the only company to have done this, which reflects the remarkable dedication the company has demonstrated in pursuit of a more sustainable business model since the 1990s. From its long-term Mission Zero strategy focused on having a fully closed-loop approach to industrial production to its current Climate Take Back campaign, stakeholders point to a range of actions and commitments to back up their belief that Interface is a beacon of leading-edge sustainability leadership. These include:

- The company embeds "sustainability into the ethos and purpose of the company – [it's] not an 'add on,'"
- It has "created a circular system to use waste for production,"
- The company "sets aggressive, long-term goals and is transparent in process and progress in achieving those goals," and
- It is "an exemplary example of a total rethink of a company based on their sustainability strategies."[9]

Three eras of leadership

The 2017 survey results show that consumer-facing companies with powerful visions and values presently dominate the Leaders Survey. But it wasn't always like this.

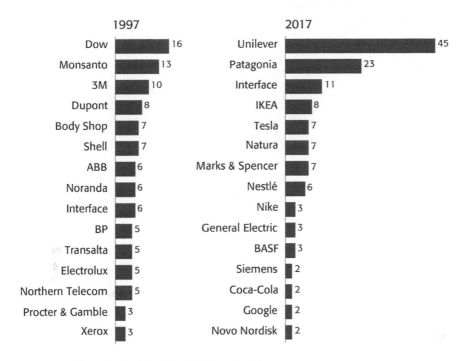

Figure 1.4 Top Ranked Leaders 1997 vs. 2017
% of Experts, Total Mentions, Unprompted

When we asked our experts which companies were leaders in sustainability in 1997, a very different set were identified. Twenty years ago, the leading companies included Dow, Monsanto, 3M, DuPont, The Body Shop, Shell, ABB, Noranda, BP, and Interface. These companies were at the top of the rankings because they were identifying their negative impacts, largely in the environmental arena, and working to reduce these externalities. This represented a significantly different and more limited approach to sustainability than the leaders of today (please see Figure 1.4).

The research tells us that corporate sustainability leadership has evolved over the years, shifting with changing expectations, opportunities, and challenges. We have identified three distinct eras of leadership between the late 1990s and today. Each era had leading companies with unique expressions of sustainability leadership.

In the first period, the **Harm Reduction Era**, running from 1997 to 2005, companies that identified the most material negative impacts of their actions on the environment and society, and committed to reducing the harm they were causing, topped the survey.

The second epoch, the **Strategic Integration Era**, began circa 2006 and lasted about a decade to circa 2015. During this time, the highest expression of leadership was built around the development of more detailed strategies or plans to drive performance.

Today we find ourselves in the third age of corporate sustainability leadership, the *Purpose-Driven Era*, which we believe began circa 2016. While still nascent, leadership companies of this era are approaching sustainability through an aspirational and mobilizing purpose.

Let's take a look at each of these eras in more detail.

1   Harm Reduction Era: 1997–2005

The fundamental approach during this period was to reduce risk and minimize negative social and particularly environmental impacts. It was very much inspired by a growing realization that industry was a notable cause of degradation to water, air, and nature, with significant health and safety impacts.

Environmental consciousness grew thanks to things like the publication of Rachel Carson's *Silent Spring* in 1962, which documented the adverse effects of pesticide use on nature, to the first pictures of the earth from space in 1972. The rapid increase in regulatory activity in the 1970s and 1980s across the world, followed by the Earth Summit in Rio de Janeiro in 1992, started to put sustainability on the map for a growing number of companies. (Please see Figure 1.5 for a list of top ranked leaders during this period.)

The early leaders tended to be industrial business-to-business (B2B) companies such as Dow, Monsanto, 3M, and DuPont, who took on the responsibility of understanding and measuring their environmental impacts and developing programs to reduce them over time. From Dow's 10-year 2005 Environment, Health and Safety (EH&S) goals (launched in 1996), to 3M's Pollution Prevention Pays, to DuPont's The Goal is Zero initiative, these companies took the lead in identifying and reducing their negative environmental impacts.

The key driver of these commitments was the need to retain a social license to operate in the face of growing public environmental consciousness and regulatory pressures. The outcome was more responsible behavior that preserved a license to trade as well as delivered significant monetary savings for the leading companies through eco-efficiency.

For the first time, executives and investors, especially in the form of growing socially responsible investment funds, began to see that sustainability was not only a moral challenge but could also affect profitability. Companies began to see that ambitious goals could be set and met, building confidence for greater mitigation. Neil Hawkins, Dow's current Chief Sustainability Officer, commented that the company's first set of EH&S Goals resulted in significant impact: "The result was incredible: not only were we able to significantly improve our EH&S results, we were also able to demonstrate the financial benefit to the company – resulting in approximately $5 billion savings with a $1 billion investment."[10]

	1997	1998	1999	2000	2001	2002	2003	2004	2005
1	Dow	BP	Shell	Shell	Shell	Shell	Shell	BP	BP
2	Monsanto	Shell	BP	BP	BP	BP	BP	Shell	Interface
3	3M	Interface	Interface	Interface	Dupont	Dupont	Dupont	Interface	Shell
4	Dupont	Dow	Dow	Dupont	Interface	Interface	Novo Nordisk	Novo Nordisk	Toyota
5	Body Shop	Monsanto	Dupont	Dow	The Body Shop	Novo Nordisk	Interface	Toyota	Dupont
6	Shell	Dupont	The Body Shop	The Body Shop	Dow	The Body Shop	IKEA	DuPont	Novo Nordisk
7	ABB	Novo Nordisk	Novo Nordisk	Toyota	Novo Nordisk	Unilever	Unilever	Unilever	Unilever
8	Noranda	The Body Shop	3M	Ford	Ford	Dow	Suncor	Body Shop	Nike
9	Interface	3M	Volvo	3M	Unilever	Procter & Gamble	The Body Shop	IKEA	HP
10	BP	Procter & Gamble	Monsanto	Suncor	Toyota	Suncor	Johnson & Johnson	Dow	General Electric
11	TransAlta	BT	Procter & Gamble	TransAlta	Suncor	Johnson & Johnson	Toyota	Co-operative	Starbucks
12	Electrolux	Electrolux	Electrolux	Volkswagen	3M	Toyota	Dow	BT	Alcan
13	Northern Telecom	Noranda	Suncor	Novo Nordisk	IKEA	Patagonia	Ford	Nike	Johnson & Johnson
14	Procter & Gamble	Unilever	TransAlta	Unilever	Patagonia	Novartis	Procter & Gamble	Philips	3M
15	Xerox	SC Johnson	Toyota	Electrolux	Nike	Baxter	BT	Suncor	The Body Shop

Figure 1.5 Annual Top Ranked Leaders in Harm Reduction Era (1997–2005)
Company Ranking, Based on % of Experts, Total Mentions, Unprompted

3M also made progress, especially through its Pollution Prevention Pays program. According to Jean Sweeney, 3M's recently retired Chief Sustainability Officer, the company "prevented 4.5 billion pounds of pollution since 1975 and a grand total saving to the company of $2 billion dollars."

Chad Holliday, DuPont's CEO in the Harm Reduction Era, described the breakthrough thinking of their "The Goal is Zero" initiative. He shared with us that Paul Tebo, one of his team members, was instrumental in building on the company's safety record and applying it to environmental issues:

> Paul said "I don't know why we just don't set the goal at zero." . . . I said "We can't get there, that is why we don't set it at zero." He said "We have individual sites that get to zero, we have individual countries that get to zero . . ." And so it seemed a little nonsensical to the engineer in us to not push for zero on environmental issues, and it really kind of caught on and it just set a higher bar.[11]

One of the exceptions to the large industrial companies in the Harm Reduction Era was The Body Shop. Anita Roddick, the iconoclast socially minded entrepreneur and The Body Shop founder, with her husband Gordon, approached business as an activist, trying to catalyze change through sourcing (The Body Shop was an early supporter of Fairtrade[12]), animal welfare (the company campaigned for a ban on animal testing in the cosmetics industry), and transparency (The Body Shop was among the first to release a verified report on its social and environmental impacts). David Wheeler, who was then on The Body Shop executive team, told us about the significant commitments the company made during this time period:

> I do think that was a significant contribution, making the triple bottom line real through an externally verified reporting mechanism. I think the carbon offset was unique at the time. . . . About a third of the company's emissions were offset by an investment in a windfarm in Wales in 1994. That was a first. That was when climate change was only beginning to be talked about, but we thought this was a tangible manifestation of corporate values because it also required the company to invest in cash to the windfarm . . . I also think fair trade was important and there is still a significant amount of sourcing from fair trade providers in the global supply chain. So that was a brilliant idea by Anita in the late eighties.[13]

Over the course of the Harm Reduction Era, corporate sustainability leadership, as recognized by Leaders Survey respondents, came to be dominated by two of the largest energy companies on the planet. Between 1998 and 2004, BP and Shell traded positions as the number one and two highest ranked businesses.

Both companies were run by charismatic CEOs, John Browne at BP and Mark Moody-Stuart[14] at Shell. Browne and Moody-Stuart were at the forefront on some of the most pressing sustainability challenges of the day, including climate change and human rights. It was striking to have two such high-profile leaders of big oil companies speaking out about the importance and strategic value of sustainability.

John Browne gave a seminal speech at Stanford University in 1997 admitting that climate change was real and that the oil industry had a responsibility to address it.[15] He later took this further and boldly rebranded BP as "Beyond Petroleum," launching a high-profile advertising campaign that reinforced the notion that the future would require greener energy and that the world needed to pull away from fossil fuels over time. David Rice, a senior BP executive at the time, explained:

> We produced a booklet called "What We Stand For" and it included Human Rights, Ethics and so on: and it was fundamentally about, what is the nature of this company? We were having one meeting at some town hall somewhere and a member of staff stood up and said "Well, BP should be beyond petroleum" and people internally liked the phrase so it ended up being used internally a lot. For the staff, it didn't mean not doing petroleum, it meant looking to the future and it kind of resonated.[16]

Shell took a different but equally bold approach. After its "annus horribilis" in 1995 due to Brent Spar and Nigeria, which we discuss in more detail in Chapter 2,[17] the company began to embrace the concept of sustainable development. This included more transparent communications and engagement with external stakeholders, bringing sustainable development to a more mainstream audience.

Shell's first sustainability report was published in 1998, covering 1997.[18] Its origins can be traced to the crises of 1995. Sir Mark Moody-Stuart, Shell's Group Managing Director at the time, shared with us how this commitment to transparency and engagement came about:

> I think the major change was a drive to get people in Shell to consult with people – we used to say whatever you do whether internally or externally, sit down and make a list of all the people who will be impacted by whatever you're planning to do and then go and talk to them, and don't just talk to them, consult with them, say "this is what we are planning to do" rather than "this is what we are going to do" several times and really try and understand what their concerns are – and out of that you really do get some very good ideas. So we tried to translate that into action – we had a sort of sustainability system loop:
>
> - Step one is what are you going to do;
> - Step two is who does it affect;
> - Go out and talk to people about it;

- Modify what you are going to do;
- Do it; and
- Go back to the people and go around the sustainability loop again.[19]

The reputation of both BP and Shell suffered tremendously in the mid-2000s. BP had a series of serious safety breaches in its American operations, starting with the Texas City oil refinery in 2005 that killed 15 people, then the oil pipeline leak in Alaska in 2006, and culminating in the Macondo Well catastrophe in the Gulf of Mexico in 2010.[20] This series of disasters destroyed the legacy of Beyond Petroleum. For Shell, it was a reserves scandal in 2004 that began to erode the company's credentials as an ethical and sustainable leader. This ultimately led to the resignation of its chairman at the time, Philip Watts, as well as numerous fines paid to authorities and shareholders.[21]

Another company gaining recognition for its leadership toward the end of this era was Novo Nordisk. The Danish pharmaceutical company was a pioneer in taking a broader approach to sustainability and especially involving external stakeholders in the process. Because of its commitments and approach, the company was one of the leading companies in the Leaders Survey from 2002 to 2004. Lise Kingo, who was the executive responsible for sustainability and stakeholder engagement while Executive Vice President and Chief of Staff at Novo Nordisk during this time, shared with us the company's approach: "To make sure that the driver of everything we did was adhering to our values of being open and honest but also trying to connect the three bottom lines that we had developed and being able to report on our work in an integrated way."[22]

As the Harm Reduction Era ended, a number of blue-chip companies were beginning to approach sustainability in this more systematic way. These included companies like Interface, GE, Walmart, M&S, and Unilever who were working hard to embed sustainability more deeply into corporate strategy. Their efforts heralded our next era.

2   Strategic Integration Era: 2006–2015

The decade between 2006 and 2015 was a volatile one economically and politically. On the back of the flood of corporate scandals of the early 2000s (e.g., Enron, Parmalat, Royal Ahold, Tyco, and others),[23] distrust in big business was taking hold across the world.

The iPhone was launched in 2007, accelerating the social technology revolution. A year later, the worst global recession since the Great Depression began, leading to growing populism such as the Occupy movements. Together, disruptions rooted in technology and changing societal expectations brought transparency into the mainstream as a driver of corporate responsibility. A range of new indices and rankings by NGOs aimed at measuring corporate performance were launched or gained prominence during this time, including Greenpeace's the Guide to Greener Electronics Index (launched 2006) and Oxfam's Behind the Brands Index (launched 2013), which assesses the sustainability performance of food companies.

At the same, governments became highly preoccupied with terrorism and national security, especially after 9/11, and from 2008 found themselves in deep recession, leading to an era of public sector austerity. It is in this context of growing instability that leading companies began to see a need for a more comprehensive response to the economic, environmental, and social challenges that were not only affecting their current social license to operate, but also their ability to exist in the future. The only way to secure stable supply chains in an age of increasingly frequent extreme weather and social dislocation, to attract and retain the best talent in a highly competitive world, and to innovate efficient ways to deliver more with less in an economic system that was using 1.65 times the earth's resources[24] was through a more comprehensive integration of sustainability into the enterprise.

Doing less harm was no longer nearly enough to satisfy external stakeholders or build an enduring business. Enlightened leaders saw that a more comprehensive response from business was required to create the conditions for stable, long-term growth. The Strategic Integration Era was a time when companies began to respond to environmental, social, and economic challenges in an enterprise-wide fashion, with many or all parts of businesses working toward outcomes that had much more significant impact and scale than previously.

One of the earliest examples of a more systemic approach to sustainability came from GE's *ecomagination* program. Launched in 2004, *ecomagination* was an extension of GE's long-standing corporate tagline "Imagination at Work." In response to better science and technological innovation, and as a result of reputational challenges it faced because of the Superfund cleanup in the Hudson River, GE designed *ecomagination* as a strategic means to create solutions to some of the great environmental challenges of the day. GE was recognized as one of the top three most sustainable companies in the Leaders Survey between 2007 and 2012 and remains in the top ranked group today. (Please see Figure 1.6 for list of leaders mentioned in the Strategic Integration Era.)

Another example of deepening integration of sustainability into core business came from Walmart. In the mid-2000s, Walmart was viewed by many as the embodiment of much that was wrong with business – too focused on hyper growth and cost efficiency and too little space for environmental or social concerns. Yet there was a deep transformation underway in the Bentonville C-suite, and in 2005 Walmart published three stretch, aspirational goals: 100% renewable energy, zero waste, and evermore sustainable products.

While skeptical at first, Leaders Survey experts quickly realized the implications of Walmart's goals, especially how they would radically transform the playing field for sustainable sourcing and manufacturing among those who wanted to sell their goods in Walmart's stores. Consequently,

	2006	2007	2008	2009	2010	2011	2012	2013	2014	2015
1	BP	Interface	Interface	Interface	Walmart	Unilever	Unilever	Unilever	Unilever	Unilever
2	Interface	Toyota	Shell	General Electric	General Electric	General Electric	Interface	Patagonia	Patagonia	Patagonia
3	Shell	General Electric	General Electric	Toyota	Interface	Interface	General Electric	Interface	Interface	Interface
4	General Electric	BP	Toyota	Walmart	Marks & Spencer	Walmart	Walmart	Walmart	Marks & Spencer	Marks & Spencer
5	Dupont	Dupont	BP	BP	Unilever	Marks & Spencer	Patagonia	General Electric	Nestlé	Natura
6	Novo Nordisk	Walmart	Unilever	Unilever	Toyota	Patagonia	Marks & Spencer	Marks & Spencer	Natura	IKEA
7	Toyota	Shell	Novo Nordisk	Marks & Spencer	BP	Toyota	Novo Nordisk	Puma	Nike	Nestlé
8	Alcan	Novo Nordisk	Dupont	Patagonia	Patagonia	Natura	Toyota	Nike	General Electric	General Electric
9	Unilever	Unilever	Marks & Spencer	Shell	Shell	Novo Nordisk	Natura	Coca-Cola	Walmart	BASF
10	Suncor	BT	Walmart	Co-operative	Nike	Co-operative	Nike	Natura	Puma	Nike
11	Dow	Rio Tinto	Patagonia	Dupont	Natura	Shell	Siemens	IBM	IKEA	Coca-Cola
12	BHP Billiton	Patagonia	SC Johnson	Novo Nordisk	Google	Coca-Cola	IBM	Google	Coca-Cola	Walmart
13	Walmart	Philips	Johnson & Johnson	BT	Co-operative	Dupont	Nestlé	Nestlé	Novo Nordisk	Tesla
14	SC Johnson	Alcan	IKEA	Nike	HP	Ford	Dupont	Novo Nordisk	Shell	Novo Nordisk
15	Whole Foods	IKEA	Microsoft	Natura	Coca-Cola	IBM	IKEA	Starbucks	Dupont	Google

Figure 1.6 Annual Top Ranked Leaders in Strategic Integration Era (2006–2015)
Company Ranking, Base on % of Experts, Total Mentions, Unprompted

Walmart was first recognized by experts in 2007 and was the top ranked company in the 2010 Leaders Survey. Today, it continues to impress with bold targets such as its commitment to taking a gigaton of carbon out of its supply chain.[25]

Kathleen McLaughlin, Walmart's Chief Sustainability Officer, told us about a pivotal moment when the company's CEO, Lee Scott, decided to put a stake in the ground on corporate sustainability leadership:

> In 2005, Lee Scott gave a speech called 21st Century Leadership in which he set out broad sustainability goals for Walmart. These days the phrase "21st century leadership" may sound a little clichéd, but back then it was a relatively new idea, and sustainability definitely wasn't a household word. So there was Lee – he literally put on a suit and tie, called the Bentonville associates into the home office auditorium, and gave this speech. It was a head turner. Several people had told him not to give that speech. He called for a re-examination of the federal minimum wage and an overhaul of healthcare to make it affordable and accessible for all. He talked about climate change, and biodiversity, and pollution. And he set out three big aspirations for sustainability at Walmart: to be powered 100% by renewable energy; to generate zero waste; and sell more sustainable products.[26]

The impact of the launch of this strategy, which came to be known as Sustainability 360, had a catalytic impact inside the company. According to McLaughlin:

> That really set people on the path toward sustainability – not just at Walmart but in waves across suppliers of the categories we sell, across the markets where we operate. People felt a sense of excitement and inspiration – unleashed to work on something big and meaningful, not as a side project, but rather through the core business. That idea of shared value took hold and has grown and grown. It is the reason that I came to Walmart. It runs very deep in the company: the idea that you can only maximize the business value of a company if you are addressing the fundamental social and environmental issues of our time, and you need to do it through the business proposition. It is not CSR, it is not philanthropy (although they are important components); it really is central to the business itself. By improving the social and environmental systems that your business relies on, you maximize business value in the long term; and by going about your business in a good way you can really strengthen social and environmental systems. Social, environmental, and economic issues are all intertwined.[27]

Interface, a company that has been commended in every year of the Leaders Survey, had its largest share of mentions from 2007 to 2009 when it was viewed as the undisputed leader. In many ways, Interface embodied the Strategic Integration Era, demonstrating this more comprehensive approach to sustainability to others. This was the period when the company began to operationalize its founder, Ray Anderson's, vision. The company championed the notion of a fully sustainable company, and climbing "Mount Sustainability" became the corporate strategic imperative.

The company launched Mission Zero, its commitment to a closed-loop manufacturing process that was in many ways one of the earliest manifestations of what has now become circular economy thinking. Interface also searched for new ways of producing carpet by embracing biomimicry, a discipline based on looking for innovative solutions from nature.

A focus on technological innovation is also the reason why experts highlighted Toyota as a leader in the early part of this period. Toyota's market leadership in hybrid technology vehicles pushed it to third place in the Leaders Survey in 2007. As Stephan Herbst, Technical General Manager, Hydrogen Strategy at Toyota Motor Europe, told us: "We felt looking at the data, looking at societal needs, that the hybrid was an appropriate solution to decarbonize transport to move into the future, so we took that decision years ago, and today it is a success story."[28] The level of disruption and impact its Prius vehicle has had on the entire automotive sector is clear.

In 2007, one of the most comprehensive approaches to sustainability was launched by the UK-headquartered retailer Marks & Spencer (M&S). The company called the strategy Plan A. Plan A was a transformative approach to how business is conducted, providing a robust framework within which to operate a progressive and modern company for the long-term. It initially involved 100 commitments that covered all aspects of its business. Because of Plan A, M&S received ever-greater recognition as a leader. In 2008, the company broke into the top 10 on the Leaders Survey and has remained there ever since.

Mike Barry, M&S's Chief Sustainability Officer, shared with us his perspective on how Plan A is also about systemic change:

> [Plan A] . . . is this very pragmatic, down to earth approach to sustainability which is about changing systemically all the things you do; for example helping all the suppliers that we do business with improve their food factories so that they are all on a bronze, silver, gold ladder to improve systemically their sustainability – we are buying more products from those guys who achieve silver and gold than we are from those who achieve bronze so again, it's not saying we have an elite, organic supply chain made up entirely of perfect factories and farms and so on; it's about having a systemic approach to helping every bit of our supply chain to improve and grow their business with us. I do think we are doing a very good job at systemizing sustainability across every product, factory, farm, raw material and store, literally everything that we touch.[29]

The most recognized culmination of the thinking around the strategic integration of sustainability during this era was Unilever's Sustainable Living Plan (SLP). The company launched the SLP in 2010 with very aggressive 2020 goals: to improve the well-being of one billion people, to have all of its raw materials sustainably sourced, and to double the business while halving in absolute terms its environmental impacts. Importantly, this was not a compartmentalized sustainability program being run by the sustainability department: it was the company's corporate strategy. An enterprise-wide approach, with the CEO advocating for it, needed a new level of integration, coordination, measurement, and conviction. Its audacity and scale captured the imaginations of experts, vaulting Unilever to the highest levels of recognition seen in the 20 years of the Leaders Survey. The company took top position in 2011 and has remained there since, steadily growing its share among stakeholders.

In our interview, Paul Polman, Unilever's CEO, shared with us his early thinking when he joined the company in 2009:

> I thought if we want to be on the right side of the statistics or to avoid being one of those companies that doesn't exist anymore after a few years, we had to become a positive contributor to society, and give instead of take. We said, why don't we make a business model or try to make a business model where everything we do is actually a positive contribution towards the world's challenges . . . then we said, well let's go all the way and let's totally decouple growth from environmental impact. Let's also then maximize our overall social impact so that it really has the three-legged stool of John Elkington – social, environmental and economic. We said we want to reach one billion people and improve their health and wellbeing.[30]

The badging of these integrated strategies – GE's *ecomagination*, Walmart's Sustainability 360, Interface's Mission Zero, M&S's Plan A, and Unilever's Sustainable Living Plan – illustrated ever greater ambition for the sustainability agenda and has shifted stakeholder expectations. Being largely consumer facing-companies gives these businesses a knack for story-telling and a flare for marketing, more at ease with stretch goals and targets than are industrial companies. They understood that to engage and mobilize employees, customers, and the public at scale meant they needed to simplify their narratives and strategies to bring them to life, make them memorable and compelling.

The implication of a more comprehensive strategy, complete with measurable targets and timelines, was the requirement to integrate sustainability across the business. As a result, it meant more internal collaboration and coordination to identify goals, and the mechanisms needed to achieve them, from functions that hitherto were absent or absolved from involvement in sustainability.

The Strategic Integration Era demonstrated a more serious approach to sustainability, leveraging the scale of the enterprise to achieve the type of results necessary for a transition to a sustainable economy. We don't believe there is any turning back to the days of sustainability being devised, managed, and executed by a small function on the periphery of the organization, looking only to reduce harm. Instead we see a growing number of examples of strategic integration as a way to future proof business, remain competitive, and drive innovation.

3   *Purpose-Driven Era: 2016–present*

So, where does this leave us today? From Harm Reduction to Strategic Integrations and all the advances that these brought to corporate sustainability, we are now in a new Purpose-Driven Era of leadership.

Purpose is the centralizing force that extends and embeds a company's engagement with a sustainable future deeper inside the organization and externally. The need to collaborate and advocate for sustainability requires more people inside and outside companies to understand intentions and strategy. Sustainability has always been a highly complex and often technical subject, making it difficult to fully engage employees and external stakeholders, especially consumers. But as the world tries to bring the UN Sustainable Development Goals to fruition over the next decade, there is a necessity for societal engagement at scale.

The rise of the millennial generation, the values they hold, and their expectations of brands are helping to create a stronger business case, showing companies that purpose can deepen consumer loyalty and help attract the best talent. A new and growing consumer segment, "the Aspirationals," reflects the opportunity for business today, as nearly four in ten of the global population are defined by their love of shopping, desire for responsible consumption, and their trust in brands to act in the best interest of society. They are among the most likely to "support companies and brands that have a purpose of making a positive difference in society through their products, services, and operations."[31]

Purposeful companies increasingly focus all that the business does, from innovation to supply chain to manufacturing to marketing, through a lens of having positive impact in the world. When done effectively, this commitment requires the company to make decisions through a purposeful framework that drives stronger performance across virtually every aspect of the business.

The timeliness of the Purpose-Driven Era is evidenced by stakeholder views of what comprises leadership today, with "values" now the most important reason Leaders Survey respondents identify companies as leaders (see Figure 1.7). Perhaps in response to the growing and often negative populism[32] that is dominating politics around the world, there is a stronger impetus for companies to declare and lead with values and purpose.

Subtle but significant changes in how leading companies articulate and mobilize around sustainability have resulted in the new Purpose-Driven

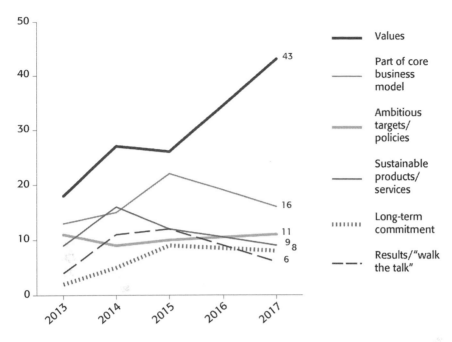

Figure 1.7 Drivers of Corporate Leadership (2013–2017)

% of Experts, Reasons Why They Mention Leadership Companies, Unprompted

epoch. The top companies identified by experts as sustainable leaders in 2016 and 2017 – Unilever, Patagonia, Interface, IKEA, Tesla, Nestlé, Natura, and M&S – have all placed greater emphasis on purpose in the recent years. (Please see Figure 1.8 for a list of leaders in this era to date.)

Unilever continues to dominate in the Purpose-Driven Era, building on the strength of its Sustainable Living Plan to embrace purpose as a driving force in how it approaches business and system change. Making "sustainable living commonplace" has become the rallying cry internally to mobilize all corporate functions across its hundreds of product brands to engage society. This has also been good for business – according to Unilever's CEO, "Our brands that are more purpose-driven are also brands that are growing faster and they are actually also more profitable."[33]

Another company that has embraced purpose is IKEA. Since 2014, we have seen IKEA's reputation as a recognized sustainability leader grow significantly. IKEA's purpose to "create a better everyday life for the many people" has become a potent framework inside and outside the organization to help amplify and drive its signature People & Planet Positive sustainability strategy.

Nestlé's purpose continues to evolve around its Creating Shared Value framework, which helped inform the shared value concept that catalyzed a wave of other businesses to engage in sustainability.[34]

	2016	2017
1	Unilever	Unilever
2	Patagonia	Patagonia
3	Interface	Interface
4	IKEA	IKEA
5	Tesla	Tesla
6	Nestlé	Natura
7	Natura	Marks & Spencer
8	Marks & Spencer	Nestlé
9	General Electric	Nike
10	Google	General Electric
11	Coca-Cola	BASF
12	BASF	Siemens
13	Nike	Coca-Cola
14	Walmart	Google
15	Novo Nordisk	Novo Nordisk

Figure 1.8 Annual Top Ranked Leaders in the Purpose-Driven Era (2016–2017)
Company Ranking, Based on % of Experts, Total Mentions, Unprompted

Natura, another company making headway on the Leaders Survey, is built around its purpose of Bem Estar Bem (which translates to the harmonious relationship with oneself, with others, and with the whole) that at its core is about taking care of life in all its forms, including the Amazon rainforest.

Similarly, BASF, the largest chemical producer in the world, has begun to appear on the list of leaders in this Purpose-Driven Era, in many ways because of its more purposeful approach to its business framed around the concept of "We create chemistry for a sustainable future."

The newest company to make the top echelons of the Leaders Survey is Tesla. Run by serial entrepreneur Elon Musk, it was founded with the very purpose "to accelerate the advent of sustainable transport by bringing compelling mass market electric cars to market as soon as possible".[35] The focus, disruption, and single-mindedness of the company's purpose addresses a fundamental element in the transition to sustainable mobility.

The future of leadership: a Regenerative Era

The current state of sustainability leadership has been built on the shoulders of pioneering companies. Even where there have been failures or an inability to sustain leadership, the initiatives these pioneers developed and the approaches they took inform and inspire today's leaders.

From the diligence of the heavy industrial companies like Dow, DuPont, and 3M that worked to minimize negative environmental impacts in the Harm Reduction Era; to companies like BP (Beyond Petroleum), GE (*eco-magination*), and Nestlé (Creating Shared Value) that had the courage to brand their approaches to sustainability in ways that mobilized support internally and externally; and the comprehensive strategies of M&S (Plan A), Interface (Mission Zero), Unilever (Sustainable Living Plan), and IKEA (People Planet Positive) during the Strategic Integration Era; to the purity of purposeful companies like Patagonia, Natura, and Tesla who stand out in the Purpose-Driven Era, all have contributed to where we are now.

The question is: What's next? What does the future of corporate sustainability leadership look like? What is required of business to ensure that we deliver the world we want for future generations and provide the opportunity for shared prosperity?

We believe that the next epoch of corporate sustainability leadership will be the Regenerative Era. We expect this new era of leadership to fully become visible in the next five years or so and to herald a new, more radically impactful approach to business. The Regenerative Era will be characterized by commitments to the circular economy, including highly designed and efficient, fully closed-loop inputs and outputs. We also believe Net Positive business models will emerge and apply full cost accounting to all business impact in the environmental, social, and economic spheres. A "do no harm" mentality will soon feel highly antiquated, as expectations will be for leading companies to maximize their positive impacts with nearly zero downside.

Imagine a food and agriculture company that grows crops while replenishing biodiversity and watersheds and sequestering carbon at the same time. Or a financial institution so expert at impact investing that exponential social returns become the expected norm alongside traditional wealth creation.

Looking forward, the characteristics that experts believe will matter the most over the next decade are captured in the five *All In* leadership attributes: Purpose, Plan, Culture, Collaboration, and Advocacy. These attributes are the foundational pillars of the type of corporate leadership required to take us to 2030. We explore these attributes in detail in Part 2 of *All In*. Before that, however, we consider triggers that enabled companies highly ranked in the Leaders Survey over the last twenty years to cross the sustainability leadership threshold.

Notes

1 Business and Sustainable Development Commission, *Better Business, Better World*, 2017, http://report.businesscommission.org/ accessed Mar 29 2018.
2 Eccles, R., Ioannou, I., and Serafeim, G., "The Impact of Corporate Sustainability on Organizational Process and Performance," Harvard Business School Working Paper Number: 12-035 2011. See also an *Arabesque and University of Oxford academic literature review on sustainability and corporate performance, which found that 90% of 200 studies analyzed conclude that good ESG standards lower the cost of capital; 88% show that good ESG practices result*

in better operational performance; and 80% show that stock price performance is positively correlated with good sustainability practices. Quoted in Whelan, T. and Fink, C., "The Comprehensive Business Case for Sustainability," *Harvard Business Review*, Oct 21, 2016.

3 GlobeScan Radar, 2017.

4 We have interviewed someone who held a leadership position in each of these 13 companies as part of our *All In* research.

5 For an explanation of methodology, see Appendix.

6 Please note that dozens of other companies are mentioned by stakeholders.

7 P&G was however among the Global Leaders for several years in the early 2000s.

8 Please see Chapter 8 on the Unilever case study for more details on the Sustainable Living Plan.

9 For more on Interface's approach to sustainability, please see Chapter 9.

10 How Dow Chemical Ingrained Sustainability into the Company's DNA, June 3, 2014, www.uschamberfoundation.org/blog/post/how-dow-chemical-ingrained-sustainability-companys-dna/31788

11 Authors' interview, Aug 21 2017.

12 Anita Roddick herself did not like the term FairTrade. She started instead with "Trade not Aid" and later used "Community Trade" – David Wheeler: Email exchange with authors Jan 2018.

13 Authors' interview, Aug 11th 2017.

14 Mark Moody-Stuart was Group Managing Director (1991–98), Chairman of the Committee of Managing Directors of the Royal Dutch/Shell Group (1998–2001) and remained on the Shell board until 2005. He was succeeded by Philip Watts.

15 Castillo, C., "British Petroleum CEO Browne Says Firm Will Respond on Global Warming," *Stanford News*, Jan 21st 1997, https://news.stanford.edu/news/1997/may21/bp.html accessed Jan 29 2018.

16 Authors' interview, Sept 19th 2017; David Rice, Director, Policy Unit, and Chief of Staff for Global Government and Public Affairs, and the BP Group Policy Adviser on Development Issues, from 1998–2006. See further: Chapter 5 on Culture and Chapter 7 on Advocacy.

17 Over rival views as to the best environmental means of disposal of a redundant North Sea oil installation.

18 "Profits and Principles: Does There Have to Be a Choice?" Shell Sustainability Report, www.shell.com/sustainability/sustainability-reporting-and-performance-data/sustainability-reports.html

19 Authors' interview, Sept 19th 2017.

20 See, for example, The Spill, PBS: A joint investigation by FRONTLINE and ProPublica into the trail of problems – deadly accidents, disastrous spills, countless safety violations – which long troubled the oil giant, BP, www.pbs.org/wgbh/pages/frontline/the-spill/ accessed Jan 29 2018.

21 Callus, A., Shell under the Skin, 10 Years after Crisis, *Reuters*, May 30, 2013.

22 Authors' interview, Aug 30th 2017.

23 See, e.g., "The World's Biggest Accounting Scandals," www.theguardian.com/business/2015/jul/21/the-worlds-biggest-accounting-scandals-toshiba-enron-olympus

24 Global Footprint Network, www.footprintnetwork.org

25 Walmart Launches Project Gigaton to Reduce Emissions in Company's Supply Chain, Apr 19, 2017, https://news.walmart.com/2017/04/19/walmart-launches-project-gigaton-to-reduce-emissions-in-companys-supply-chain

26 Authors' interview, Oct 31st 2017.

27 Ibid.

28 Authors' interview, Jan 22nd 2018.

29 Authors' interview, Sept 5th 2017.
30 Authors' interview, Aug 11th 2017.
31 The Aspirationals Are a Joint Project by BBMG and GlobeScan, https://globescan.com/aspirational-consumers-are-rising-are-brands-ready-to-meet-them/
32 For a powerful analysis of underlying drivers of populism see, for example, Goodhart, D., *The Road to Somewhere: The Populist Revolt and the Future of Politic* (2017), C Hurst & Co Publishers Ltd.
33 Authors' interview, Aug 11th 2017.
34 Porter M., Kramer M., "Creating Shared Value," *Harvard Business Review* January–February 2011, https://hbr.org/2011/01/the-big-idea-creating-shared-value
35 Musk E., "The Mission of Tesla," Nov 18 2013, www.tesla.com/en_CA/blog/mission-tesla

2 Crossing the threshold to corporate sustainability leadership

"It always seems impossible until it's done."

Nelson Mandela

Over 20 years of tracking, we have seen a diverse set of companies identified as corporate sustainability leaders, a status some held for long periods of time. How did these companies cross the threshold to become recognized and what were the drivers behind their transformation? We found three catalysts or triggers of sustainability leadership: **The 3 P's – Pressure, Perspective, and People** (please see Figure 2.1).

While in rare cases it takes only one of these three catalysts to create the dynamics for leadership transformation, in most instances of companies rising to the top of the Leaders Survey all three catalysts have been present in some capacity (please see Figure 2.2, which showcases 10 sustainability leadership threshold case studies).

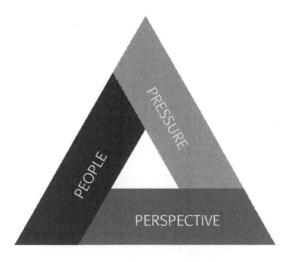

Figure 2.1 Catalysts for Crossing the Sustainability Leadership Threshold

Company	Pressure	Perspective	People
3M	Staying ahead of new regulations (e.g., US Clean Air and Water Acts)	Scientific, innovation-focused culture Understanding customers' needs, both articulated and unarticulated	Dr. Joseph Lim, VP of Environmental Engineering in the 1970s, instigated a program to reduce emissions
BP	Growing pressures around climate change and human rights issues	Significant opening up to and engagement with environmental and social NGOs	CEO John Browne, who believed the oil & gas industry had to change to maintain its license to operate; David Rice, who led Public Affairs
BT	Consumer pressures (e.g., relating to chat lines, child-protection, premium rate adult-lines, etc.) as well as growing sense of responsibility for business impacts	Legacy of ex state-owned enterprise carrying over in strong sense of social responsibility and commitment to earn and maintain license to operate	Chris Tuppen, one of the world's first CSOs; Ben Verwaayen (BT CEO 2003–2008)
DuPont	Getting off the EPA's 'sin list'	Scientific culture of the company; safety commitment and ability to apply culture of absolute goals (its pursuit of zero safety incidents) to sustainability	Paul Tebo, Corporate Vice President - Safety, Health and Environment, Linda Fisher (the world's first CSO of a public company), and Chad Holliday, CEO
GE	Hudson River Superfund reputation crisis	A commitment to understanding the science Highly customer-centric, looking for opportunities and means to anticipate and meet customer needs	Jeff Immelt, new CEO, who was open to making money by solving society's problems and who believed "green is green"
IKEA	A number of reputation challenges from taxation issues to Eastern European labor that lead to an impact on brand equity	Scandinavian values and a natural affinity toward sustainability Founder, Ingvar Kamprad, had an early Purpose for the company Foundation ownership sheltered company from short-term market pressure	Steve Howard, activist CSO, working together with CEOs Mikael Ohlsson and Peter Agnefjall
Interface	Financial pressure, resulting in an openness to a different approach to business Pressure from customers on environmental policies	External advisory group to help them see new opportunities	Ray Anderson epiphany ('spear through the chest') after reading Paul Hawken's *Ecology of Commerce*; Dan Hendrix CFO then CEO and now Chairman; Erin Meezan current CSO
M&S	Successive "responsible business" awards and pushing themselves for more	Long corporate history / sense of stewardship / Al Gore's *An Inconvenient Truth*	CEO Stuart Rose (inspired by Al Gore) and his successors; Mike Barry, CSO

Figure 2.2 Catalysts for Crossing the Sustainability Leadership Threshold: Case Studies, Part 1

Company	Pressure	Perspective	People
Natura	Global ecological crisis amplified through Brazilian lens i.e., Amazon as lungs of planet and Natura's sourcing raw materials from there as means to preserve it.	Brazilian context of both Amazon and great inequality Certified B Corp	Founders Antonio Luiz Da Cunha Seabra, Guiherme Leal and Pedro Luiz Passos
Nike	Epiphany moments as a result of being seen as the sweatshop poster child in the 1990s	A culture of performance Openness to the science and how it fits with innovation agenda	Phil Knight, Founder and Chairman; Hannah Jones, CSO; Mark Parker, CEO
Novo Nordisk	Reputation crisis after Ralph Nader launched campaign against enzymes in detergents & company's perception in 1990s of threat of history repeating itself	Danish heritage Triple Bottom Line philosophy introduced in 1997 to maximize value to all stakeholders Ownership i.e., a foundation committed to addressing diabetes	Lise Kingo, SVP Stakeholder Relations, and and Steen Riisgaard, Head of Enzymes Division
Patagonia	Global environmental crisis as seen through eyes/experience of Founder and other early employees who were also "outdoors" people	Experience of mountain climbing and other outdoor activities and seeing the natural environment changing in real-time Privately held company	Founder Yvon Chouinard as passionate advocate; Rick Ridgeway, VP Environmental Initiatives
Shell	Annus horribilus of Brent Spar in North Sea and human rights issues in Nigeria in 1995	Deep commitment to listening, stakeholder engagement and scenarios-based planning	Sir Mark Moody-Stuart, CEO, who opened up the company to external perspectives; and Cor Herkströter, who preceded him
Unilever	Financial pressure, introspection and biggest customer (Walmart) shifting expectations for its suppliers around sustainable products	Looking at mega trends and implications in the future Heritage as an Anglo Dutch company with deep historic commitment to social and environmental responsibility	Paul Polman, CEO, building upon the work of previous Unilever leaders, including: Niall FitzGerald and Patrick Cescau
Walmart	Pressure on social license to operate because of perceptions of its growth and business model Hurricane Katrina and its catalytic impact on how the company contributes to society	A culture of efficiency and looking to reduce waste A commitment to doing the best thing for families and communities traditionally expressed in economic terms (lower prices) and extended to address sustainability writ large The Walton family as stable long-term shareholder	CEO Lee Scott, along with external influencers, such as EDF's Fred Krupp

Figure 2.2 Catalysts for Crossing the Sustainability Leadership Threshold: Case Studies, Part 2

Pressure: helpful tension

Pressure relates to the external conditions that drive companies to embrace sustainability. The components of Pressure are multifaceted and generally arise from three types of circumstances: growing or impending policies and regulations by governments, a crisis of reputation that forces a company to re-examine its approach to business, or an external incident such as an extreme weather event or a natural disaster. These represent shocks to business as usual and can catalyze an embrace of sustainability.

New governmental policies or regulations often force companies to change their behavior and provide an incentive for possible first-mover advantage when committing to sustainability. For example, 3M looked at the growing number of environmental regulations in the United States and decided that it needed to get ahead of these and embrace stronger sustainability performance to remain competitive in the long-term.

In our interview with Jean Sweeney, the recently retired Chief Sustainability Officer at 3M, we learned that the introduction of the Clean Air and Water Acts by the US Environmental Protection Agency in the mid-1970s provided an important stimulus to begin taking environmental issues more seriously within the company. This external pressure, combined with an inspired VP of Environmental Engineering, Joseph Ling, who believed that it was better for the company to reduce pollution rather than clean it up, catalyzed the company's early leadership in sustainability and resulted in it being viewed as a model company in the Harm Reduction Era.

Similarly, regulatory pressure was a factor in helping DuPont commit to sustainability. As Chad Holliday, the company's former CEO, explained: "We were number one on the EPA's top ten toxic chemicals list and we wanted to be off the list. We were just tired of being criticized so much."

Another driver of Pressure is reputational crisis: For Shell, as we mention in Chapter 1 and discuss later, the twin challenges presented by Brent Spar in the North Sea and Nigeria in 1995 caused a critical pivot for the organization. Sir Mark Moody-Stuart, former Shell CEO, described the impact of these crises: "We thought we were doing alright, then all of a sudden we found out that people, even those who had sympathy with us, didn't think we had handled it very well. Hence, being a rather rational kind of organization, we asked this question of what are the corporate responsibilities of a global organization in the 21st century."[1]

Nike went through a significant reputation crisis in the 1990s when it was reported that some of its garments were being produced in sweatshops. The company initially denied responsibility for these bad practices in its supply chain, but soon responded by deeply looking at its purpose and how it operated. The result was a stronger commitment to sustainable business, including addressing global systemic challenges such as human rights and climate change. Nike's present Chief Sustainability Officer, Hannah Jones, shared with us her perspective on the challenges the company went through then and how it was a catalyst for sustainability leadership:

> Hindsight is a beautiful thing. Being in the public eye in the early nineties on the issue of working conditions in supply chains was one of the most searing experiences the company has gone through, and yet also potentially one of the great gifts that we've been given.[2]

The gift, in many ways, was a greater consciousness and appreciation of the requirements and opportunities for sustainable and innovative business. Jones continued:

> At first, we were defensive, and we wouldn't directly acknowledge the allegations. Then, we pivoted. I always look to these pivots, these *inflection moments* in our story, and I'd say that May 1998 was an inflection point. That was when Phil [Knight] stood up at the National Press Club in Washington and confirmed our commitment to improving working conditions; talked about expanding independent monitoring; and acknowledged that this was going to be the new license to operate for business in the future. Why is that important? It is important because it opened up the company's eyes to the fact that doing the right thing is a strategic imperative. We were at the forefront of what would become a massive movement. The role of corporations now includes setting environmental and social standards around the world, and actually changing the nature of how business thinks about what it is accountable for, and what its footprint should be.[3]

A final Pressure factor that has been a catalyst for sustainability leadership is an unexpected momentous external experience such as an extreme weather event or a natural disaster. We have noticed that these events have been significant in several corporate transformational journeys. For example, Hurricane Katrina had a catalytic impact on Walmart. The company was already beginning to explore how it could better respond to rising societal pressure for corporate responsibility and Lee Scott, the then CEO, was undergoing a deep rethink of Walmart's strategy. But when Hurricane Katrina hit, the company responded immediately to provide people in the American Gulf states with food, water, and other necessities. The impact of this on internal morale and pride was difficult to overstate, and Lee Scott was convinced of the value of being a more responsible company. Walmart Chief Sustainability Officer Katherine McLaughlin told us:

> Walmart began focusing on sustainability in earnest around 2005, precipitated by a couple of things – one of which was Hurricane Katrina. Walmart found itself in the middle of that storm in some ways as both a victim of the disaster and also as a responder. We had hundreds of stores, millions of customers, and thousands of associates all throughout the Gulf Coast region. It was a devastating storm and the company sprang into action pretty reflexively. We were on the ground: we had trucks, we had distribution centers and stores, we had products. There are stories people tell to this day, about associates commandeering bulldozers and busting out the front of stores so people could get products, others sheltering people in place or taking supplies to shelters, and associates rescuing people with trucks and administering first aid. We have an

iconic picture hanging in the Walmart home office lobby: a convoy of Walmart trucks waiting to be released to go into New Orleans, when everybody else was going out of New Orleans. That is just such a great symbol of Walmart using its strengths in a different kind of way to help people beyond the business.

At the time, Lee Scott was the CEO. In the aftermath of the storm, people were calling in from all the regions in the Gulf Coast and asking for permission: "Is it okay if we give away all of these diapers," or "What about this infant formula," and "We want to use the distribution center to stage product for the shelters, is that okay?" Finally, Lee just said, "Don't ask for permission – just do whatever you think needs to happen and we will figure it all out later." Katrina had, I think, a pretty deep effect on Walmart culture and the psyche of associates – suffering loss alongside others, but then also seeing the impact of using Walmart's strength in this way. It got Lee thinking, "What if we were that kind of company every day? What else could we do with our assets that would serve others in new ways?"[4]

Perspective: peripheral vision

Perspective is the second catalyst for sustainability leadership transformation that we have identified. Perspective is critical for allowing a company to look at and respond to the new opportunities that sustainability brings.

There are three components of Perspective. First, an ability to plan long-term, largely connected to the nature of ownership, capital investments, and the degree of short-term financial pressure faced. Second, the origin and heritage of a company and how organizational longevity can develop a worldview that lends itself to sustainability. Third, the ability to see the world as it is evolving, not how it has been, and take an evidence-led, non-ideological view of the challenges and opportunities.

Long-term perspective has been an important enabler for many of the enduring companies in the Leaders Survey. This has often manifested itself in the level of exposure the company has to short-term financial pressures. Being privately held or having a significant portion of the company owned by a patient family or foundation owner has been indispensable in allowing companies like IKEA, Novo Nordisk, Patagonia, and Walmart to commit to a long-term sustainable business model.

For IKEA, having the company owned by a foundation has protected it and has made it easier to make long-term decisions such as investing in wind farms to produce renewable energy and becoming a founding funder of coalitions such as We Mean Business, a business group committed to driving policy action to drive the transition to a low-carbon economy.[5]

One of the reasons Walmart has been able to go *All In* on sustainability has been its ownership structure too. The Walton family still owns a sizable proportion of the company, and the family has been clear that it believes in a long-term strategy for the company that includes a strong commitment to sustainability. This has allowed the company to make significant commitments, including a \$2.7 billion investment in training and wage increases across the company in 2015, which had negative short-term impacts on share price. With patient and supportive shareholders in the Waltons, the company was able to make these forward investments, even with some blowback from Wall Street. Kathleen McLaughlin, Walmart's CSO, told us: "We were fortunate in that we had the family as a major shareholder saying we totally support this; let's do it; we know it will prove to be right in the end. And it has."[6]

A second pillar of Perspective is a company's heritage. The culture and origin of a company has often been a powerful enabler of stronger sustainability leadership. A good example of this is Novo Nordisk, where the Danish values of the company were instrumental in driving a commitment to responsible business, especially in the area of stakeholder engagement. Lise Kingo, who led Novo Nordisk's sustainability function while Executive Vice President and Chief of Staff, spoke to us about the importance of Scandinavian culture as a driver of the company's ability to become a more committed leader: "I mean this Scandinavian culture, this sort of democratic open culture, was a prerequisite for developing the stakeholder engagement strategy at Novo. It was a sort of natural evolution. I think the openness and the whole idea of governance and democracy which characterised the Scandinavian society at that time and still does today was an excellent backdrop for the strategy we developed."[7]

A third expression of Perspective is mindset. This is the distinctive ability to truly see the world as it is, with unbiased understanding. GE's commitment to *ecomagination* provides a good case study for Perspective. Looking to science, especially in the wake of reputational challenges related to the Hudson River Superfund cleanup, became an important contributor to GE seeing opportunities for sustainable product and service offerings. As Jeff Immelt, GE's former CEO, tells it:

> I was curious about the science itself. So, we created a couple of internal teams to [go] through the science of global warming and we said go study what has been written; what do you guys see in the research and things like that. We created a group that was focused on the public policy side – what was the state of play vis-à-vis the EPA, renewable portfolio standards and things like that. Then we had a team that did outreach to see what our customers' awareness was. . . . We studied what BP did, what Ford did, what a bunch of other companies did. We put it in our own context and we formulated what we called *ecomagination* which was really built around a focus on innovation . . . to reduce the carbon footprint of the technologies we have, partner with customers, and reduce our own carbon intensity but as a way to drive productivity

and outreach both to the NGO community and also to government. Our notion was really that green is green.[8]

Patagonia provides another example of how openness and the enthusiasm to understand the context within a company operates help drive sustainability leadership forward. Rick Ridgeway described Patagonia's approach:

> In the early years we figured as we started to become aware of these changes we had to do our homework. We had to go into self-learning mode and we would bring in experts and people who were much wiser than we were and much better informed to guide and teach us. Some of them were leading environmental thinkers like David Brower[9] who was head of the Sierra Club or the great ecological philosopher Arne Næss[10] . . . You know we started really following and learning from these guys. Yvon's close friend and my close friend, Doug Tomkins, was a real mentor for us as well.[11]

People: the power of one

The third catalyst for companies to break through the sustainability leadership threshold is People. While plural, "People" often comes down to one committed leader or a few key players who have significant impact during company transitions to sustainability leadership status. This often comes from a strong founder or CEO who has awakened to the opportunity or necessity of sustainability, galvanizing the entire organization's commitments to new levels. It can also come from an effective and courageous Chief Sustainability Officer. Or, in some cases, this transformation can in part be facilitated by external provocateurs.

Visionary leaders have always created change in the world and this is no less true when it comes to sustainability leadership. There are many examples we have already mentioned: Anita Roddick at The Body Shop, Ray Anderson at Interface, and Paul Polman at Unilever.

In IKEA's case, however, the Chief Sustainability Officer, Steve Howard, an outsider to the company, provided additional leadership that catalyzed greater commitment to sustainability. Howard, while being recruited, ensured that he would have a mandate before accepting the job. Here is what he told us:

> I actually found within my first day that a lot of people wanted to ask the question, are we okay? Is what we do okay or are we part of this turbo consumerism exploitative world? I spent a lot of time saying to people, actually you know we are good and we can be great. . . . The preconditions were there, it was in the culture and the people were well disposed to doing the right thing. Then obviously, you could then amplify

things. . . . So, I came in and I knew I had a lot to learn about the core business. I knew other stuff but I was not an expert on home furnishing manufacturing and retailing. You have to have some humbleness in that situation knowing you've got this world class company with people with the expertise that you lack. I was purposefully acknowledging the good things I saw and the expertise and the competence around me where people had driven successful initiatives in sustainability. So, you could say "we've already made progress but now it is time for the next big step." I think the honest truth is I came in as a campaigning sustainability person really and the company was receptive to that. Then you looked at how do you drive leadership really hard and go after all of the material areas with a relentless campaigning approach. . . . It is a battle against the status quo. You are just trying to drive change.[12]

We were intrigued to find a number of examples where external instigators had a catalytic impact on spurring sustainability leadership. An example of this is how Lee Scott, Walmart's former CEO, became convinced of the imperative of sustainable business. Kathleen McLaughlin, Walmart's current CSO, shared with us the impact external thought leaders had on Scott's journey:

Lee Scott had already been doing a lot of thinking that year anyway . . . by 2005 Walmart had become a pretty significant business. It had grown by leaps and bounds through its first 20–30 years and like any big company it started to come under a lot of criticism for unintended consequences of this huge growth. . . . He had been having a lot of conversations (what Lee called "listening sessions") with critics – thought leaders from social and environmental circles – people like Fred Krupp from Environmental Defense Fund, Peter Seligmann from Conservation International, Amory Lovins[13] and Paul Hawken[14] and many other people who had very useful and valid critiques of Walmart.[15]

Similarly, M&S's former CEO Stuart Rose, who was instrumental with others in defining and birthing M&S's sustainability strategy, was inspired by Al Gore. Mike Barry told us:

Stuart instinctively got that the world is changing and said "*We must not rest on our laurels*" – it's all about the definition of being a responsible business. Without being able to annunciate the narrative as we can now 10 years on, Stuart instinctively got that we had to change and was very personally influenced by Al Gore's work *An Inconvenient Truth* . . . he took an entire leadership team to see it at a private cinema screening and got everybody the book and everybody read it, and there is an interesting aside to this. I was talking to Steve Rowe the current CEO of M&S at a stakeholder event this summer, and he got out a copy of the book that Stuart had personally given him 10 years earlier when Steve was the director of home business with the personal handwritten note that said "*We have to do things differently, read this – the world is changing*". So the baton was passing 10 years ago to the CEO who is just emerging now.[16]

Another powerful example of how external stakeholders were able to influence sustainability performance is Novo Nordisk. In speaking with Lise Kingo about her time leading the sustainability function at Novo, she referenced external thought leaders such as John Elkington as critical prognosticators who spurred the thinking of internal executives such as Steen Riisgaard, who led the company's Enzymes division in the 90s:

> One of the things that John Elkington suggested that we would start doing was to invite a quite large group of critical NGOs to come and visit the company for a couple of days which became a sort of annual tradition. I think for top management and those of us that worked on the sustainability agenda that was a very, very important learning process. In conversations over a couple of days they also made us aware about perspectives of the business, about upcoming issues that I think we would never have thought about. For example, the whole issue around biodiversity was an issue we had no knowledge or no attention on at all. I mean we had great attention on environmental management and so on, but the biodiversity issue and the fact that the company was actually gathering genetic materials from different parts of the world in order to research and produce new enzymes was a completely new perspective. Based on this very creative input from stakeholders we were able to be very proactive and ahead of other companies I think in the way we grew and developed our sustainability agenda. So, your question on why was it that your agenda was broader and more inclusive? I think it was very much due to the stakeholder engagement and actually spending time with stakeholders to listen to their points of view. Also, to have top management being part of that and I have to say somebody like Steen Riisgaard at that time was absolutely amazing. He was a biologist himself which many of the NGOs were too so I mean it just became a very interesting dialogue, between professionals in an area.

Conclusion

Understanding the kind of catalysts that can trigger a company to cross the leadership threshold, embed sustainability within their day-to-day operations and become role-models will hopefully help more companies to follow suit.

We move now to Part Two of the book, to explore in further detail the five interlocking leadership attributes for sustainable business.

Notes

1 Authors' interview, Sept 19th 2017.
2 Authors' interview, Oct 19th 2017.
3 Ibid.
4 Authors' interview, Oct 31st 2017.
5 We Mean Business Coalition of coalitions, www.wemeanbusinesscoalition.org/
6 Authors' interview, Oct 31st 2017.
7 Authors' interview, Aug 30th 2017.
8 Authors' interview, Oct 13th 2017.
9 David Brower (1912–2000) was a prominent environmentalist and the founder of many environmental organizations, including the John Muir Institute for Environmental Studies, Friends of the Earth, the League of Conservation Voters, Earth Island Institute, and Fate of the Earth, https://browercenter.org/about/who-was-david-brower/
10 Arne Næss (1912–2009) was Norway's best-known philosopher who developed the concept of "deep ecology."
11 Authors' interview, Aug 31st 2017.
12 Authors' interview, Aug 10th 2017.
13 Amory Lovins (1947–) is cofounder and Chief Scientist of Rocky Mountain Institute; energy advisor to major firms and governments in 65+ countries for 40+ years, https://rmi.org/people/amory-lovins/ accessed Jan 30 2018.
14 Paul Hawken (1946–) is an environmentalist, entrepreneur, author, and activist, www.paulhawken.com/biography/ accessed Jan 30 2018.
15 Authors' interview, Oct 19th 2017.
16 Authors' interview, Sept 5th 2017.

Part two
Going *All In*

The attributes of corporate sustainability leadership: introduction

In Part one, we shared a history of the last twenty years of corporate sustainability leadership.

Now, in Part two, we explore each of the five interlinking attributes that are essential for enduring leadership going forward. These are:

PURPOSE: Why we do what we do; the organizing idea for why the business exists

PLAN: What we do and what we aspire to do as an organization

CULTURE: How we do things around here

COLLABORATION: Who we work with in other businesses and other sectors of society to be more effective

ADVOCACY: Where we use the authority of the business to encourage others to act to advance social justice and sustainable development.

We have arrived at these five interlinking attributes based on our analysis of the two decades of input representing the opinions of the thousands of experts who have responded to the Leaders Survey over the years. Additionally, in 2017, we asked an open-ended question about the required attributes for sustainability leadership in the coming decade. The experts' answers – and our own experience and views – inform the five attributes as we have defined them.[1]

There are, of course, other models for understanding and embedding sustainability in business. London Business School Professor Ioannis Ioannou and his co-researchers propose a responsible business model which has four pillars:

- Corporate governance
- Stakeholder engagement
- Time-horizon of decision-making
- Transparency and accountability.[2]

Further, John Browne, Tommy Stadlen, and Robin Nuttall offer their connect model for businesses to reconnect with society:

- Identify most material impacts
- Adopt a societal Purpose beyond just making a profit
- Apply world-class management skills
- Radically engage with critical stakeholders.[3]

We agree with both analyses. Identifying material impacts is a critical step in creating a Plan. We have a similar view to the Connect model about the centrality of Purpose. Likewise we endorse world-class management skills and believe these now crucially include Collaboration and Advocacy. We also consider radical engagement with stakeholders to be a fundamental element of an *All In* Culture. However, we suggest that, for businesses wishing to become sustainability leaders in the future, all five of our attributes need to work together and reinforce each other. Purpose is the foundation for why the business exists; it requires a Plan to bring it to life, a Culture that supports it, Collaboration to scale, and Advocacy to amplify and nurture the conditions that favor sustainability. (Please see Figure 3.1.)

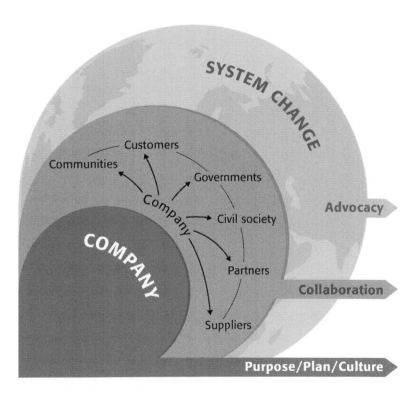

Figure 3.1 All In Leadership Attributes

After looking at each of the five attributes in turn in Chapters 3–7, we examine how they come together in case studies of Unilever – the company which has dominated the Leaders Survey since 2011 – and Interface – the one business which has featured in all twenty years of the Leaders Survey – in Chapters 8 and 9.

We conclude Part two with a checklist of the key actions required of any company now aspiring to be an enduring leader in sustainability. This present Best Practice Checklist comprises Chapter 10.

Notes

1   Our understanding of the Attributes also builds on the work of GlobeScan and Sustainability on the Regeneration Roadmap: Changing Tack, Extending Corporate Leadership on Sustainable Development, 2013, http://theregenerationroadmap. com/files/reports/Changing-Tack.pdf accessed Feb 11 2018.
2   Ioannou, I., "Big Ideas to Change the Way We Do Business," *London Business School*, Jan 2018, www.youtube.com/watch?v=7EquLX6mwbg&t=519s accessed Jan 31 2018.
3   Browne, J., Nuttall, R. and Stadlen, T., *Connect: How Companies Succeed by Engaging Radically with Society* (2015). WH Allen.

3 Purpose

"My belief is that the purpose of economic life is to meet the social needs of people."

Maurice Strong

Our first attribute is Purpose. Purpose is the foundation for why the business exists; it requires a Plan to bring it to life, a Culture which supports it, Collaboration to scale, and Advocacy to amplify and nurture the conditions that favor sustainability.

Enablers

The essential enablers of Purpose are:

- Being authentic and believable; corresponding to what the company is about
- Linking to business performance and social good, and guiding decision-making
- Having senior leadership buy-in and being supported by their evangelism
- Building understanding, increasing engagement and mobilizing actions among employees and other stakeholders
- Demonstrating flexibility in order to stay relevant as societal expectations and needs shift over time.

Clear purpose

Purpose, the most foundational of the *All In* leadership attributes, is about answering these questions: What is the social aim of business? Why does your company exist? Is it to make a profit or maximize shareholder value? The *Financial Times* columnist Martin Wolf framed it this way: "Almost nothing in economics is more important, than thinking through how companies should be managed, and for what ends. Unfortunately, we have made a mess of this; this mess has a name, it is Shareholder Value Maximization. Operating companies in line with this belief not only leads to misbehavior but may also lead to militate against the true social aim, which is to generate greater prosperity."[1]

The great social philosopher and management guru Charles Handy was clear: "The principal purpose of a company is not to make a profit – full stop. It is to make a profit in order to continue to do things or make things, and to do so even better and more abundantly."[2]

There are myriad definitions of Purpose, ranging from emphasis on branding and marketing to drivers of corporate strategy. In the context of corporate sustainability leadership, we gravitate to the latter and define Purpose in a comprehensive way:

> Purpose is an explicitly stated vision and authentic belief that defines the value that the company seeks to create for itself and society, directs key business decisions in the way value is created, aligns everyone in the business towards a common goal, guides how the company engages its stakeholders, and provides the organization with courage to foster positive change.

At its core, Purpose is the deepest expression of a company's ability to make the world better with its business solutions. But to be a catalyst and foundational element of corporate leadership, Purpose also needs to act as the blueprint for a fully integrated and comprehensive approach to sustainability. Having a pro-society Purpose means that you need to be committed to sustainability because that is essential for people and the planet. Purpose is important across all cultures and industry sectors and applicable to B2B companies as well as to B2C brands.

The case for purpose

Purpose in business has received increasing attention in recent years.[3] While it has been a subject of management theory at least since Peter Drucker declared the purpose of business is to create a customer,[4] it has taken on a new life over the past few years and has a contemporary and emerging quality to it. We have come a long way from Milton Friedman's view that the only purpose of business is to maximize profits for shareholders, with more and more business leaders and management theorists arguing that there is a greater Purpose for companies than simply making money. It aligns with a growing search for meaning across society, expressed most widely at present by the millennial generation, and with a growing understanding that long-term success depends on a sustainable ecosystem, economy, and society.

One of the reasons why companies are taking sustainability more seriously today and embedding it into their core business, is that they now see social and environmental issues as critical elements of their strategy and business Purpose. As companies think deeply about what they stand for, and put this in the context of optimizing shareholder and stakeholder returns in the long term, the value and necessity of strong sustainability commitment becomes obvious. If a company's Purpose goes beyond the pursuit of profit and takes into consideration the value created for society, then sustainability strategies, commitments, and goals become critical vehicles for delivering this. In many ways, sustainability has become the most important vehicle for proving the substance of a company's Purpose. Rethinking Purpose has helped an increasing number of businesses and investors to understand the value of sustainability.

There is a growing and multifaceted business case for how Purpose can create value for companies. First, Purpose drives financial performance. According to a study by Deloitte, strong core beliefs drive up to 17% of the variation in financial performance in leading European companies.[5] Similarly, Havas's Meaningful Brands research showed purposeful brands outperformed the stock market by 133%.[6] Second, Purpose is a powerful vehicle to drive consumer engagement. A GlobeScan and Sustainable Brands study from 2016 showed that 65% of consumers across 22 countries try to support companies that have a strong Purpose.[7] Third, Purpose supports talent acquisition, especially with millennials.[8] And fourth, a Harvard/EY Beacon Institute survey of executives demonstrated the value of Purpose with over eight in 10 saying that it contributes to employee satisfaction, business transformation, and customer loyalty.[9]

A trend that supports the business case is the growing number of purposeful businesses that are being acquired by leading companies. Unilever, for example, has now acquired five companies that are B Corp certified[10] (four within 2017 alone): Sundial, Seventh Generation, Pukka, Mae Terra, and Ben & Jerry's.

Unilever is not alone in its pursuit of benefit corporations. SC Johnson bought Method and Ecover, both certified B Corps, in 2017. Natura acquired The Body Shop from L'Oréal in 2017 in large measure because of the company's purpose, and Natura plans to "unleash the company and help it get back to its activist roots."[11] Another example is the 2013 acquisition of Plum Organics, another B Corp, by the Campbell Soup Company, which in many ways marked the beginning of that company's Purpose journey which revolves around "Real food that matters for life's moments."

Many if not all current companies in the Leaders Survey have a clear, authentic, and public Purpose statement. This is no coincidence, as Purpose enables overall performance and is a key reason expert survey respondents identify them as leaders. The following table outlines the Purpose statement of each of the top companies in the 2017 Leaders Survey (please see Figure 3.2).

Company	Purpose
Unilever	To make sustainable living commonplace.
Patagonia	Build the best product, cause no unnecessary harm, use business to inspire and implement solutions to the environmental crisis.
Interface	Lead industry to love the world.
IKEA	To create a better everyday life for the many people.
TESLA	To accelerate the advent of sustainable transport by bringing compelling mass market electric cars to market as soon as possible.
Natura	Bem Estar Bem.
M&S	Plan A is our way to help build a sustainable future by being a business that enables our customers to have a positive impact on wellbeing, communities and the planet through all that we do.
Nestlé	Enhancing quality of life and contributing to a healthier future.
Nike	Bring inspiration and innovation to every athlete* in the world. (*If you have a body, you are an athlete).
GE	GE's mission is to invent the next industrial era, to build, move, power and cure the world.
BASF	We create chemistry for a sustainable future.
Google	Since the beginning, our goal has been to develop services that significantly improve the lives of as many people as possible. Not just for some. For everyone.
Coca-Cola	To refresh the world in mind, body and spirit. To inspire moments of optimism and happiness through our brands and actions.
Walmart	We save people money so they can live better.

Figure 3.2 Purpose of Top Ranked Leaders (2017)

Pioneers in purpose

Let's go back to the early corporate sustainability leaders in the Leaders Survey to explore the origins of Purpose as a part of the sustainability agenda.

One of the reasons why DuPont could break through during the Harm Reduction Era in the late 1990s was because it approached sustainability through Purpose. The technical elements of its sustainability performance were strong, but it was the application of its "The goal is zero" mantra, which originally applied to safety and the pursuit of zero incidents, to sustainability goals like getting to zero emissions, that truly catalyzed the company's leadership. As Chad Holliday, then DuPont's CEO, described it: "We made a step change improvement in safety not just because it was a goal but because we put different things in place. . . . And then we thought, why should we have any environmental spills? And it just fell over from there and so our commitment to sustainability just built from that first goal on safety."[12]

This more purposeful approach to business evolved further into innovation and product development. According to Holliday, "We started looking at the percentage of R&D investment going towards sustainable products that were significantly more sustainable than the product they were replacing."[13] Further, new employees who joined the company added purposeful fuel to the fire at DuPont:

I found that our younger people – engineers, scientists and sales folks – just naturally wanted to put more attention here, so there was a natural evolution towards more focus on sustainability. Because we had a pretty good reputation . . . we tended to attract people that wanted to . . . be more focused on sustainability, and we had to give those people a chance to make a difference and work on sustainability projects.[14]

DuPont demonstrated early on how Purpose can be a way to drive a culture of sustainability commitment, and how that can galvanize the broader enterprise to achieve great things, such as hitting ambitious stretch sustainability targets.

Interface also provides an early example of a purposeful company. In 1994, Ray Anderson, the company's founder, had his epiphany moment and challenged the company to "Be the first company that, by its deeds, shows the entire world what sustainability is in all its dimensions: people, process, product, place, and profits – and in doing so, become restorative through the power of influence."[15]

The power of this quote stems from its comprehensiveness and its orientation toward the development of a restorative business model and being an influential beacon to change the world. Erin Meezan, Interface's Chief Sustainability Officer, describes it this way: "It was fundamentally at its heart about how we transform our business to be something different."[16]

Ray Anderson's vision went beyond the company's business objectives, and Interface's Purpose, then and now, takes the company's strategy beyond the walls of its factories to the products and services it delivers its customers, looking to create the systemic conditions required for sustainable development. It is this type of catalytic and inspiring Purpose that drives significant sustainability commitment and performance. As Dan Hendrix, Interface's Chairman, said, its Purpose gives the company the courage to believe that "This little carpet company could actually change the world."[17]

Interface recently re-framed its Purpose as *Lead Industry to Love the World*. This new Purpose inspired the company to dedicate itself to Climate Take Back, the company's commitment to reversing global warming through its actions and the actions of others. Meezan says this is a new chapter, an evolution from "doing no harm, you know the zero footprint days, to an evolved thinking of, how does a business do more good? How do we become a positive instrument?"[18]

Originally purposeful

Some companies were purposeful at their founding, an increasingly relevant dynamic given start-up culture around the world. Two long-standing companies in the Leaders Survey that embedded purpose right from their beginnings are Patagonia and Natura.

Patagonia was founded by Yvon Chouinard in 1973 to provide rock climbers with outdoor apparel. The name was chosen to reflect the values of the company as it evoked "romantic visions of glaciers tumbling into fjords, jagged windswept peaks, gauchos and condors."[19] Patagonia's mission statement defines the company's Purpose in terms that align its business with solving the world's environmental challenges: *Build the best product, cause no unnecessary harm, use business to inspire and implement solutions to the environmental crisis.*

The power of this Purpose has driven the company relentlessly. According to Rick Ridgeway, Patagonia's VP of Environmental Initiatives and someone who has been with the company since its founding, "If you are in business you use your business as an agent or tool for doing something about a problem like that. That is a moral obligation for us and that is where it came from. . . . Our sustainability programs and commitments all have their origin in this concern about the state of the planet; about the state of the wild places that remain on the planet. That has informed everything in our thinking going back to the very beginning."[20]

Patagonia's Purpose has enabled a remarkable range of commitments, from donating 1% of the company's sales to a network of environmental NGOs to a commitment to have 100% of its products sourced from facilities practicing or aligning with fair labor practices to new regenerative protocols to create net positive impacts in all that it does (e.g. farming cotton, wool, etc.).

Another company that had similarly deep founding passions was Natura, the Brazilian cosmetics company. Natura was started in São Paulo in 1969 by Antônio Luiz Seabra, who committed to selling cosmetic products made from natural substances and chose a name that expressed this explicitly. Natura's CEO, João Paulo Ferreira, explained the origins of the company: "Mr Luiz Seabra . . . decided from the beginning that . . . cosmetics was a means to touch people's lives and transform them and . . . that it would have to happen in communion with nature somehow."[21]

Ultimately, Luiz Seabra linked beauty to *Bem Estar Bem* and this became the company's Purpose. As Ferreira describes it, *Bem Estar Bem* means

> By being well in ourselves, we can feel well with the world, the environment, other people and society. This is both the *raison d'être* of Natura Brasil and a broader philosophy – the search for those moments when the body and the mind fuse and we become one with the rest of the world. It is all about balance – work and family, community and country, the planet, nature, even the divine.[22]

Natura's expression of its Purpose evolved over the years, especially when Guilherme Peirão Leal joined the company in 1979, as he pushed Natura toward deeper expressions of *Bem Estar Bem*. This included not only sourcing natural products, but also committing to care for the ecosystem that provided them in the Amazon rainforest. Natura also extended its Purpose in the social arena by looking at ways to address poverty through its consultants – its sales team who are largely women from lower income backgrounds.

Purpose in Silicon Valley

Two contemporary Leadership Survey companies from the technology sector, Google and Tesla, also fit into this category of companies that were founded with an original and clear Purpose. Google's "Do no evil" framing was baked into the company's ethos from the beginning. The now famous Founders' IPO Letter in 2004 uses the language of purpose: "Our goal is to develop services that significantly improve the lives of as many people as possible. In pursuing this goal, we may do things that we believe have a positive impact on the world, even if the near term financial returns are not obvious."[23]

Over time, the company has been working to fill in the Purpose with more substantive impact. As one of the founders, Larry Page, described it in 2014, "We're in a bit of uncharted territory. We're trying to figure it out. How do we use all these resources . . . and how do we make a much more positive impact on the world?"[24]

Google's original mission – "Organize the world's information and make it universally accessible and useful" – only takes the company so far. Google's website describes the company's Purpose more fully: "Since the beginning, our goal has been to develop services that significantly improve the lives of as many people as possible. Not just for some. For everyone."[25] This purposeful approach is driving Google's commitments in renewable energy and its $1 billion social investment strategy over the next five years.

As Kate Brandt, Leader for Sustainability at Google, framed it: "I think for us the core is that we believe that global businesses should lead the way in improving people's lives while eliminating our dependence on virgin materials and fossil fuels, and that we truly believe this can be done in a way that will make business sense, but also has economic return in positive social and environmental terms."[26]

Tesla, the automaker, energy storage company, and solar panel manufacturer, is another example of a Silicon Valley company that put Purpose front and center in its founding strategy. The company's Purpose is *To accelerate the advent of sustainable transport by bringing compelling mass market electric cars to market as soon as possible*. It is based on disruption and addressing the climate change crisis.

Tesla's commitment to its Purpose has led it to grow from an automaker into a more diversified company also pushing frontiers on energy storage in the form of batteries and power generation via solar power – Tesla is at the forefront of the transformation from an economy based on fossil fuels to one based on renewables. The clarity and conviction of its Purpose has been part of what has driven external interest from consumers and investors.

Purpose redux

A good number of today's Leadership Survey companies are institutions with long histories that have recently rediscovered their Purpose. This is one of the defining features of the Purpose-Driven Era of corporate sustainability. Companies from Unilever to Nestlé to BASF, all of which started in the nineteenth century, to IKEA, a 75-year old company, have in many ways gone back to their original Purpose and updated them to align with twenty-first century sustainable development imperatives. As the top-ranked company in the Leaders Survey the last seven years, readers will not be surprised to hear that Unilever is one of the most Purpose-driven companies we have encountered. Similarly, although younger, Interface is clear and consistent on this attribute. But because we have case studies on each company later in *All In*, we focus here on what makes Nestlé, BASF, and IKEA stand out in Purpose terms.

The world's largest food and beverage company, Nestlé, was founded in 1866 and has a long history of being purposeful. The company's Purpose is: *enhancing quality of life and contributing to a healthier future*. Through its purpose, Nestlé aims to deliver sustainable, industry-leading financial performance and earn trust.

The company is increasingly driving all its activities, from R&D to how it sources its products to how it engages consumers around health and well-being via its Purpose. Nestlé calls the framework for its long-term business activities "Creating Shared Value," and the framework is highly integrated with the company's Purpose. As the Nestlé website states:

> Our purpose allows us to take Creating Shared Value a step further, while adhering to our fundamental belief that our business will be successful in the long term by creating value for both our shareholders and for society where it intersects with our business. Our positive impact on society focuses on enabling healthier and happier lives for individuals and families, on helping the development of thriving and resilient

communities and, finally, on stewarding the planet's natural resources for future generations, with particular care for water.[27]

The balancing of the short-term and long-term is something many fast-moving consumer goods firms, including Nestlé, have struggled with. The mark of leadership today relates to the ability to manage this, to be successful financially while ensuring the long-term value the company creates for society is nurtured. Paul Bulcke, Nestlé's Chairman, notes "The top line of it is that for a company to be successful over time . . . it has to create shareholder value, true, but at the same time what it does and what it stands for should also create value for society."[28]

Bulcke believes that Purpose is "not something that is on the sideline; it is something that is intrinsically built into our business strategy . . . I think that a strength of a company like ours is that we have scale and can impact widely."[29]

In our interview, Bulcke paid special attention to the notion of leadership and the need for executives to fully embrace and drive Purpose:

> First you speak out of conviction, to make clear that it is the right thing to do, but then you don't leave it to words, you make it part of your operations, you operationalize purpose. You operationalize it so that three hundred and thirty thousand employees and . . . suppliers and everyone upstream and downstream . . . understand what the company stands for and how they fit into it. . . . At the end of the day the job of a Chairman and a CEO and of management in general is to have a healthy company and to keep it healthy. This is best done when its purpose is framed by the company's values.[30]

Another example of long-established company that has recently re-emphasized Purpose is BASF, the German chemical company that was founded in 1865. We interviewed Dirk Voeste, BASF's VP Sustainability Strategy, and he explained how the company had always aspired to be purposeful:

> If you look at BASF, we are now 152 years old, and even one year after the foundation of BASF we already had occupational health for employees on our site, so we said there is a dimension of sustainability in taking care of social aspects; taking care of the people and employees in a certain way which was part of the DNA. If you then look at how BASF is set up in what we call the 'Verbund system',[31] which is the interconnected system to optimize resources . . . right from the beginning there is a kind of sustainability thinking already embedded into BASF.[32]

Building on the company's history of strong social and environmental commitments and performance, in 2011 a new approach was adopted to develop and commit to an even stronger Purpose, which required a deeper and more expansive approach to sustainability. Voeste explains the journey BASF went through:

> If you then look at the challenges we are facing and have been observing for a few decades, that we see we will have more people on the planet; we fight for resources; we see climate change coming; we see that people all over the world struggle with quality of life, defining quality of life differently . . . you see that sustainability is ongoing within this. It became even more obvious when we wrote our [new] strategy in 2011. We call it the Re-Create Chemistry Strategy and within the strategy we didn't give ourselves [a] vision which is normally something you do in strategic process . . . [instead] we at this point in time gave ourselves a purpose. We said, why are we here? What is the purpose of BASF? What is our purpose in terms of society [and] stakeholder demand, [and] also in terms of contribution to Planet Earth? The purpose is "We create chemistry for a sustainable future." By having this purpose, it is not only that sustainability gets a very high awareness and recognition in . . . external communication and internal engagement, it also becomes an imperative of how you look at your business.[33]

The impact of Purpose on BASF's sustainability performance is apparent in several enterprise-wide initiatives: an assessment of 60,000 products through 180 workshops worldwide, redesigned annual performance reviews embedding sustainability as a key criterion, and the development of a new methodology to assess BASF's overall contribution to sustainability called Value to Society.[34]

An example of how BASF is now approaching sustainability through the lens of its Purpose, and the challenges and opportunities this presents to the business, relates to a review they undertook on polyfluorinated substances in take-away drinking cups. These substances are what make the cups leak-proof and grease resistant. They are fully legal and regulated, but they didn't live up to BASF's aspirations. This led to a difficult internal discussion given the ongoing revenue this product generated. As Voeste describes it:

> That was a tough discussion because if you have certain sales with such a substance in certain markets your sales guys say: "Come on this is business, why do you take it out?" This has been identified as a "challenge" product. It is a legally compliant product but we believe challenge products shouldn't be on our journey into the future. That is why we took them out and that was a tough discussion. We started an R&D project to identify whether we could find other products . . . which have similar characteristics but a completely different profile. If you look at the waste generated . . . of these paper cups you see that we [have] a huge problem and [so] we found a substance which is biodegradable and we found a substance which is made out of recycled material. So not only did we get rid of the polyfluorinated substances but we also put in something

which is much more environmentally favorable and a better contribution to a sustainable future.[35]

Finally, while not a company with as long a heritage as Nestlé or BASF, IKEA, founded in 1943, has also recently reinforced the power of its Purpose. In founding the company, Ingvar Kamprad (whose initials make up the first letters of IKEA; the last two come from the farm – Elmtaryd – and village – Agunnaryd – where he grew up in Sweden) had a vision to meet consumer needs at reduced prices. Access and affordability were at the heart of his vision[36] when he started the company in the 1940s, then codified in his 1976 treatise "Testament of a Furniture Dealer".[37] The first page of this document begins with the Purpose statement: *To create a better everyday life for the many people.*

IKEA has had a long history with sustainability – its first environmental policy was launched in 1990 – but it took a much more comprehensive approach when it created its People & Planet Positive strategy in 2012. It was 2015 when IKEA became recognized as a one of the top companies in the Leaders Survey, which we see resulting in good part from the company recommitting to its Purpose.[38]

The rediscovery of IKEA's Purpose has had a catalytic affect internally. The entire enterprise has begun to apply the Purpose as a mobilizing concept, bringing it to life from design to distribution to consumer experience. It is through Purpose that the company finds the confidence to be a true sustainability leader and to engage internally and externally more effectively.

Steve Howard, IKEA's Chief Sustainability Officer during this time, commented:

> What we identified was that there was a disconnect between the company's purpose and the day-to-day business. Right at the start of our People & Planet Positive strategy, we baked in "create a better everyday life for the many people." So, delivering super-affordable LEDs for everybody was consistent with the purpose. Making sure that we were using Better Cotton, and that kids in cotton communities were going to school and farmers were receiving better pricing was consistent with the purpose. It was a hugely powerful thing to connect things in that way. We constantly referenced the purpose and brought people back to it. Because it was the Founder's concept, it explicitly gave us permission to pull our business closer to living up to the purpose. I didn't know that "purposing" could be a verb until I had been through that process.[39]

Connecting the founder's Purpose with a comprehensive sustainability strategy proved compelling. According to Howard:

> Our sustainability strategy allowed a humanistic business with a strong vision to become purpose-driven. . . . A vision is a nice idea without

strategies, actions and plans behind it. When you have a vision with strategies, actions and plans that are up to the task, then it becomes purpose. We brought the company's purpose alive through the sustainability strategy and found that IKEA was far more powerful with purpose.[40]

At the end of our conversation, Howard took the idea of Purpose further, telling us he sees it having the potential to reshape business at scale: "There is the potential that we see a reinvigoration of values-driven capitalism where businesses are fully thoughtful about their total impact on the world. The product offerings they have, the business models they have, the way they treat people through their value chains."[41]

How to develop purpose

Developing a Purpose must be a process that is owned by the leadership of the company: the board, CEO, and other senior leaders. Typically, it is an iterative process involving workshops with employees. A new resource based in the UK is Blueprint for Better Business – a relatively young charity that grew out of an initiative of the Roman Catholic Archbishop of Westminster and a group of corporate CEOs. They have developed a blueprint in the form of two A4 sheets: one covering a blueprint framework,[42] and the other articulating a series of guiding principles[43] for better business.[44] Companies are using both to help them review their current portfolio and current ways of working, then coming to an articulation of their Purpose and how it relates to society – a "social Purpose" if you will. In some cases, businesses are seeking help from an internal taskforce or external advisers to help them facilitate their Purpose journey.

Organizations that can trace a social Purpose from their founder's vision or in their history and heritage are well-placed to draw on these in articulating a refreshed Purpose for today. However a revised Purpose is developed, it is essential to communicate it widely and thoroughly. Employees need sufficient opportunity to test out their understanding of the Purpose and what it means to them, how they behave, and what they do in the company. This needs to be an ongoing process.

Conclusion

Purpose is an old idea, with even more history behind it than we realized. We see it in companies that have been in business for over 150 years and in those that have just come into existence.

The power of Purpose from a sustainability perspective is that, because of its all-encompassing nature, it can engage the entire enterprise. This integrated approach ensures that sustainability performance – the vehicle for creating societal value, which is required to be truly purposeful – is embedded across the company. With Purpose, sustainability moves from being a set of programs managed by a distinct function, to become a unifying means to create value throughout the entire business and for society.

The power of Purpose has been demonstrated by a variety of companies – old and new, B2B and B2C – operating in diverse locations worldwide. It is a universal attribute for corporate sustainability leadership that is growing in importance. In short, in the words of a blogger: "Purpose = shared value + authenticity + action."[45]

We turn next to Plan.

Notes

1 "Opportunist shareholders must embrace commitment," *Financial Times*, 26 Aug 2014
2 Handy, C., "What Is a Company for?" *RSA*, 1990, www.growthinternational.com/resources/Charles+Handy+1990.pdf
3 In the UK, for example, public conversation about purpose, between 1995 and 2016, has increased five-fold: Oxford University and Ernst and Young, 2016.
4 Drucker, P., *The Practice of Management* (1954).
5 Deloitte, *Core Beliefs & Culture Survey* (2013).
6 Havas, *Meaningful Brands* (2016).
7 GlobeScan, *Public on Purpose Survey* (2016).
8 Deloitte, *The Deloitte Millennial Survey* (2016).
9 EY/Harvard, *The Business Case for Purpose* (2016).
10 B Corps are for-profit companies certified by the non-profit B Lab to meet rigorous standards of social and environmental performance, accountability, and transparency, http://bcorporation.eu/what-are-b-corps accessed Feb 8 2018.
11 In our interview with João Paulo Ferreira, Natura's CEO, on Sept 27th 2017, he shared with us that it was very much the opportunity and perhaps even obligation to rekindle Anita Roddick's activist legacy through The Body Shop that convinced the Natura Board to buy the company.
12 Authors' interview, Aug 21st 2017.
13 Ibid.
14 Ibid.
15 Interface, www.interfaceglobal.com/sustainability.aspx
16 Authors' interview, Aug 21st 2017.
17 Ibid.
18 Ibid.
19 Patagonia, www.patagonia.com/company-history.html
20 Authors' interview, Aug 31st 2017.
21 Authors' interview, Sept 29th 2017.
22 Ibid.
23 Page L. and Brin S., "An Owner's Manual" for Google's Shareholders, https://abc.xyz/investor/founders-letters/2004/ipo-letter.html#_ga=2.207908564.790345074.1515963583-469950629.1515963583
24 Waters R., "FT Interview with Google Co-Founder and CEO," *Financial Times*, Oct 31, 2014.
25 Google, "Our Company," www.google.com/intl/en/about/our-company/ accessed Feb 9 2018.
26 Authors' interview, Sept 14th 2017.
27 Nestlé, www.nestle.com/csv/what-is-csv
28 Authors' interview, Oct 10th 2017.
29 Ibid.

30 Ibid.
31 Verbund refers to BASF's principle of efficiency: The Verbund Principle Enables Us to Add Value as One Company through Efficient Use of our Resources, www. basf.com/en/company/about-us/strategy-and-organization/verbund.html
32 Authors' interview, Aug 28th 2017.
33 Ibid.
34 BASF's Value to Society is an attempt to take a wholistic measurement of the impacts, positive and negative, it has in the world. Voeste describes this process: We Embarked on a Project and Started to Calculate our Monetized Impact on Society based on our Business Activities from All of our Supply Chain Down to our Customer and Calculated This, www.basf.com/en/company/sustainability/management-and-instruments/quantifying-sustainability/we-create-value/impact-categories.html
35 Authors' interview, Aug 28th 2017.
36 Ingvar Kamprad died just as we were completing *All In*. As Steve Howard tweeted on the news: "Brilliant entrepreneur, founder of IKEA and someone who always 'dared to be different.'"
37 IKEA, www.ikea.com/ms/en_CA/pdf/reports-downloads/the-testament-of-a-furniture-dealer.pdf
38 It should be noted that in Swedish, the "the many people" is very closely associated with common people, reinforcing the egalitarianism at the heart of the company's founding and ongoing Purpose.
39 Authors' interview, Aug 10th 2017.
40 Ibid.
41 Ibid.
42 Blueprint for Better Business, www.blueprintforbusiness.org/framework2/
43 Blueprint for Better Business, www.blueprintforbusiness.org/explore_principles/
44 Blueprint for Better Business draws on Catholic social justice teaching, the teaching of other faiths and the great philosophical traditions, as well as the latest insights from neuroscience about individuals and what motivates us.
45 Afshar, P., Fleishman Hillard's Purposeful Business Blog, Jan 22, 2018, www. edie.net/blog/A-powerful-man-wants-purpose-What-next/6098443 accessed Jan 30 2018.

4 Plan

> "One's philosophy is not best expressed in words; it is expressed in the choices one makes . . . and the choices we make are ultimately our responsibility."
> Eleanor Roosevelt

Our second attribute is Plan. A successful Plan brings Purpose to life, reinforces a Culture that can deliver the Plan, and is strategic about the Collaboration and Advocacy needed to support implementation of the Plan

Enablers

The essential enablers of Plan are:

- Being comprehensive and internally consistent; covering all core business activities; being integrated across functions, strategic business units, and markets
- Articulating a compelling business case based on sustainability
- Including stretch goals based on science and aligned with the SDGs as well as clear metrics and measurement, and timely reporting and disclosure
- Ensuring that it is championed and driven by top leadership who are constantly re-selling the Plan with the new data and examples required to keep it fresh
- Pursuing it persistently, even through adversity, and being responsive to changing societal expectations
- Ensuring organizational rewards and resources are aligned with delivery of the Plan.

Pioneering Plans

The dozens of *All In* interviews revealed that at least some elements of the best Plans have been in play for decades. During the Harm Reduction Era, for example, 3M's high GlobeScan-SustainAbility Leaders Survey ranking in the late 1990's was driven partly by the company's attentiveness to shifting societal demands. Instead of waiting to see how new EPA rules and oversight would affect them, 3M moved ahead of the regulatory curve, defining and implementing a "Pollution Prevention Pays" (PPP) program over four decades ago that outpaced regulation, reduced emissions and waste, and saved the company several billions of dollars.

In her *All In* interview, Jean Sweeney, 3M's recently retired Chief Sustainability Officer, emphasized the importance of 3M having very senior sustainability leadership as early as the 1970s. Dr. Joseph Ling, VP, Environmental Engineering, won the trust of successive 3M CEOs and is credited with PPP's creation and otherwise setting in place the conditions that led 3M to train its sales people to listen to customers differently. What they found was that customers were expressing concern for a host of sustainability challenges that 3M could solve with new products marrying environmental performance to more sustainable offerings. For 3M, strong senior leadership support, responsiveness, and rooting their efforts in science all contributed to creating a strategy that delivered real impact.

DuPont was another company that framed a strong Plan for sustainability that led to strong rankings in the Leaders Survey from the late 1990s through the mid 2000s. Chad Holliday, DuPont's CEO at that time, told us how critical it was that sustainability efforts aligned to the DuPont culture. DuPont was a safety leader, and used a "The goal is zero" mantra to encapsulate their safety ambitions. The company adopted the same phrase to describe their aims for sustainability performance, launching a quest to be a zero waste and zero emissions company under the leadership of Holliday and then CSO-equivalent Paul Tebo. Making sustainability equivalent to safety inside the company underscored to employees how important the work was at the same time as establishing an exciting aspiration, as "zero" was well beyond the clear majority of even the brightest thinkers and best performers of this era. Tebo was also a significant sustainability advocate, lending his thinking gratis to other companies like Ford Motor Company working to embed sustainability into their strategies in a similarly culture-aligned way.

DuPont's acknowledged leadership during the Harm Reduction Era depended on senior leadership support, but also alignment with its existing safety culture so as to better resonate with employees and a commitment to absolute goals at a time when most were not thinking in those terms. DuPont's Plan also demonstrated responsiveness in that they were one of the first companies to form and take input from an external stakeholder advisory committee.

Acceleration via integration

The Strategic Integration Era that followed the Harm Reduction Era of corporate sustainability leadership was defined by the advent of Plans that engaged the entire enterprise and scaled impact.

As a group, they are comprehensive – for the most part addressing all the Plan enablers we list earlier – and dynamic – adapting and evolving as circumstances in the company, the market, and society change.

Unilever's Sustainable Living Plan (SLP) is the consensus gold standard of the moment, both for its quality and how it connects to the other four leadership attributes of Purpose, Culture, Collaboration, and Advocacy.[1] The SLP, however, followed a series of detailed Plans launched earlier by the likes of GE, Walmart, and M&S.

A simple Plan: meet needs, make friends, and make money

We spoke with Jeff Immelt, GE's CEO from 2000 to 2017, about GE's emergence and persistence as a sustainability leader under the banner of its *ecomagination* program. Immelt told us he is uncomfortable with the terms "sustainability" and "sustainable development," finding them complex and almost distracting in a business context. While citing huge respect for his peer Paul Polman at Unilever and other more "zealous" corporate sustainability leaders, Immelt said positioning *ecomagination* for success inside GE meant a more measured approach.

Immelt himself was central to *ecomagination*'s 2004 launch, so the senior leadership support aspect was certain, but making the Plan stick within the GE Culture was not. Immelt set corporate social responsibility and citizenship buzzwords aside to instead talk about "making money while solving society's greatest problems"[2] as well as developing necessary partnerships and "making more friends." And he constantly reminded executives and employees that GE would succeed only if the company could make money addressing environmental challenges, by demonstrating that "green is green."

Immelt described how *ecomagination* was embedded into the company after a close study of science, policy, and customer needs. The GE team concluded, based on an extensive study in 2003, that the science behind climate change was real but that related policy was an ineffective jumble. Most important to the business perhaps was the realization that customers were still unaware of the implications of climate change, which opened the door for GE to provide them with more efficient products they did not yet know they needed.

GE's *ecomagination* thus set out to innovate and bring customers better products, and to partner with customers and others – including competitors and NGOs when appropriate. They also worked to increase the efficiency of GE's own operations, and to engage in outreach – most notably in the form of the US Climate Action Partnership (USCAP)[3] mentioned previously – to try to spur better policy on climate and other issues.

Critical in Immelt's mind to making the effort enduring was ensuring it was not marketing-led and that the goals they made public from the start were business-oriented – *ecomagination* products would be at least 25% more efficient than those of their predecessors, with revenue from those products amounting to billions of dollars and expected to comprise a portfolio that would outperform the rest of the company. The *ecomagination* program was customer-focused in that it was all about providing more efficient products, from locomotives to turbines. It was also agnostic in terms of current partner performance: Immelt and GE were happy to work with utilities to make coal-fired generation more efficient at the same time as working to expand its renewables business lines. This broad church approach is what Immelt means by "making friends" to "solve society's problems" and "make money." He believed in working with everyone trying to push forward from where they are, no matter their history or current performance, partly because of the difficulty of building coalitions like USCAP without such a perspective.

The launch of GE's *ecomagination* was a significant moment for corporate sustainability, marking the emergence of the kind of comprehensive sustainability approach addressing to considerable degree all five leadership attributes we view as critical simultaneously. While we note GE's struggles in the marketplace today, *ecomagination* has endured for well over a decade and remains a best-in-class approach even as the company transitions leadership and re-shapes its portfolio of businesses.

A Plan for everything

Walmart is one of the iconic companies of our time. It's polarizing, with many believing its business model and approach are part of the problem, while others – including Leaders Survey respondents over several years in the Strategic Integration Era – credit it for having emerged as a corporate sustainability champion.

This polarization may reflect something Joel Makower of GreenBiz said in conversation with us during *All In's* development: it is harder than ever to say who precisely is "a good company," as every institution is part of the problem and (at least potentially) part of the solution. But whatever your view, it is true that Walmart doesn't do anything by half; now that they have made sustainability a priority, they are developing plans – sometimes alone, often in partnership – for literally every aspect of their business, at a dizzying pace.

As described earlier, Walmart and its then CEO Lee Scott hit their "threshold moment" in 2005 with Hurricane Katrina. Kathleen McLaughlin, Walmart's present Chief Sustainability Officer, told us in her *All In* interview that after the storm "the company sprang into action reflexively," with Scott giving permission to Walmart personnel in affected regions to do whatever they perceived to be needed and right for their communities without worrying about how the company would judge it or account for it later.

Even before Katrina, Scott had started a series of "listening sessions" (sessions that current Walmart leaders continue today) with critics and experts like Fred Krupp of the Environmental Defense Fund. McLaughlin related how Katrina pushed Scott to the next level, to ask "What would it take for Walmart to be that company, at our best, all the time?"

More than ten years later, Walmart continues to work on its Plan. It has been refined – McLaughlin emphasized the way Walmart's view of sustainability has expanded beyond its direct operational impacts to a perspective that takes in the entire value chain – but it remains focused on what the company can accomplish using its commercial strengths, with McLaughlin holding "It is only possible to maximize the business value of a company if it is addressing the fundamental social and environmental issues of our time via the core business."[4]

McLaughlin expanded on how Walmart tries to maximize value in such a manner, providing this overview of the company's comprehensive approach:

> Our core business is about bringing people safe, affordable food, apparel [and] household goods in many countries around the world. That in and of itself solves a social need for access and affordability, food safety and so on. We are trying to do it in a way that uses our strengths to create additional shared value – simultaneously creating value for business and for society.
>
> First, we aim to use our jobs and purchase orders to create *economic opportunity* for associates and suppliers from farmer to manufacturer. Second, we are working on *sustainable supply chains*. In every single chain, whether it is shrimp, apparel, tuna, palm oil, tomatoes, electronics, you name it, there can be social and environmental hotspots – externalities of consumption. By working with others, not only can we reduce emissions, create a more circular economy, move to more sustainable chemistry, and so on – in doing so, we can improve product quality, enhance availability, manage risk, improve cost structure, enhance customer trust and loyalty, etc. That is how we try to approach things – very much from a whole system, shared value point of view, leading through the business, and collaborating with others to accelerate systemic change. The third big area for us is *local community* where, because we are a retailer and we have physical presence with people, products, and assets on the ground, we can make a difference on things like disaster relief or hunger relief. For example, as a food retailer, donating unsold food reduces food waste and it also provides charitable meals. And we can strengthen local community cohesion through volunteerism and community grants. We are a mass retailer – we have people of all walks of life come through our doors. We can help build bridges.[5]

Today Walmart is applying its core business strengths to issues as diverse as: wages and workforce success based on more and better training and development, higher starting wages, and quicker raises; reducing fleet emissions by doubling efficiency in the ten years to 2015 through a combination of initiatives including driver behavior, engines, fuels, and cab redesign; waste, where the company has realized 77% waste diversion in its own operations thanks to interventions like shifting food labels from "best before" to "use by"; chemicals, where all Walmart suppliers will be required to disclose their use of chemicals of concern by 2018; and so on. McLaughlin says everything Walmart does, especially in leveraging supply chain partner contributions through The Sustainability Consortium (in which the clear majority of Walmart suppliers participate) "is about system acceleration."[6] This commitment to acceleration and the true scope of their ambition and the comprehensiveness of their Plan is maybe best represented by Project Gigaton.[7]

Announced in April 2017, Project Gigaton aims to do exactly what the name implies for climate and carbon dioxide equivalent (CO_2e). By providing an emissions reduction toolkit and working with suppliers, Walmart is committed to eliminating a gigaton of Scope 3 emissions (indirect emissions that occur in the value chain) between 2015 and 2030 – "equivalent to taking more than 211 million passenger vehicles off of U.S. roads and highways for a year."[8] Project Gigaton is not all Walmart is doing, not by far, but the initiative sums up the strengths of its Plan: hugely ambitious and purposeful, science-based, launched with full institutional support, rooted in value chain collaboration, and material to the business in that it will build supply chain resiliency, save money, improve reputation, and more. And Walmart has promised to pursue Scope 3 progress not just on energy, but also on agriculture, waste, packaging, deforestation, and product use and design. The company indeed seems to have a "A Plan for Everything."

No Plan B

Since its launch in 2007, Marks & Spencer (M&S) has referred to its sustainability strategy as Plan A – "Because there is no Plan B."

Don't let this flippant phrase fool you. Plan A is 100% serious to M&S's CSO Mike Barry and the CEOs who have led M&S over the decade since Plan A first launched under then CEO Stuart Rose.[9] Following its second comprehensive refresh and relaunch in 2017, this time as Plan A 2025, Barry assured us in our conversation that M&S believes Plan A is the right thing for society and the planet – and *essential* for the company's long-term commercial success.

We asked Barry what differentiates Plan A. He said that Plan A's effectiveness and longevity stem from its *completeness* (Plan A covers the entirety of M&S operations and stretches further to ensure value chain activation), *transparency*, *integration* (M&S has a small sustainability team; Plan A depends on the whole business being involved), and *the quality of the business case* underlying it (Barry stressed that an essential factor in Plan A's continuity has been identifying how it contributes to M&S's competitive advantage).

As admired and successful as Plan A has been, Barry pointed out that Plan A is only a necessary condition for success, not a guarantee, saying "Success on sustainability gives a company a fighting chance"[10] in ever evolving and extremely competitive markets, but no sustainability plan assures market success. In fact, just before *All In* was completed, M&S had a very difficult 2017 Christmas season in commercial terms, underscoring Barry's point that sustainability is only part of the answer and that traditional business performance norms and demands always apply.

Plan A is clearly comprehensive. When it was launched in 2007 it aimed "to address the key environmental, social and ethical challenges facing M&S."[11] Progressively since, and explicitly within the Plan A 2025 relaunch, the company has extended its perspective beyond its own operations, through its value chain and to the customer.

Plan A 2025 is billed as "an ambitious, customer focused plan that builds on the success of the first 10 years of Plan A and will support 1,000 communities, help 10 million people live happier, healthier lives and convert M&S into a zero-waste business."[12] Barry argues that customer focus is the essential element for the next phase of this work, the piece that will really determine if Plan A 2025 reaches its ambitions. He believes this will happen only if customers "see the personal benefit of the product, see that it is cheaper, better, tastier, etc., not just some green option that's nice but not improved."[13] And he believes that there is a huge audience for this; while just 10% of M&S customers might be deep green consumers, Barry says "at least 80% – deep greens, light greens, and those who will act as "part of a tribe" – are convincible if you offer them the right thing in the right way."[14]

Changing consumer behavior is famously difficult, and business is often afraid to try. Sustainability is challenging in this regard – complex, remote, and scary – so Barry urges making it "local and personal."[15] For this reason, Barry says M&S "works on systemic food waste but does not talk about it at store level," instead focusing on food bank donations and helping customers save money by wasting less food at home. And M&S carefully picks the things people care about most to use as examples: for instance, M&S customers currently care more about the source of their coffee than where palm oil comes from, so information on packaging and in store is about the former.[16]

M&S has rare strengths. It had an enviable reputation to build upon even before Plan A launched in 2007, having won the UK's Business in the Community *Responsible Business of the Year* award in 2004 and 2006. It has managed extremely careful baton-passing from CEO to CEO since Plan A launched, ensuring Plan A consistency through leadership changes. Its products are almost all private label, so the M&S brand is on everything, which Barry claims enables "deeper relationships with suppliers and partners."[17] The company is more than 130 years old and has a wealth of experience, including its part in the 1940s war effort, that has taught it to appreciate the value of contribution and the power of collaboration. But for all that may be inimitable about M&S, Barry stressed that the absolute key to sustainable business – or to business becoming sustainable – is replicability. And that's why Plan A emphasizes transparency and value chain Collaboration. While M&S wants to win in the marketplace, it knows its sustainability Plan is only as good as the system in which it operates, which involves business brass tacks like supply chain continuity.

As we closed our interview, Barry warned that things will only get harder from here, as the low hanging fruit has been picked. But he is hopeful that by

2030 we will see thousands of businesses meaningfully involved in this agenda, which is why M&S is committed to Advocacy, especially demonstrating that the best corporate sustainability thinking is based on "sound science and stakeholder engagement," or, as we might say context-based and responsive.

Plans – and Master Plans – fit for the future

Tesla is unique and perhaps the best example of a Plan for the Purpose-Driven Era of corporate sustainability leadership likely to endure well into the Regenerative Era that we predict will follow. The company vaulted into the Leaders Survey based on the responses of sustainability experts in 2016 and in 2017 ranked among the top five. Perhaps not coincidentally, this time period also saw Tesla acquire SolarCity, the launch of the more affordable Tesla Model 3, and the moment in April 2017 when Tesla's market capitalization first exceeded that of each of the traditional US automaker heavyweights GM and Ford. While occurring after the 2017 Leaders Survey closed, we expect that Tesla's delivery of the world's largest battery[18] – capable of powering 30,000 homes – to the state of South Australia, where it will help the region manage its plentiful but intermittent wind power, along with exciting new vehicle announcements (both a semi and a sports car) in late 2017, will do nothing but boost its reputation.

When contacted for an interview for *All In*, Tesla's press team referred us to Elon Musk's infamous Tesla Master Plan[19] (2006) and Tesla Master Plan Part Deux[20] (2016). The Master Plans' presentation of Tesla's intention is audacious, not to mention hugely ambitious and deceptively simple at the same time, with the original and the update each concluding in just four bullets summarizing "everything" Tesla will accomplish by first building a single – very expensive! – electric car.

Amazingly, especially since the integration of SolarCity and the launch of the Model 3, it feels Tesla's Purpose and Plan might reasonably boil down to just one point rather than four: designing and delivering an affordable, reliable low-carbon lifestyle. For a California automaker, this is genius; an updated version of The Beach Boys *Fun Fun Fun* car romance songs of the 1950s and 1960s, without the tailfins or the emissions.

Tesla is without doubt a company to watch. They have senior leadership support and Purpose in abundance. They position the entire business model as responsive to societal needs (in terms of accelerating the transition to a low-carbon economy) and rooted in science. But the proof of their Plan will come in execution, including getting to millions of cars sold annually (GM and Ford together today produce about 16 million cars per year to Tesla's few thousand). Tesla also must make the Gigafactory a success in terms of both volume and quality of batteries produced, deal with an expanding and more complex supply chain, and become a leader in dealing with the e-waste EVs will generate.[21] All in all, Tesla's vision is remarkable; now they need to show markets and consumers they can deliver against the ambitions they have shared.

Making the old new again

As we transition from the Purpose-Driven Era towards the Regenerative Era of corporate sustainability leadership, more Tesla's, with business models designed to be sustainable from the outset, will emerge and (we hope) flourish. At the same time, given the sheer scale of the systemic challenges standing between today's realities and a truly just and sustainable society, it is critical to rapid market transition that today's incumbents successfully reinvent themselves as evermore sustainable enterprises also. This may lead to a remarkable twist given current perspectives on certain industries and companies that are often said to be foot-dragging at best and actively opposing change at worst.

One example of an incumbent – historically controversial but highly ranked in the Leaders Survey during the Harm Reduction Era – perhaps signaling business model transition is energy giant Royal Dutch Shell. When we talked to Chad Holliday about DuPont's sustainability leadership when he was DuPont's CEO, we also asked also where he believes future leaders will emerge from now through 2030.

While Holliday is presently the Chair of Royal Dutch Shell and thus has a natural bias, he suggested that we not overlook the potential for Shell and other traditional fossil fuel energy companies to return to the leadership positions they held in the Leaders Survey ten to twenty years ago. As evidence, in late 2017, Shell Chief Executive Ben van Beurden announced industry-leading and Paris Agreement-exceeding (in terms of the glide path required to stay below 2 °C warming) carbon intensity reduction targets applying to all Shell's Tier 1, Tier 2, and Tier 3 emissions, and a commitment to invest at least $2 billion a year in its New Energies business.[22]

Whether Shell and other energy giants will shake off the big oil dinosaur label many apply to them and show new life and leadership remains to be seen, and some immediate responses to Shell's plans included criticism that the company aims only for a 50% reduction in carbon *intensity* by 2050. Still, in this announcement, we see the senior leadership support, responsiveness, context or scientific basis, clear goals and a system of measurement, customer linkage (in addressing Tier 3 emissions), and certainly the business relevance essential to building a robust and enduring corporate sustainability leadership Plan.

For the economy to transition, it will be at least as important for companies like Shell to embrace and lead change as it is for companies like Tesla to disrupt. For this reason, we are equally excited and welcoming of the sustainability efforts of all types of companies, and simply wish for more to tackle sustainability quickly, seriously, and at scale.

Conclusion

Companies that want to go *All In* on Plan will identify their material impacts and develop a comprehensive Plan with stretch goals based on societal context and the best available science.[23]

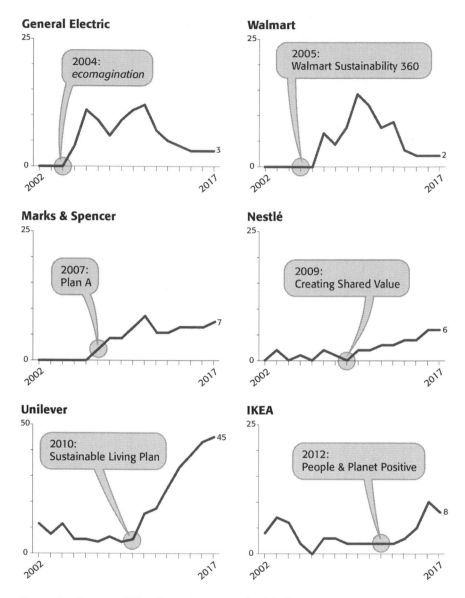

Figure 4.1 Impact of Plan Launches on Leadership Reputation
% of Experts, Total Mentions, Unprompted, 2002–2017

Their progress will be demonstrated with metrics and performance measurements that show sustainability Plan impact on commercial success as well as positive impact on reputation (see Figure 4.1). Such plans will be fully integrated and indeed *become* the business strategy over time.

Notes

1 Unilever's Plan is described in detail Chapter 8 as part of a comprehensive case study.
2 Authors' interview, Oct 13th 2017.
3 United States Climate Action Partnership, www.merid.org/en/Content/Projects/United_States_Climate_Action_Partnership.aspx accessed Dec 3 2017.
4 Authors' interview, Oct 31st 2017.
5 Ibid.
6 Ibid.
7 "Walmart Launches Project Gigaton to Reduce Emissions in Company's Supply Chain," Walmart Press Release, April 19 2017, https://news.walmart.com/2017/04/19/walmart-launches-project-gigaton-to-reduce-emissions-in-companys-supply-chain accessed Dec 2 2017.
8 Ibid.
9 CEO 2004–2010 as well as Executive Chair from 2008–2011.
10 Authors' interview, Sept 5th 2017.
11 M&S Plan A Report 2017, http://planareport.marksandspencer.com/ accessed Dec 2 2017.
12 "M&S LAUNCHES PLAN A 2025 – AN AMBITIOUS, CUSTOMER FOCUSED SUSTAINABILITY PLAN," Press Release, June 1 2017, https://corporate.marksandspencer.com/media/press-releases/2017/plan-a-2025 accessed Dec 2 2017.
13 Authors' interview, Sept 5th 2017.
14 Ibid.
15 Ibid.
16 Ibid.
17 Ibid.
18 Chappell B., "World's Largest Battery Is Turned On In Australia As Tesla Ties Into Power Grid," NPR, December 1, 2017, www.npr.org/sections/thetwo-way/2017/12/01/567710447/worlds-largest-battery-is-turned-on-in-australia-as-tesla-ties-into-power-grid accessed Dec 2 2017.
19 Musk E., "The Secret Tesla Motors Master Plan (just between you and me)," Tesla Blogs, Aug 2nd 2006, www.tesla.com/en_CA/blog/secret-tesla-motors-master-plan-just-between-you-and-me?redirect=no
20 Musk E., "Master Plan, Part Deux," Tesla Blogs, July 20th 2016, www.tesla.com/en_CA/blog/master-plan-part-deux?redirect=no
21 Tesla Gigafactory www.tesla.com/gigafactory accessed Nov 30 2017.
22 Krauss C., "Shell, to Cut Carbon Output, Will Be Less of an Oil Company," *New York Times* Nov 28th 2017, www.nytimes.com/2017/11/28/business/energy-environment/shell-carbon-oil.html accessed Nov 29 2017.
23 An increasing number of firms are defining their science-based targets with reference to, and registering them with, the Science Based Targets Initiative. This champions science-based target setting as a powerful way of boosting companies' competitive advantage in the transition to the low-carbon economy.
   It is a collaboration between CDP (formerly the Carbon Disclosure Project), World Resources Institute (WRI), the World Wide Fund for Nature (WWF), and the United Nations Global Compact (UNGC) and one of the We Mean Business coalition commitments, http://sciencebasedtargets.org/about-the-science-based-targets-initiative/ accessed Feb 11 2018.
   The telecoms company BT, for example, is now setting itself on the path to help limit global warming to 1.5 °C through a new science-based target to reduce emissions by 87% by 2030 against a 2016/17 baseline, after reaching a carbon target four years ahead of schedule.

5   Culture

"Coming together is a beginning; keeping together is progress; working together is success."

Henry Ford

Our third attribute is Culture. Culture underpins Purpose, enables the successful implementation of Plan, supports and enhances Collaboration, and lends authority and credibility to organizational Advocacy.

Enablers

The essential enablers of Culture are:

- Building on organizational heritage and values
- Being clear, consistent, transparent, open and responsive, and building trust
- Promoting, recognizing, and rewarding behaviors and performance from top management down that reflect the desired Culture
- Engaging and empowering; supporting innovation and learning; reinforcing accountability and ethics; and fostering diversity and inclusion.

Defining Culture

Culture is an elusive concept. As author Phillip Barlag writes: "Culture is a tricky subject. It's intangible, and when something is hard to define, it's hard to address, improve, or measure."[1] With Purpose, Culture defines what a leading sustainability organization *is* and *how* it goes about what it does. Plan, Collaboration, and Advocacy on the other hand are more on the doing side, about the action. Purpose and Plan can be perfectly defined, but without the right Culture, execution is fiendishly difficult.

Academic definitions refer to culture as the "shared assumptions and values as well as expected behaviours and symbols."[2] An organization's Culture guides the decisions of its members by establishing and reinforcing expectations about what is valued and how things should be done. Over time, an organization builds up its own Culture, providing a sense of identity to its members about "who we are" and "what we do." Famously, Culture is "the way we do business around here." Equally famously – although usually erroneously attributed – "culture eats strategy for breakfast."[3] Culture and values are an often overlooked part of the ultimate accountabilities of the board.[4]

Culture in the early days

Organizations acquire and then develop a Culture from their earliest beginnings. Despite that, there was little discussion of Culture in the early years that the Leaders Survey was running. That does not mean that it did not exist, but simply that it was not generally something that got a lot of attention in sustainability circles. Perhaps unsurprisingly, the priority in those days was more about getting issues such as climate change, pollution, human rights, and sweatshops on corporate agendas; then persuading companies to pay attention to them. Perhaps too, in the Harm Reduction Era, the connection between sustainability and organizational Culture was less apparent.

Despite (or because of) this, companies ranked highly in the early years of the Leaders Survey were often ones that could connect their specific actions around sustainability back to their prevailing organizational Culture. Indeed, it might be argued that the early leaders exhibited a variety of cultures depending on their history, early leadership, and the nature of their core activities. The Body Shop, for example, was an entrepreneurial, "seat of the pants" operation, with its anti-establishment environmental campaigning and unconventional way of doing business very much reflecting its iconoclastic founder, the late Anita Roddick.

In contrast, Shell had a much more disciplined Culture. Already in the 1970s it had adopted and made public a Statement of General Business Principles, which set out an explicit mandate for Corporate Responsibility. As a result, when Shell endured its "annus horribilis" in 1995 – first the Brent Spar fiasco (a high-profile Greenpeace campaign to stop Shell's planned disposal of a redundant North Sea installation by sinking it in deep waters), and then alleged complicity in the judicial murder of Ken Saro-Wiwa and other Ogoni activists in Nigeria – there was widespread concern amongst Shell employees that they seemed to have badly misjudged popular expectations of business. Instead of pulling up the drawbridge, Shell commissioned external agents to conduct a year-long, global consultation with thought leaders and stakeholders from civil society, trade unions, academia, governments, and other businesses. The consultation exposed the top leadership to these external voices across the world in a series of no holds barred roundtables. The conclusions were distilled in a seminal speech by the then Shell chief Cor Herkstroter in October 1996.[5] They became the basis for Shell's commitment to "People, Profit, Planet"; sustainability reporting; a series of specific social, environmental and economic programs; and the appointment of their first global sustainability director – former Shell country manager Tom Delfgaauw.

Jessica Uhl, Shell's Chief Financial Officer, described what Shell's culture means to her: "I thought of Shell as a company that I would want to work for; that I could be proud to work for given its values and the way that it approached societal level issues. I don't think I would have necessarily ended up in any oil and gas company. I think this company made a difference in terms of my own relationship to the industry and ultimately my commitment to it."[6]

Chad Holliday described to us how DuPont had driven a commitment to sustainability through the operating businesses in the early years:

> At least once a year, sometimes twice, we'd review the whole strategic plan of each of our about forty different business units. Linda (Fisher)[7] would sit in, and I would sit in periodically, and what that did was create champions inside the business. A lot of them (the champions) came out of R&D but sometimes it was manufacturing, or marketing or the sales group. We let the natural champions emerge. Then we would see if the general manager needed a little bit of coaching, or the finance leader needed a little bit of help. What we found was you got a lot more done that way, rather than just setting goals and ordering people to do it.[8]

Cultural clashes

As companies merged and acquired, there was sometimes a mélange of cultures even within the same legal entity. One under-explored question about the fall from sustainability (and market) grace of the long-cited Leaders Survey company BP is how a Culture clash contributed to the Texas City refinery fire, the Alaskan pipeline accident, and ultimately to the company's near-death experience after the Deepwater Horizon disaster in the Gulf of Mexico in 2010. It has been suggested that the original BP Culture, corporate HQ apparently expected pushback from the field if managers there felt proposed budget cuts were going too far. In contrast, the prevailing corporate Culture in both ARCO and ARAMCO (which BP acquired in the 1990s) was reputedly that, even if the field felt HQ was cutting back into operational muscle rather than fat, it would just shrug and defer to the authority of HQ.

There was a bold attempt in 2000 to create a new narrative for BP and start to build a new, common Culture. This was "Beyond Petroleum," discussed in Chapter 2. Over the years, each of the three authors of this book have spoken to individuals who were either inside BP or working with the company at the time of Beyond Petroleum and the years thereafter. From these disparate conversations, it seems that Beyond Petroleum quickly came to mean different things to different people. It was clearly always much more than changing the name from "British Petroleum" to "BP" and a re-branding exercise (replacing the old BP shield – which was viewed negatively in some markets – in favor of a stylized yellow sun with green edges that could just as easily have been a flower). For some, it represented a statement of intent. Having broken ranks with the rest of the oil industry by accepting the reality of man-made climate change and embracing the Kyoto Protocol, then CEO John Browne was already signaling a new BP commitment to renewable energy. BP was going to become an energy company, not only an oil business.

Not everyone inside BP was enthusiastic. Some, both inside and outside, misunderstood the extent of the commitment. It is easy to forget now, but back in the early 2000s, John Browne and Beyond Petroleum attracted idealistic, talented young people to work for BP, much as Paul Polman and the Sustainable Living Plan attract talent to Unilever today. According to the renowned educational psychologist Howard Gardner, BP became a "learning company," ". . . for example, BP executives spent a great deal of time in strategy sessions – reflecting on the current state of the petroleum industry as well as the opportunities available, the possible pitfalls, and alternative courses of action."[9]

BP also invested in renewables. According to John Browne many years later:

> Most importantly of all, BP changed the debate on climate change. With Shell, it led the oil industry from a position of vehement denial to an acceptance that the status quo was unsustainable. Today every international oil company acknowledges man-made climate change. Instead of arguing with the energy sector over the science, governments and NGOs can now concentrate on working with industry to develop solutions. It was this realisation that Big Oil must move towards a low carbon world that motivated me to change the firm's tagline to Beyond Petroleum.

Browne added, however, that:

> In hindsight this went further than the public could then accept. It was a mistake to push so hard. Beyond Petroleum should have been a sub-heading, not a main line. The renaming symbolised the shortcomings in our climate strategy. In essence, the company had got ahead of itself and ahead of where industry and government were willing to go at that time. Beyond Petroleum was never meant to be literal – not yet, anyway – but there was still too much of a gap between the aspiration and reality, which I now regret. The actions we took were bold, but they could have been bolder. Ultimately that was my fault, and the barriers I failed to overcome provide a useful lesson for today's CEOs as they attempt to change the status quo.[10]

Browne's commitment did not outlast him. His successor, Tony Hayward, swiftly dismantled the BP renewables business, famously observing in a lecture at Stanford Business School in 2009 that, when he became CEO, BP had "too many people working to save the world."[11] BP's Culture had not been lastingly changed. Nevertheless, the importance of Browne's Advocacy both at the time and since should not be underestimated, as we discuss further in the Advocacy Chapter.

The power of heritage

Where an organization has been able to retain the spirit of a powerful founder's Culture, emphasizing societal purpose and responsibility to what we now call "stakeholders," this has proved an enduring quality – an intangible but amazingly valuable asset. One such company is Tata Group, which has ranked in the Leaders Survey amongst Asian respondents for several years. Tata is a conglomerate spanning more than 100 companies (such as Jaguar Land Rover and the Taj hotels chain) that does business in 150 countries around the world. By Asian standards, Tata is a veritable newcomer – celebrating only its 150th anniversary in 2018.[12]

Dr. Mukund Rajan, Chairman, Tata Global Sustainability Council told us:

> In many Tata offices and plants, you will see a very famous quote of our founder Jamsetji Tata, which actually tells you about the way we think about the role of corporates and business in the community. The quote states:
>
> "In a free enterprise, the community is not just another stakeholder in the business, but is in fact the very purpose of its existence."
>
> So for us it has always been an article of faith in that the way you think about business, you have to look at the way you are responsive to what the community needs. If you do not have the community supporting you, you will not have critical stakeholder groups who are essential for your survival, not just your customers but indeed other groups including the people who work for you, investors in your corporation and so on. So that is the starting point for the way we have thought about our role within the community and our responsibility, not just in the social sense, but also in respect and care for the environment. . . . The tone at the top and the commitment to the long term and the tremendous legacy that we have had from the time of our founder, which has inspired and continues to inspire the business philosophy, all of these have integrated very nicely in more recent years into such things as our code of conduct and into the commitments that we make when we enter the Tata Brand Equity and Business Promotion agreements.[13]

Other things, of course, have contributed to this enduring culture, including long-term leadership: Tata has had only seven Chairmen in its 150 years. Today, Tata uses a variety of tools to maintain its Culture. These include the deployment of a sustainability team which was carved out from the Tata Business Excellence Group (TBEG), measuring and then monitoring resource consumption, particularly in connection with climate change and on water consumption; a cohort of climate and water champions; an annual global sustainability summit; a sustainability month to raise awareness; and internal competitions and widespread use of the Group intranet and webinars to share experiences and good sustainability practices across the Group.

One of the areas where Tata could have an important part to play in changing the Culture of corporations and financial markets more widely, according to Dr. Rajan is "firmly establishing the culture of long term investment – to be deployed both within the organization but also to be understood equally well by the outside stakeholders. So Tata has been a founding member of Focusing Capital on the Long Term (FCLT), an initiative to encourage long-term behaviour in business and investment decision making."

Toyota too has the advantage of family business heritage and long-term focus. Stephan Herbst, Toyota Motor Europe's Technical General Manager told us: "One of the challenges our Board has is to prepare the company for the next one hundred years. The Chairman [and] some of the EVPs have to come up with a concept about how can Toyota sustain in the next one hundred years? That gives a completely different perspective on how actually you do business, with which technologies and how to operate."[14] Herbst further explained:

> We are not just preparing the future for the company but also for the network, the companies who rely on Toyota. It is also part of the sustainability of the company that we don't just look at the low hanging fruit, but for solutions that help us and the supply chain sustain . . . for the next 100 years. Long-term shared destiny relationships with different stakeholders. The leaders we have had from Shoichiro Toyoda, then Cho-san,[15] until Akio Toyoda[16] today all have this long-term vision and actually their role is to give the overall guidance and strategic direction. Cho-san has fundamentally laid the foundations for the Toyota Way in the fundamental management principles. Now we want to be able to change Toyota into a mobility company.[17]

As the authors of *All In*, we have found ourselves asking a question as we have examined both the historic Leaders Survey results and some of the newer Chinese, Asian, and other fast-growing economies' businesses that are now engaging more in international sustainability fora. Will some of these businesses, if they can maintain the stewardship values and culture of their founders, become prominent in the Leaders Survey and other sustainability rankings in the 2020s?

Sustainability Culture today

According to the experts consulted for the Leaders Survey, certain dimensions of sustainability Culture stand out amongst the businesses now ranked highly. These include: innovation, engagement, intrapreneurism, transparency, openness, stewardship, ethics, responsibility, and accountability.

An **innovation** culture is essential because the business must make radical changes to what the business does and how it does it to become sustainable. **Engagement** is needed because sustainability must become everybody's business to ensure coherence and consistency in what the business does. Engagement can in some cases create **intrapreneurism** because the business wants employees with ideas to run with them to advance sustainability. **Transparency** is no longer optional. In an age of global connectivity and social media, everything is ultimately on the record, so a business might as well embrace the inevitable and capitalize on this, especially as this helps a business to be **open** to ideas and insights from both inside and outside. Sustainability also means being **responsible** and **accountable** for impacts; to do this, everyone in the organization needs an **ethical** framework, providing clarity as to how they are expected to behave.

We now explore each of these dimensions in turn, but emphasize that it is the interlinking and reinforcing between *all* of them that creates a Culture conducive to sustainability.

Innovation

Hannah Jones[18] leads Nike's Sustainable Business & Innovation team, with a goal to decouple growth from constrained resources through sustainable innovation. She explained how sustainability has become innovation in Nike and vice versa:

> We have worked to embed sustainability into the core of the Nike business for more than 10 years in order to drive collective decision-making and accountability across the company. This approach has delivered a pipeline of products, technologies, and manufacturing and business model innovations to help create our vision for a sustainable future. We have cross-functional teams of innovators, designers, engineers, scientists and others from inside and outside the company that work together. In addition to integrating into Nike's innovation strategies, we've also built a business development function that hunts partnerships, potential joint ventures, acquisitions and investment opportunities, building our muscle as a best of class innovation team. We continue to do that work today. The second piece is our belief that if innovation doesn't go to scale, it's not innovation. Anybody can be an inventor in their garage, but we aim to create breakthroughs that will improve our world – while also being better for athletes and consumers. It's about finding a solution that has the potential to obsolete the past and become the new normal.[19]

Jones has been with Nike for twenty years, so she has a deep understanding of their organization's Culture. She explained to us:

> What one does as a practitioner must be reflective of the culture and the behavior of the company. At Nike, we've grown up with a reverence for

irreverence, and we're driven by an entrepreneurial spirit. . . . When we focus on the "responsibility" of corporate responsibility, and when we keep going on about being "less bad," it doesn't capture the imagination of the company in the way that "innovate for a better world," or "be an agent of change" can. We knew that if we were going to be successful in our corporate culture, we had to harness the inventiveness and the innovation genes in the company. So, we got rid of the title of corporate responsibility. We actually held a wake at a jazz bar over whiskey, to say goodbye to corporate responsibility and welcome "sustainable business and innovation."[20]

But she also nuanced the sustainable innovation Culture they are trying to build in Nike:

I think one of the misplaced notions out there is that innovators do best when they are just allowed to wander about and be creative. Frank Gehry the architect once said: "Give me a timeline and a budget, and I do my best work." So I have this kind of guiding principle, which is that for every act of creativity that I am trying to stimulate, there is a constraint that has to be put on people as well. I think designers and innovators do best when they have a tight constraint around them and when their performance is measured.[21]

Engagement and intrapreneurism

Daniel Pink wrote in his remarkable book *Drive* about what motivates people, saying it boils down to three things. "It's about autonomy, the desire to steer your own ship; it's about mastery, the ability to be able to steer that ship well; and it's about purpose, knowing that your journey has some wider, broader meaning."[22] Engagement also requires that people feel they are treated fairly; that they are listened to; and that they are cared for.

Google is a company that has been built on a culture of radical, constant innovation. In 2017, it topped the *Fortune* "Best Places to Work" list for the sixth year in a row. A range of programs and benefits help foster what employees say is a "safe and inclusive" workplace at this hive of high performers.[23] Employees can make use of any of a number of channels of expression to communicate their ideas and thoughts. These include Google+ conversations, a wide variety of surveys, Fixits (24-hour sprints wholly dedicated to fixing a specific problem), TGIF's (Google's weekly all-hands meetings, where employees ask questions directly to the company's top leaders and other executives about any number of company issues), and even direct emails to any of the Google leaders.[24] Employees are empowered (both equipped and encouraged) to take initiative and bring forward new ideas. Google provides its employees with 20% of their work time to be spent on their own projects.

One of us (David) has previously written about the potential of social intrapreneurs, who are:

> People within a large corporation who take direct initiative for innovations that address social or environmental challenges while also creating commercial value for the company. . . . They leverage existing infrastructures and organisational capabilities to deliver social value on a large scale. . . . Social intrapreneurs aim to generate entirely new forms of commercial value through significant innovations in products, services, processes or business models for their employers.[25]

Social intrapreneurism is likely to be a powerful extra force driving progress toward the UN Sustainable Development Goals.[26] Some companies are now putting selected employees through Intrapreneur Labs and other training programs, running "Dragon's Den" style competitions where intrapreneurs can pitch their ideas, and have established Intrapreneurs' Innovation Funds. Google was one of the first companies to send young leaders with intrapreneurial potential to the Aspen Institute for Business & Society's First Movers program.[27] Several well-known Google products originated with intrapreneurs including Google News, Gmail, AdSense, driverless cars, Google Glass, and the pioneering use of Google mapping tools to help landmine clearance and to prevent illegal logging.

Transparency and openness

When we ask what is driving businesses around the world to take more responsibility for their environmental, social, and economic impacts, one thing that is invariably mentioned is social media and intensifying global connectivity. Don Tapscott discusses this in his book *The Naked Corporation*.[28] He argues that if businesses are going to be naked, then they had better be buff! In this context, "buff" means being responsible, coherent, and consistent in the way they do business.

Another element of a sustainability Culture, therefore, is fast becoming a willingness to embrace transparency. Over the lifetime of the Leaders Survey, we have seen an explosion not just in the percentage of large companies producing annual sustainability reports, but also in their quality and rigor. The consulting firm KPMG has tracked the trends in corporate responsibility reporting since 1993. In their latest analysis they conclude that: "Corporate Responsibility reporting is standard practice for large and mid-cap companies around the world. Around three quarters of the companies studied in this survey issue CR reports."[29]

Companies such as Nike and M&S now publish details of all their suppliers' factories. SC Johnson's "What's Inside" initiative[30] publishes comprehensive details of all its product ingredients. Companies like Legal & General, the insurance giant, publish exhaustive details of and rationale for their corporate tax strategy.

For all their imperfections and susceptibility to "free-rider" criticisms, the explosion of standards, certification schemes, and industry codes of practice are also contributing to the inexorable growth of this culture of transparency. We also see transparency becoming more common in the actions of corporate sustainability leaders. For example, Google's Executive Chairman shares with all Google staff practically the same material that the Board of Directors saw at their most recent meeting, including launch plans and product roadmaps.[31] Rick Ridgeway shared his view that Patagonia has only been able to achieve all that it has because it has always remained a family-owned business and had the freedom to pursue long-term strategies including transparency, which he suggests encourages innovation.

> In our internal operations, top management will work as a group, and with maximum transparency. This includes an "open book" policy that enables employees easy access to decisions within normal boundaries of personal privacy and "trade secrecy." At all levels of corporate activity, we encourage open communications, a collaborative atmosphere, and maximum simplicity while we simultaneously seek dynamism and innovation.[32, 33]

Transparency alone, of course, is of limited value without a parallel commitment to engage with critics; what John Browne, the former CEO of BP describes in his 2015 book *Connect* as "radically engaging."[34] Other sustainability leaders also share openly. Tesla made its battery technologies available to competitors: According to Elon Musk in June 2014, "Tesla will not initiate patent lawsuits against anyone who, in good faith, wants to use our technology."[35] Another example is GSK sharing its compounds library with other bona fide researchers.[36] We recognize in some cultures such transparency represents more of a stretch. It is going to be fascinating to see how corporate cultures of transparency and accountability develop in societies with less of a tradition of either transparency or accountability.

Transparency can enhance openness if a business is receptive to ideas from disparate sources from outside as well as inside an organization. As author and sustainability facilitator Phillip Barlag writes:

> The best companies often are the ones that know that they still have a lot to learn. Only by letting go of the need to be seen as the best can companies have enough collective humility to build a culture of learning and intellectual curiosity. Bring fresh perspectives into your company to keep the ideas flowing.[37]

We are struck by how many of the top ranked companies in the Leaders Survey have some form of regular forum to listen to critical voices and gather external insights. Nestlé, for example, has had an annual convening with civil society since 2012.[38] Novo Nordisk has run a similar event since the

1990s.[39] Similarly, a number of companies such as M&S and Unilever have Sustainability Advisory Panels to advise their boards and senior management teams. Syngenta CEO Eric Fyrwald repeatedly emphasized the range and frequency of the dialogues that he and his senior colleagues have with NGOs on critical issues affecting the business. For example, Syngenta and the Nature Conservancy have worked together over the past decade in Brazil and the United States on nutrient stewardship, floodplain restoration, and habitat enhancement. They are now expanding this work to improve the environmental footprint of Syngenta's products and services while also building unprecedented access to the agriculture community to drive agricultural sustainability more broadly.

Transparency, of course, also has to be coupled to a readiness and willingness to rectify poor corporate behavior. Nevertheless, transparency is a *sine qua non* for a truly engaged Culture.

Ethics, responsibility, and accountability – shared values

The final dimension – but in many respects the most fundamental – is an ethical lens capable of guiding principles for decision-making. For many companies, the ten principles of the UN Global Compact[40] provide such a framework.

> By incorporating the Ten Principles of the UN Global Compact into strategies, policies and procedures, and establishing a culture of integrity, companies are not only upholding their basic responsibilities to people and planet, but also setting the stage for long-term success.[41]

Others, like Shell, developed their own framework internally. Sir Mark Moody-Stuart told us:

> We had very advanced business principles going back to the 1970s talking about Shell's responsibilities to what would now be called stakeholders (our customers, employees, suppliers, wider communities, governments and shareholders). No one took priority. It was the job of management to balance all the requirements, and to our shareholders it said it was our responsibility to deliver an acceptable return and protect the value of their investment. I still to this day think it is a very good expression for summarizing what a company's responsibilities are. . . . These (Shell General Business Principles) were well penetrated in the company . . .[42]

In 1991, Patagonia found itself expanding too quickly in a recession. It almost went bust and 20% of staff had to be laid off. Part of the rebuilding was through the articulation of Patagonia's values and the development of a series of "Philosophies" covering design, production, marketing, distribution, finance and values, HR, management, and the environment. Yvon

Chouinard started to lead week-long camping trips for employees to train them in the company's philosophies. As Chouinard writes in his memoirs:

> The goal was to teach every employee in the company our business and environmental ethics and values. When money finally got so tight we couldn't even afford buses [to take employees to places like Yosemite], we camped in the local Los Padres National Forest, but we kept training.[43]

Patagonia deemed the training crucial. "If all employees share a common understanding of the organization's values and are well trained in what it means to apply those values," write academics Mette Morsing and Dennis Oswald, "they will not have to look to formal policies nor will they be engaging in guesswork to decide how to respond to novel and/or 'sticky' problems"[44]

The passion continues today at Patagonia. "In the 45 years I have been hanging out here, I have never seen this company on fire as much as it is right now . . ." says Ridgeway. "It is fierce and it is committed to being more and more fiercely bold. . . . People are rolling up their sleeves and saying we are going to do everything we can to turn this around, and boy do people here really mean it. We would never be able to be where we are at now if it wasn't for the Chouinard's commitment to use the company for that."[45]

Being responsible is clearly easier if there is a powerful and positive heritage on which to draw to inspire and explain the company's commitment. This can particularly help in times of adversity. Stuart Rose – the CEO who launched the original M&S Plan A for Sustainability in January 2007 – was asked at the height of the Global Financial Crisis a year later whether he would continue with it. "If we don't," he replied, "why should we ever be trusted again?"[46]

Conclusion

A Culture of sustainability is "one in which organizational members hold shared assumptions and beliefs about the importance of balancing economic efficiency, social equity, and environmental accountability. Organizations with strong cultures of sustainability strive to support a healthy environment and improve the lives of others while continuing to operate successfully over the long term."[47]

We believe each enduring sustainable Culture will involve all the dimensions of innovation, engagement and intrapreneurism, transparency and openness, an ethical core of responsibility and accountability, and intergenerationality, i.e., being good stewards.

Notes

1 Barlag, P., "Five Ways to Create a Culture of Sustainability in Any Culture," *Fast Company*, Oct 17, 2013, www.fastcompany.com/3020115/5-ways-to-create-a-culture-of-sustainability-in-any-company accessed Dec 3 2017.
2 Network for Business Sustainability, Systematic Review: Organizational Culture, https://nbs.net/p/systematic-review-organizational-culture-c19ebd3b-51ff-4c61-865d-9ec4f3154a8f

3 Frequently attributed to Peter Drucker but should perhaps be attributed instead to Marc Bard, MD, CEO of the Bard Group, 2002 and popularized in 2006 by Mark Fields of Ford Motor Company, www.quora.com/Did-Peter-Drucker-actually-say-culture-eats-strategy-for-breakfast-and-if-so-where-when accessed Dec 3 2017.

4 Corporate Culture and the Role of Boards, Financial Reporting Council, 2016, www.frc.org.uk/directors/the-culture-project accessed Feb 11 2018.
    See also Grayson, D. and Kakabadse, A., "Towards a Sustainability Mindset: How Boards Organise Oversight and Governance of Corporate Responsibility 2013," *Business in the Community*, www.bitc.org.uk/resources-training/research/towards-sustainability-mindset-how-boards-organise-oversight-and accessed Feb 11 2018.

5 Dealing with contradictory expectations – the dilemmas facing multinationals. Herkstroter, C.A.J. (Shell International Limited, London, 1996) speech, The Hague, Oct 11th 1996.

6 Authors' interview, Oct 3rd 2017.

7 Head of Sustainability who became the world's first Chief Sustainability Officer in 2004 – see Chapter 11 Individual Leadership below page X.

8 Authors' interview, Aug 21st 2017.

9 Gardner, H., *Changing Minds: The Art and Science of Changing Our Own and Other Peoples Minds (Leadership for the Common Good)*. Harvard Business Review Press, 2004.

10 Stadlen, T., Nuttal, R. and Browne, J., *Connect: How Companies Succeed by Engaging Radically with Society* (2015), WH Allen.

11 Hayward, T., "Entrepreneurial Spirit Needed: Tony Hayward," *British Petroleum Stanford Graduate School of Business*, 2009, www.youtube.com/watch?v=FwQM00clxgM accessed Jan 31 2018.

12 Goyder, M., *Living Tomorrow's Company: Rediscovering the Human Purpose of Business* (2013), Knowledge Partners: see in particular, reference to Funabashi, H., *Timeless Ventures* (2009), Tata McGraw Hill: There are 600 companies in Japan more than 300 years old; 30 over 500 years old; 5 of over 1000 years.

13 Authors' interview, Nov 3rd 2017.

14 Authors' interview, Jan 22nd 2018.

15 Cho-san – Fujio Cho was only the second outsider to head Toyota.

16 Akio Toyoda, grandson of Toyota founder Kiichiro Toyoda, became CEO of Toyota in 2009, https://newsroom.toyota.co.jp/en/corporate/companyinformation/officer/operating_officer/akio_toyoda.html

17 Ibid.

18 Hannah Jones is the long-serving NIKE Inc.'s Chief Sustainability Officer and VP Innovation Accelerator.

19 Authors' interview, Oct 19th 2017.

20 Ibid.

21 Ibid.

22 *Drive: The Surprising Truth about What Motivates Us* – 2011 Paperback by Daniel H. Pink (Riverhead Books).

23 "Fortune 100 Companies Best Companies to Work For," http://fortune.com/best-companies/google/ accessed Jan 14 2018.

24 "The Google Way of Motivating Employees," Sept 25th 2014, www.cleverism.com/google-way-motivating-employees/

25 Grayson, D., McLaren, M. and Spitzeck, H., *Social Intrapreneurism and All That Jazz: How Business Innovators Are Helping to Build a More Sustainable World* (2014), Greenleaf Publishing.

26 For a succinct encapsulation of the business case for encouraging intrapreneurism see Pinchot, G., Memo to the CEO, Nov 2017, www.pinchot.com/2017/11/memo-to-the-ceo.html accessed Feb 11 2018.

27 Seth Marbin, 2011 First Movers program; Therese Lee, 2013; Renée DuPree, 2015, https://assets.aspeninstitute.org/content/uploads/2017/03/First-Movers-Fellowship-Project-Statements.2009-2016-Classes.pdf
   Samantha Hennessey, 2017.
28 Tapscott, D., *The Naked Corporation: How the Age of Transparency Will Revolutionize Business* (2012), Free Press.
29 The Road Ahead the KPMG Survey of Corporate Responsibility Reporting 2017, https://home.kpmg.com/content/dam/kpmg/campaigns/csr/pdf/CSR_Reporting_2017.pdf
30 SC Johnson, "What is Inside," www.whatsinsidescjohnson.com/gb/en accessed Dec 3 2017.
31 "The Google Way of Motivating Employees," Sept 25th 2014, www.cleverism.com/google-way-motivating-employees/
32 Authors' interview, Aug 31st 2018.
33 Extract from Patagonia's Values, drafted by Jerry Mander, adopted by its first board in 1991 and quoted in Chouinard, Y., *Let My People Go Surfing: The Education of a Reluctant Businessman*, 2nd edition (2016), Penguin, p. 63.
34 Browne, J., Nuttall, R. and Stadlen, T., *Connect: How Companies Succeed by Engaging Radically with Society* (2015), WH Allen.
35 Musk E., "All Our Patent Are Belong To You," Tesla Blogs, June 12, 2014, www.tesla.com/en_GB/blog/all-our-patent-are-belong-you accessed Jan 14 2018.
36 "GSK Announces 'Open Innovation' Strategy to Help Deliver New and Better Medicines for People Living in the World's Poorest Countries," GSK Press Releases, Jan 19, 2010, www.gsk.com/en-gb/media/press-releases/gsk-announces-open-innovation-strategy-to-help-deliver-new-and-better-medicines-for-people-living-in-the-world-s-poorest-countries/ accessed Jan 14 2018.
   Barlag, P., "Five Ways to Create a Culture of Sustainability in Any Culture," *Fast Company*, Oct 17, 2013, www.fastcompany.com/3020115/5-ways-to-create-a-culture-of-sustainability-in-any-company accessed Dec 3 2017.
38 Full disclosure: Mark's employer, SustainAbility, organizes these annual convenings.
39 Also originally organized by SustainAbility.
40 The **Ten Principles** of the **United Nations Global Compact** are derived from: the Universal Declaration of Human Rights, the International Labour Organization's Declaration on Fundamental **Principles** and Rights at Work, the Rio Declaration on Environment and Development, and the **United Nations** Convention Against Corruption, www.unglobalcompact.org/what-is-gc/mission/principles accessed Feb 8 2018.
41 The Power of Principles, UN Global Compact, www.unglobalcompact.org/what-is-gc/mission/principles
42 Authors' interview, Sept 19th 2017.
43 Chouinard, Y., *Let My People Go Surfing: The Education of a Reluctant Businessman*, 2nd edition (2016), Penguin, p. 66.
44 Morsing, M. and Oswald, D., "Sustainable Leadership: Management Control Systems and Organizational Culture in Novo Nordisk A/S," *Corporate Governance*, Vol. 9, No. 1, 2009, pp. 83–99. [Google Scholar] [Link] [Infotrieve], p. 85.
45 Authors' interview, Aug 31st 2017.
46 Rose, S., *Cranfield Lecture*, Cranfield School of Management Oct 2008.
47 Bertels S., Papania L., & Papania D., "Embedding Sustainability in Organizational Culture: A Systematic Review of the Body of Knowledge," Canada: Network for Business Sustainability, 2010, https://nbs.net/p/systematic-review-organizational-culture-c19ebd3b-51ff-4c61-865d-9ec4f3154a8f

6 Collaboration

"Alone we can do so little; together we can do so much."

Helen Keller

Our fourth attribute is Collaboration. Collaboration is aligned with and extends Purpose, supports the attainment of Plan, reflects organizational Culture, and enables Advocacy.

Enablers

The essential enablers of Collaboration are:

- Matching company and partner objectives within appropriate Collaboration opportunities
- Finding the required balance among Collaboration partners in terms of depth of commitment and abilities including time and other resources, skills, authority, and status to contribute to and ensure effectiveness
- Mapping the necessary theory of change and understanding required to achieve outcomes/bring about desired change
- Providing the required organizational input and commitment from top management and appropriate experts
- Identifying the best forms of partnership (e.g., B2B or multi-stakeholder) and ideal structure (e.g., Knowledge Network, Standard Setter or Delivery Network)
- Ensuring robust governance as well as effective facilitation/brokerage as required
- Modeling appropriate mindset/approach including patience, humility, and hunger for solutions
- Monitoring the external environment to identify, e.g., that pre-competitive collaborations do not breach competition laws.

Understanding collaboration

The top-ranked companies in the Leaders Survey have been at the forefront of creating and/or leading an increasingly complex and sophisticated range of Collaboration to improve their own, and society's, resilience. Some of these collaborations are B2B; others also involve civil society, governments, public agencies, and academia. Whilst the initial focus of the oldest collaborations, the early Corporate Responsibility Coalitions, was on mobilizing corporate community involvement to tackle social exclusion, this quickly evolved into tackling issues affecting core business operations.

Increasingly, collaborations can have a number of different functions. These include:

- To identify and disseminate good practices and encourage more businesses to adopt them
- To set and subsequently certify collective, self-regulatory standards
- To pool R&D efforts to innovate sustainable solutions to specified problems
- To create a "safe space" to explore pressing business or societal and ethical dilemmas
- To advocate jointly for public policy supportive of sustainable development
- To tackle the systemic challenges inherent to sustainability.

Early-stage collaboration

Businesses banding together to learn from each other and to press their interests is nothing new: think of medieval guilds or chambers of commerce. Since the 1980s, business-led corporate responsibility (CR) coalitions have galvanized action on economic regeneration, social inclusion, and responsible business practices.[1] Business in the Community, established in 1981 in the UK, for example, has gotten member companies, including founding members such as M&S, Unilever, and Shell, to act collectively on issues such as employability, homelessness, enterprise promotion, and, more recently, on issues like mental health in the workplace.

From the early 1990s onwards, several new CR coalitions emerged such as Business for Social Responsibility (BSR), CSR Europe, the International Business Leaders Forum (IBLF) and the World Business Council for Sustainable Development (WBCSD). These four – and later, the UN Global Compact – helped to build a global network of responsible business coalitions. These became more important as companies expanded their operations in different parts of the world – especially in regions undergoing dramatic transformation such as Eastern Europe. These coalitions became a vehicle to demonstrate that incoming companies wanted to be good corporate citizens, contribute to economic and social development, and build local relationships. They also often showed new, in-country entrepreneurs that this was part of doing business responsibly. BSR, in which many top-ranked Leaders Survey businesses have been active members over the years, for example, quickly evolved from a lobbying group of smaller, progressive businesses into a network to identify and promote global responsible business practices – not least as North

American headquartered companies moved manufacturing operations off-shore and had to assume greater responsibility for extended supply chains.

There were also early, isolated examples of industry- and issue-specific collaborations. After the Bhopal disaster in India, when a chemical plant exploded, killing hundreds immediately and many more subsequently, the chemical industry including Dow and DuPont came together to develop and promote the Responsible Care standard. The Body Shop was an early supporter of the fair trade movement. Unilever teamed up with the World Wildlife Federation (WWF) in 1996 to launch the Marine Stewardship Council to develop sustainable fishing standards and a certification scheme. BP and Shell were amongst the founders of the Extractive Industries Transparency Initiative, which began as a campaign to encourage extractive companies to publish details of the taxes and royalties they paid to individual governments, and has evolved to become a global standard to promote the open and accountable management of oil, gas, and mineral resources.

Developing collaboration from the Harm Reduction Era to the Strategic Integration Era

Increasingly, generalist corporate responsibility coalitions, open to businesses from any industry and tackling a range of responsible business issues, have been supplemented by collaborations focused on particular industry sectors, or on specific issues including water or human rights. These issue-specific and industry-specific coalitions of companies include the CEO Water Mandate and the Better Cotton Initiative.

In addition, some of the leading international corporate responsibility coalitions (BSR, CSR Europe, and WBCSD) also now support specialist industry coalitions such as Better Coal (BSR); European Automotive Working Group on Supply Chain Sustainability (CSR Europe), which has now evolved into Drive Sustainability;[2] and the Tire Industry Project (WBCSD).

Many of these collaborative ventures served to pool existing knowledge and identify and disseminate good practice. Some provide a safe space for participants to explore business-society dilemmas. Vodafone, for example, established the "Telecommunications Industry Dialogue on Freedom of Expression and Privacy," after its difficulties in Egypt in early 2011, when the former Mubarak regime forced it and other mobile phone providers first to take down their networks, then to restore them – but to transmit only pro-regime messages. By collaborating with other telecom companies, the hope is that it will help them prepare better for any similar events in the future.

In some cases, companies began collaborating with competitors as well as NGOs and public sector bodies, to develop new technological solutions to address specific problems. Refrigerants Naturally, for example, brought together Unilever, Coca-Cola, PepsiCo, and Red Bull in an alliance with Greenpeace and the UN Environment Programme (UNEP), to develop more sustainable refrigeration technologies.

Some collaborations have been designed to give companies a "seat at the table" to co-create future regulation and the infrastructure to support this. BMW and other European automakers realized that enlightened self-interest was a good thing, giving them a chance to help shape the direction of EU Extended Producer Responsibility regulations that now require all auto companies selling cars in Europe to take back their cars at the end of their life. Savings from their investments in designing cars to be remanufactured and effective disassembly infrastructures are now in the hundreds of millions of dollars annually. BMW took a leadership role first amongst German automakers and then across Europe.[3] It took almost ten years for a team of negotiators from BMW and EU regulators to complete the End of Vehicle Lifetime directive in 2004. It required continual education around the practical realities of car design, production, and recovery. The prize was that participating automakers – by having a seat at the table – had time to redesign their vehicles for easy disassembly and recycling.

Several business representative organizations such as the Consumer Goods Forum (CGF)[4] are also increasingly facilitating collaboration for sustainability among their members (see Figure 6.1). M&S and Unilever have led a growing

Figure 6.1 Five Strategic Initiatives of the Consumer Goods Forum

CGF focus on sustainability since it was created in 2009. Unusually for a trade association, CGF works with its members at a pre-competitive stage so that they can improve their business efficiency while driving positive change for the planet and its people. Nestlé leads the CGF health pillar. CGF members have committed, for example, to halve food waste globally by 2025.[5]

The Ellen MacArthur Foundation coordinates the CE (circular economy) 100 network of companies and partners, addressing the challenges of switching from the old linear model of "take, make, use and waste." The CE 100 is a pre-competitive innovation program established to enable organizations to develop new opportunities and realize their circular economy ambitions faster. It brings together corporates, governments, cities, academic institutions, emerging innovators, and affiliates in a unique multi-stakeholder platform. Specially developed program elements help members learn, build capacity, network, and collaborate with key organizations working on the circular economy. It includes several Leaders Survey ranked companies including Dow, Google, IKEA, M&S, Unilever, and Walmart.

In recent years, collaborations have been established to advocate for pro-sustainable development public policy. The insurance company Aviva Investors convened the Corporate Sustainability Reporting Coalition to influence the UN Rio+20 Sustainability Summit in 2012 in favor of greater reporting requirements for businesses on their social, environmental, and economic impacts, and helped in shaping an EU directive on this topic. Similarly, the We Mean Business initiative is a coalition of seven leading corporate responsibility and sustainability groups including BSR and WBCSD. Its objective is "catalyzing business action and driving policy ambition to accelerate the low-carbon transition."[6]

In 2009, Patagonia and Walmart came together to initiate the Sustainable Apparel Coalition (SAC) to address "the urgent, systemic challenges that are impossible to change alone."[7] The Coalition's vision is of "an apparel, footwear, and textiles industry that produces no unnecessary environmental harm and has a positive impact on the people and communities associated with its activities." Rick Ridgeway from Patagonia explains SAC's theory of change

> is straightforward and profound: putting standardized sustainability in the hands of key decision-makers in the apparel and footwear value chain will incentivize them to make better decisions that collectively reduce the environmental impact and increase the social justice of the entire industry.

The rationale for SAC was spelled out in a joint letter signed by Patagonia's Yvon Chouinard and John Fleming, who was then Walmart's Chief Merchandising Officer, inviting CEOs of some of the world's biggest clothing companies to collaborate. Chouinard and Fleming wrote:

> Creating a single approach for measuring sustainability in the apparel sector will do much more than accelerate meaningful social and environmental change. Standardization will enable us to maximize sustainability benefits for all buyers

---

Figure 6.2 Sustainable Apparel Coalition

without investing in multiple sustainability technologies and certification processes and ultimately empower consumers to trust claims regarding sustainably sourced apparel. Finally, as an industry, we will benefit from the unique opportunity to shape policy and create standards for measuring sustainability before government inevitably imposes one. . . . The time is right and the need is great for the apparel sector to move forward now, without further delay, in unison, with strong partners like you.

SAC now has more than 200 members worldwide including major brands and retailers like M&S, Disney, and Burberry, manufacturers, and academic, government and NGO affiliates. At the heart of the Coalition is the Higg Index – "a suite of tools that enables brands, retailers, and facilities of all sizes – at every stage in their sustainability journey – to accurately measure and score a company or product's sustainability performance."[8]

Another top ranked Leaders Survey company, Nike, is active in the SAC, and early on was persuaded to donate the Nike Considered Index to the coalition. It became the Materials Sustainability Index, now one of the tools in the Higg Index suite.

The creation and early evolution of the SAC is well told in a short article by a leading sustainability commentator Marc Gunther. Drawing on Gunther's piece and other materials, it is possible to discern several critical success factors for SAC that are highly relevant to other business collaborations today.

- The initial pairing of Walmart and Patagonia was engineered by a trusted intermediary – Jib Ellison, the founder of consultancy BluSkye – who advised Walmart and its CEO, Lee Scott, on sustainability. Ellison is also a longtime friend of Rick Ridgeway
- Unlike conventional trade associations which typically operate at the "lowest common denominator," SAC focused on a set of companies that they were confident would want to set a high bar and move fast
- They established a rule of engagement that companies designate one person to work on the coalition and send that person to all its meetings; this ensured continuity and that individuals had authority to commit
- As with most – if not all – of the best coalitions over the years, there was a credible facilitator to hold the ring, cajole, and keep moving things forward: in this case, John Whalen, a principal at BluSkye
- At the outset, Walmart and Patagonia worked hard to attract other sustainability leaders who would make this "a club you wanted to be invited to join." Nike had to be convinced that Walmart was serious before it agreed to participate
- The initial participants took the time to build trust and to share tangible signs of their commitment. As Gunther relates: "The group held a get-acquainted dinner in New York early in 2010. Walmart's representative took them on a tour of Walmart's office and showroom in the Fashion District and reflecting 'My competitors, Target, Kohl's and J.C. Penney, couldn't believe that I was taking them around the office'"[9]
- SAC brought in critical external friends such as Michelle Harvey of the Environmental Defense Fund, as a member of the SAC's board
- They were willing to build on existing good practice such as the Nike Considered Index
- There was a clear common need and purpose: "when it came to labor and workplace issues, they had already learned how wasteful and messy it is to go it alone. Virtually all of the big apparel companies – to the dismay of their suppliers – have their own code of conduct, inspectors and reporting system. This means that a single supplier with many customers can be inspected and audited numerous times. The retailers and brands didn't want to duplicate efforts all over again when it came to setting environmental standards."[10]

Figure 6.2 (Continued)

Collaboration: a more sophisticated space today

Collaborations today serve many different functions such as: pooling R&D efforts; persuading others in an industry value-chain to change;[11] generating a critical mass of influential businesses to give authority to setting and enforcing standards; creating economic muscle to convince others to take desired action and speeding up the adoption of more sustainable practices; and/or to be a valuable interlocutor for governments and civil society.

As Al Gore has said: "We must abandon the conceit that individual, isolated, private actions are the answer. They can and do help. But they will not take us far enough without collective action. Let us say together: 'We have a purpose. We are many. For this purpose we will rise, and we will act.'"[12]

Companies wishing to collaborate on sustainable development today have no shortage of options. Indeed, the sheer number of potential collaborations can be daunting. Corporate sustainability leaders are in demand as "anchor members" for particular coalitions and initiatives. Companies, therefore, need to approach Collaboration for sustainability in the same way as other potential partnerships. What are the objectives? Which forms of Collaboration and what type of vehicle for it are most likely to be effective? Which organization can best address this?

Business-initiated and business-led collaborations are now part of a wider Collaboration "universe." Two leading international management thinkers, Don Tapscott and Roger Martin,[13] are behind a major research project, led by the Martin Prosperity Institute at the Rotman School of Management in Toronto, which is mapping and exploring the potential of what they call "Global Solution Networks" (GSN) (see Figure 6.3).[14] The GSN project has produced a taxonomy of ten different types of networks including:

- Global Standards Networks
- Governance Networks

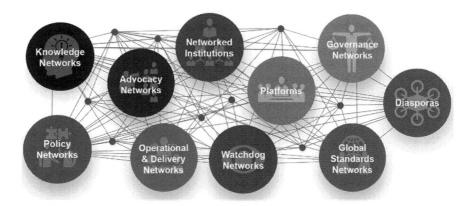

Figure 6.3 Global Solution Networks Taxonomy

- Knowledge Networks
- Watchdog Networks
- Operational and Delivery Networks[15]

Hannah Jones, Nike's global head of sustainability and innovation, has commented:

> We believe that the innovations required to create the future won't come from a single source. Not from science. Not from technology. Not from governments. Not from business. But from all of us. We must harness the collective power of unconventional partnerships to dramatically redefine the way we thrive in the future.

Her boss, Nike CEO Mark Parker, has added: "Our future depends heavily on innovation, collaboration and transparency."

Jones told us:

> I remember Simon Zadek[16] once telling me, "If all you do is create an oasis in the middle of the desert then you would have failed," and I agree with him wholeheartedly. It became very clear to us that we needed to have strategies that would act as levers with broader systems that would in turn enable us to do our work more easily. . . . If you think about the issue of working conditions in the supply chain, and the fragmented nature of our supply chain, then clearly there needs to be collaboration with other brands – in ways this very competitive industry has never collaborated before.[17]

We agree with Walmart's Kathleen McLaughlin who told us:

> We can't solve deforestation as a single company. We can't solve waste as a single company. We can't solve forced labor on our own. These are broad systemic challenges that need to be addressed through collaboration not only within the private sector but across sectors. So there isn't anything we do that doesn't involve all sectors. There is some government, some civil society, and some private sector engagement in all of these things. As a society, we need more collaboration and more effective collaboration to accelerate sustainability.[18]

We also share the view of Johnny Kwan, recently retired chairman of BASF Greater China who told us:

> Global companies must seek cooperation with newly evolved local business partners to generate new sustainability business solutions that are both global and yet local. For example, cooperating in the areas of clean energy like solar and wind. . . . My vision is [that] global leading

companies will transform not only their own business sustainability proposition, but a collective and collaborative transformation through diverse partnerships.[19]

Confronted with a plethora of corporate responsibility coalitions, multi-stakeholder initiatives, and ad hoc cooperative ventures,[20] businesses need to strategically prioritize engagement with collaborations where they can contribute and learn the most. This is especially important for the more strategic and significant collaborations that involve CEOs or other C-suite executives committing their organizations to stretch targets.

Collaboration playbook

As sustainability leaders realize that they have secured the "low hanging fruit" and they need partners for what comes next, Collaboration moves from "nice to do" to "have to do." Business then need to pay serious attention to the leadership and management skills required to make these collaborations work – both for their own employees; but also for third-party staff who may be needed to run a Collaboration as an independent entity. Some scholars and practitioners have described a whole new role of "Partnership broker," defined as:

> an active "go-between" who supports partners in navigating their collaboration journey by helping them to create a map, plan their route, choose their mode of transport and change direction when necessary. They can both "serve" and "lead" as the situation requires and as the needs of the partnership change over time.[21]

A specialist NGO, The Partnering Initiative, suggests that there are four partnership skills: understanding other sectors, technical knowledge of partnering, people and relationship skills, and, underpinning it all, a mindset for partnering. (Please see Figure 6.4.)

Companies such as Microsoft, Shell, and Nestlé have integrated partnership training into their executive development programs. For individual managers, this means acquiring additional skills. Specifically, the ability to listen actively; put yourself into other people's shoes; understand the real interests, needs, and constraints of others; the ability to communicate your organization's interests; relationship-building and trust-building; being able to distill and synthesize views, and to achieve balance between your organization's own interests and those of the partnership; being well-researched about other partners and the overall context; and having interest-based negotiating skills.

Collaborations fail for many reasons: unclear, conflicting, unrealistic goals; insufficient capacity to implement; or the absence of senior leadership and essential skills. Developing the next generation of leaders with the ability

Mindset

- Humility to realize others may have more appropriate knowledge/resources
- Inclination to reach out to work with others
- Willingness to give up autonomy of decision-making
- (Measured) risk taking
- Propensity for innovation
- Ability to work for the benefit of the partnership as a whole

Understanding other sectors

- Values and culture
- Interests
- Motivations and drivers
- Resources and capabilities
- Systems and processes
- Capacity limitations
- Legal limitations
- AND Understanding of your own!

Human/relationship Skills

- Ability to look from others' perspectives
- Networking and connecting
- Approaching and engaging potential partners/selling ideas
- Relationship/trust building
- Interest-based negotiation
- Facilitation
- Communication
- Coaching/mentoring
- Mediation/conflict resolution/troubleshooting

Technical partnering knowledge

- Understanding the partnering lifecycle
- Key principles and building blocks of partnerships
- Best practice approaches to setup and governance
- Ability to assess critically when and when not to partner
- The partnering black box of trust, equity, and power
- Partnership agreements
- Reviewing partnerships
- Exit strategies

tpi
THE
PARTNERING
INITIATIVE

Figure 6.4 M.U.S.T.-Have Partnering Competencies

to work across boundaries to tackle global challenges is a key priority. (See Chapter 11 on Individual Leadership, pages 153.)

Collaboration benefits and challenges

Competition will stimulate innovation in sustainable products, services, and business models. However, as Unilever's Paul Polman has observed: "In areas where big breakthroughs are needed, we must step up joint working with others."

Sir Mark Moody-Stuart gave us the specific example of the development of the mining supplement for the Global Reporting Initiative (GRI), the independent international organization that has pioneered sustainability reporting since 1997:

> I remember when the GRI did a mining sector supplement – that was because if you talk about waste in a mining sector GRI indicator, waste is not about how much paper you recycle, it's how many million tons of earth you leave lying around and so on and what do you do with your other forms of waste – so you need a sector supplement that standardizes the form in which mining companies should report for comparability. I spoke to the guy from BHP who ran this process and I said "How did it go?" and he said "Well, it probably took us an extra year because of the consultation with civil society; it would have been quicker if we had just done it ourselves – it had some incremental costs; we had to support the presence of civil society and fund the GRI to help do this and so on, but those were trivial." He said the enormous benefit of it was an unanimous agreement from business and civil society – so by working together you get a more solid conclusion.[22]

David Rice, BP's former Policy Director[23] argues that standard-setting collaborations like the Extractive Industries Transparency Initiative and the Voluntary Principles on Security and Human Rights[24] can help to change an industry but also help to consolidate change in the initiating companies too:

> If you change your sector, your industry, the world around you, that is a change that is very difficult to undo – if you just make a change internally, that can be undone by the next wave of leadership.
>
> The thing I am most proud of for my time at BP was the Voluntary Principles on Security and Human Rights – we made it happen. Those are now standards for oil and gas companies around the world and I have no doubt that people's lives have been saved and made less horrible by having those standards. Now whatever happens at BP – they cannot undo that because it has become a standard in the industry. There were other things as well like the EITI (Extractive Industries Transparency Initiative) – once it's out there – that's the toothpaste out of the tube – you can't get it back in.[25]

Mike Barry, Chief Sustainability Officer at M&S told us:

> When you are doing things like palm oil or low-carbon refrigeration, no one retailer, not even a Walmart or M&S can possibly move the market sufficiently to actually change it cost effectively, so there is a strength in pre-competitive, collaborative action . . . I think the businesses that will prosper in the next decade will be those that can move smoothly between collaborating one day and competing the next, and having a leadership that is comfortable with that ambiguity and uncertainty and, therefore, able to unlock advantages in different ways.[26]

As Victor Zhang from Huawei explained,

> With a global supply chain, with almost 80% of our suppliers being out of China, it is important to have a collaborative mechanism between peers from the industry, governments, and other stakeholders to address the various issues within the supply chain. We believe a supply chain is only as strong as its weakest link. That is why we require our suppliers to cascade our requirements down through the entire supply chain, with particular focus in the areas of ethics, the environment, health and safety, and labor conditions.[27]

External commentators, too, argue the benefits of collaboration:

> "Organizations," wrote Don Tapscott and Anthony Williams in *Macrowikinomics*, "that make their boundaries porous to external ideas and human capital outperform those that rely solely on their internal resources and capabilities, and outmoded ways of working."[28]

Others argue, however, that these voluntary partnerships reward free-riders that don't contribute to their development or observe the higher voluntary standards that are often a part of the membership requirements for the partnership.

Nike's Hannah Jones had a robust response to the free-rider argument:

> You know once I was talking to Phil [Knight] about this. . . . His perspective to me was: "We are number one in the industry, this is the mantle of responsibility you hold." We see that sometimes our responsibility is to be the risk taker that makes others feel that it is safe to come out about something or to use their voice to stand for what matters.[29]

Collaborative commitments

We could speculate about how addressing sustainable development could be radically accelerated if different actors – businesses, governments, NGOs, regulators, international development agencies, etc. – could develop their work and programs with reference to each other. Even better would be if these different actors deliberately designed their own interventions so as to encourage others to bring forward/expand their own contributions. Elsewhere, this has been described as the process of "collaborative commitments."[30]

A number of major companies have committed to the UN Sustainable Development Goals (SDGs), aligning their strategies and seeking out new collaborations to make their commitments as impactful as possible. We see considerable potential in the idea of collaborative commitments to accelerate chain reactions around implementation of the SDGs.

Conclusion

As collaboration becomes more important for business and for the successful execution of sustainability strategy so does deciding what issues to prioritize, in which order, and with which partners.

All In businesses are increasingly likely to favor collaborations with other purposeful organizations, with compatible cultures. And as Collaboration becomes more essential for mainstream business success, constraints on legitimate Collaboration such as the inappropriate application of anti-trust laws will become an increasingly important topic for corporate Advocacy, which is the final attribute we turn to now.

Notes

1 Grayson, D. and Nelson, J., *Corporate Responsibility Coalitions: The Past, Present & Future of Alliances for Sustainable Capitalism* (2013), Stanford University Press and Greenleaf Publishing.
2 Drive Sustainability, https://drivesustainability.org/ accessed Feb 11 2018.
3 Quoted in Senge, P., "How Individuals and Organizations Are Working Together to Create a Sustainable World," *The Necessary Revolution* (2006) Broadway Business.
4 The CGF is a global, parity-based industry network that is driven by its members to encourage the global adoption of practices and standards that serve the consumer goods industry worldwide. It brings together the CEOs and senior management of some 400 retailers, manufacturers, service providers, and other stakeholders across 70 countries. Its member companies have combined sales of EUR 3.5 trillion and directly employ nearly 10 million people, with a further 90 million related jobs estimated along the value chain.
5 Corporate Citizenship Briefing June 26th 2015.
6 We Mean Business, www.wemeanbusinesscoalition.org accessed Jan 2 2018.
7 Sustainable Apparel Coalition, https://apparelcoalition.org/the-sac/ accessed Jan 2 2018.
8 See Sustainable Apparel Coalition website, https://apparelcoalition.org/the-higg-index/ accessed Jan 2 2018 – called Higg according to the Coalition's Executive Director, Jason Kibbey, inspired by the Higgs Boson search. The name Higg also met other key criteria: it was short, easy to pronounce, and was able to clear trademark registration in 120 countries. Godelnik, R., "Interview: New Tool Will Measure Sustainability across Apparel Supply Chain," *TriplePundit*, July 27, 2012 accessed Jan 2 2017.

9 Sustainable Apparel Coalition website: "Our History," https://apparelcoalition. org/behind-the-scenes-at-the-sustainable-apparel-coalition/

10 Gunther, M., Ibid.

11 See, for example, Crets, S., True Sustainability Leaders Don't Try to Dominate Sector Peers, Jan 10, 2018, www.linkedin.com/pulse/true-sustainability-leaders-dont-try-dominate-sector-peers-crets/ accessed Feb 11 2018.

12 Quoted in Grayson, D., "Companies' Collective Action Shapes Way Forward," *Financial Times*, June 2, 2015 accessed Nov 28 2017.

13 Tapscott was named second and Martin as first in the Thinkers50 listing of top global management thinkers in 2017.

14 The GSN project follows earlier work by Rischard, J.F., *High Noon 20 Global Problems, 20 Years to Solve Them* (2002) Basic Books; and Waddell, S., *Global Action Networks* (2011) Palgrave Macmillan.

15 Global Solution Networks, http://gsnetworks.org/ten-types-of-global-solution-network/

16 Simon Zadek is an independent advisor and author on business and sustainability.

17 Authors' interview, Oct 19th 2017.

18 Authors' interview, Oct 31st 2017, Kathleen McLaughlin is senior vice president, chief sustainability officer for Walmart Stores, Inc., and the president of the Walmart Foundation.

19 Authors' interview, Dec 7th 2017 and subsequent email exchange Jan 2018.

20 For an indication of the sheer range of collaborations today, see: Nelson, J., Partnership for Sustainable Development: Collective Action by Business, Governments and Civil Society to Achieve Scale and Transform Markets, Corporate Responsibility Initiative, Harvard Kennedy School of Government for Business and Sustainable Development Commission, 2017, www.hks.harvard.edu/centers/mrcbg/programs/cri/research/reports/report73 accessed Feb 11 2018.

21 Partnership brokers, http://partnershipbrokers.org/w/brokering/ The term "partnership broker" is increasingly used across the globe but, if problematic, there are a number of alternative terms that work just as well – these include: process manager, change maker, intermediary, bridge-builder, animator, or connector. They can be either "internal" (from within one of the partner organizations) or "external" (independent specialists called in to undertake specific tasks) – See: What is a partnership broker? Partnership Brokers Association.

22 Authors' interview, Sept 19th 2017.

23 BP's Director, Policy Unit, and Chief of Staff for Global Government and Public Affairs, and the BP Group Policy Adviser on Development Issues (1998–2006).

24 www.voluntaryprinciples.org/

25 Authors' interview, Sept 19th 2017.

26 Authors' interview, Sept 5th 2017.

27 Email interview, Jan 2018.

28 Tapscott, D. and Williams, A., *Macrowikinomics* (2016) Portfolio.

29 Authors' interview, Oct 19th 2017.

30 "Collaborative commitments" are agreements made voluntarily between individuals and organizations from business, the public sector, and civil society to achieve positive social impacts which would not be possible for one sector acting alone to obtain. Grayson, D., *"Collaborative Commitments": Prime Minister's Council on Social Action* (2008), https://www.catch-22.org.uk/wp-content/uploads/2018/02/Collaborative_commitments_3_FINAL-1.pdf

7 Advocacy

"Life's most persistent and urgent question is, 'What are you doing for others?'"
Dr. Martin Luther King Jr.

Our fifth attribute is Advocacy. Advocacy promotes conditions that favor sustainability in line and consistent with organizational Purpose, Plan, Culture, and Collaboration.

Enablers

The essential enablers of Advocacy are:

- Ensuring consistency with company conduct, e.g., the business model (from sourcing and product development to end of life) applies and advances sustainability best practice, there is no egregious behavior in the recent past to undermine company positions, and operational and financial performance are sufficient to make Advocacy credible
- Making sure that it is justifiable to investors, employees, customers, and other stakeholders because it is in the long-term interest of the business and society without being selfish or narrowly self-interested
- Having clear and transparent objectives
- Being proportionate, i.e., not grandstanding nor deliberately distracting
- Embracing appropriate context and rooted in the best available scientific knowledge
- Having consistency with the Advocacy of the business coalitions and membership organizations in which the company is a member
- Applying and making public the right mix of advocacy techniques
- Respecting alternative views

Understanding advocacy

When companies raise their voices, there are almost always voices raised in opposition, claiming businesses speak only out of their self-interest – classic lobbying, if you will. That does happen; corporations too often only speak up to address issues narrowly affecting them. But, increasingly over the last two decades, and especially in the last few years, leading companies and the people running them have found both means and imperative to speak out on systemic sustainability issues. We need more of it.

We believe Advocacy is qualitatively and substantively different from lobbying and that companies committed to progressing performance in this area can lend needed legitimacy as advocates for sustainable development. Lobbying seeks changes in public policy (such as changes in tax policy, regulatory interpretations, subsidies, the awarding of public sector contracts or government grants, etc.) to the direct benefit of the lobbyist/client. Advocacy, on the other hand, is identifying and speaking up for the behavior, policies, laws, etc., associated with advancing sustainable development whether that is to the direct benefit of your organization or not. Often, sustainable development Advocacy is only indirectly in the interests of the advocate, and, even then, perhaps only in the longer term. Further, while the objects of Advocacy may be governments and/or elected politicians, and public policy may be in play, the audience may also be citizens, other businesses, or other types of organizations like NGOs, since Advocacy objectives are not limited to policy change.

Advocacy may involve Collaboration with others. Especially as ideas amplified by Advocacy mature and are more widely socialized, Advocacy may even morph into Collaboration. Indeed, the precursor to many now well-established Collaboration initiatives was Advocacy.

Part of what defines Advocacy in any era is its place on the cutting edge. Advocacy (and its close cousin activism, see below) is particularly necessary when rules and norms are not yet defined or, having been previously determined, are no longer fit for purpose because they are anything from simply out of date (and out of step with evolving societal expectations) to grossly unfair (as with laws once seen as reasonable that, from a contemporary point of view, clearly discriminate against classes of people based on race, gender, religion, etc.). We believe that Advocacy is when an individual business or business leader takes a stand for what they believe is in the public interest, and where the stance is not just cutting edge but also often controversial in the sense that it addresses issues on which societal views are divergent – often sharply so.

Advocacy is sometimes narrow and topic specific. In this form, it may introduce and endorse new issues or approaches – for example, The Body Shop's early championing of fair trade sourcing practices in the 1980s and 1990s when ethical sourcing was not even a consideration for most people. This type of Advocacy often advances an issue in line with business strategy and practice. The Body Shop was committed to fair trade as a concept, but was also an organization building a market position based on sourcing differently and communicating the rationale for and benefits of that to franchisees and customers to secure their loyalty.

Advocacy can also be about challenging the system. Contrary to Milton Friedman's view that "the only social responsibility of business is to increase its profits within the rules of the game,"[1] this type of Advocacy is about asking and testing whether the rules of the game are adequate in terms of design and sophistication to address systemic failures. This may not align directly with an individual organization's strategy and practice; instead it is about supporting the creation of the best and fairest business environment possible. Given this, such Advocacy is often interpreted as having ethical or moral as well as practical foundations. This is arguably what is behind the kind of corporate activism that sees CEOs speaking out on the need for global climate action, and that leads companies to join coalitions like We Are Still In, which formed in 2017 to protest the Trump Administration's declared intention to leave the Paris Agreement. Similarly, it's visible when CEOs weigh in on issues like immigration policy or transgender rights. These Advocacy positions may not relate directly to short-term business success, but they are about building and maintaining open, inclusive, and stable economies and societies, where all citizens have the same rights – and are free to participate equally in the economy as employees, consumers, and so on.

As much as Advocacy for system change may relate less directly to commercial success (especially in the short term), a self-interest component persists. For companies determined to be responsible leaders on sustainability issues and otherwise, better and stronger rules of the game may benefit them down the road. For example, companies that take climate change seriously and which are working to reduce their carbon footprint will be advantaged if cap and trade systems and/or carbon pricing mechanisms come into effect. There are even instances where the most audacious sustainability goals may only be achievable if system change enables their fulsome pursuit. For example, as automakers commit to eliminate internal combustion engines from their fleets, they are counting on regulation (and often subsidies) that favor hybrids and electric vehicles, on increasing consumer demand for such vehicles, and on a societal disposition to address both global climate change and ambient air pollution.

At another level, system change Advocacy does matter to corporate reputation and credibility, both of which have tangible and intangible value. For example, companies have pushed increasingly over the last few decades to put in place policies and practices on diversity and inclusion to make them more competitive by helping them attract and retain the best people regardless their differences. When companies have policies that accept and welcome people irrespective of gender, physical ability, sexual orientation, age, etc., there is a missed opportunity and maybe even internal risk in *not* advocating for recognition of the same issues and protection for people externally.

A specific example of Advocacy for system change on a social issue where the immediate benefit to the company behind it was limited comes from Australia in the early 2000s. At this time, John Pollaers, then running the Australian operations of the drinks giant Diageo, became convinced of the need for a proactive and coordinated response by the Australian alcohol industry to the widespread misuse of their products via practices like binge drinking and drunk driving. Pollaers undertook intense, personal Advocacy to convince his employer, and then industry competitors, of the need for what eventually became the responsible drinking coalition DrinkWise. While indubitably relevant to the business, Pollaers's actions and his Advocacy could easily have been seen as a threat for shining a spotlight on a dark side of the alcohol industry. His persistence wound up reducing harm for customers, after which some reputational benefits were perceived to flow back to Diageo as well, long after the public Advocacy phase, with its inherent risk, had been fully committed. With Advocacy, such commitment and risk often come well before reward.

As with all the leadership attributes addressed in *All In*, Advocacy has evolved over the two decades of the Leaders Survey. It is unique among the attributes because it necessarily consorts with issues that are themselves cutting-edge and dynamic. Advocacy more often and more rapidly than Purpose, Culture, Plan, and Collaboration tears down and rebuilds its own foundations to align with available knowledge and shifting societal expectations. While Purpose, Culture, Plan, and Collaboration approaches also evolve over time, they are more stable once established. Advocacy on the other hand only ever gets fully established as a *practice*; its focus or application is built anew in approach and intent depending on current context and the issue in question.

Below we explore leading-edge Advocacy today, what it has looked like over the 20 years of the Leaders Survey, and the role it will need to play through 2030.

CEO, CSO, or CAO? Behold the chief activist officer

Advocacy is very dependent on senior leadership inside a corporation, and CEO leadership especially. This has been starkly evident recently as CEOs have found themselves thrust into more and more complex environmental (e.g., climate), economic (e.g., inequity), and social (e.g., race, gender, and transgender rights) debates. We see what the media sometimes labels "CEO activism" as the current extension of a tradition of corporate Advocacy essential to progress on sustainable development. That historical connection being what it may, we are interested in why there has been such an increase in business activism and what makes Advocacy an essential part of strong sustainability performance today.

The Economist explored the sharp rise in corporate Advocacy in a December 2017 article, *Bosses are under increasing pressure to take stances on social issues. How should they respond?* The piece examined so-called "Rules of thumb for navigating the era of activism," suggesting that, in this charged political era, "Executives who would rather concentrate on commerce are finding it ever harder to avoid politics, in America and beyond."[2]

The Harvard Business Review (HBR) published a very similar piece in its January–February 2018 Edition, *The New CEO Activists*.[3] Its authors warn that participation in such activism is becoming an expectation or even a norm, stating:

> As more and more business leaders choose to speak out on contentious political and social matters, CEOs will increasingly be called on to help shape the debate about such issues. Many will decide to stay out of the fray, but they should still expect to be peppered with questions from employees, the media, and other stakeholders about the hot-button topics of day.

The HBR authors added:

> We believe that the more CEOs speak up on social and political issues, the more they will be expected to do so. And increasingly, CEO activism has strategic implications: In the Twitter age, silence is more conspicuous – and more consequential.

Both articles underscore a new reality: CEOs and other corporate leaders face ever-higher expectations that they speak out on policy and societal matters broadly, covering issues ranging from traditional business territory like taxes and jobs, to a middle ground where businesses have reasonable experience like globalization and environmental policy, to much less familiar and often less comfortable topics like immigration, diversity, LGBTQ rights, sexual harassment, and more.

Some take to this naturally – witness Starbucks founder Howard Schultz championing business practices and government policies related to health insurance, access to education, race, hiring practices, immigration, and inclusion over the years – but for others it must be learned over time, sometimes forged in crisis or thrust on them by stakeholders.

The Economist says that it is often internal stakeholders – employees – that demand companies generally and their employers specifically take positions on social issues. The article also underscores the point that other stakeholders, including owners, are increasingly involved, as, more and more often "shareholders are judging firms on broader criteria than financial ones."

Stakeholder alignment is critical to knowing where to draw the Advocacy line. We see a distinction between activist CEOs using their positions as platforms to promote personal beliefs and ideas and CEOs undertaking sustainability Advocacy with the support of their boards and in line with their company Purpose. In addition to board and employee support, Advocacy can be enhanced by external stakeholder engagement, e.g., stakeholder advisory panels that advise corporate leadership on sustainability issues and societal expectations. While applauding CEOs who take clear personal stands for engaging in public discourse and being transparent, only when Advocacy aligns with company Purpose, Plan, Culture, and overall direction is it really credible, enduring, and impactful.

Lonely early voices

If we now live in a world where Advocacy is a de facto CEO job requirement, it was not always so.

The Economist piece neatly summarizes some present-day Advocacy pitfalls companies must navigate and the kinds of tactics required in the tone of a primer for a topic just being introduced. *HBR* likewise states it is a new phenomenon, saying "Until recently, it was rare for corporate leaders to plunge aggressively into thorny social and political discussions about race, sexual orientation, gender, immigration, and the environment."

While such behavior used to be rare, there is a long if sparsely populated history of corporate Advocacy, with isolated examples occurring not just in the last few decades, but also over a much longer period. This includes individual merchants speaking out for the abolition of the slave trade, nineteenth century entrepreneurs like Robert Owen and the Rowntree and Cadbury families helping to define and speaking up for early responsible business, and Levi Strauss desegregating its factories in the Deep South of the US in the 1950s, and then, in the 1980s, urging for action to combat AIDS.

Instances of corporate Advocacy multiplied in the 1980s and 1990s, sometimes through cause-related marketing, but also in deeper ways such as the substantive business voices and action seen addressing issues of urban renewal and community economic development through programs like Cleveland Tomorrow in the US and local enterprise agencies and One Town Partnerships in the UK. Even more striking was the role business leaders played relative to South African apartheid, challenging discriminatory laws and pushing for – sometimes even facilitating – talks with the African National Congress.

Considering this history, we are not surprised in looking back at the twenty years of the Leaders Survey to find examples of what constitutes Advocacy and corporate activism building and becoming more numerous and complex.

HBR mentions corporate values, purpose, and personal conviction as being key reasons for CEO activism, and that we find true. Leaders Survey companies in the late 1990s were displaying all three of these elements. This aligns with the view of Jeff Immelt, the former GE CEO, as quoted in *The New CEO Activists*:

> I just think it's insincere to not stand up for those things that you believe in. We're also stewards of our companies; we're representatives of the people that work with us. And I think we're cowards if we don't take a position occasionally on those things that are really consistent with what our mission is and where our people stand.[4]

Modern trailblazers

Early examples of Advocacy that existed during and even prior to the Harm Reduction Era among companies cited in the Leaders Survey include The

Body Shop, Patagonia, and BP. We believe that their Advocacy had a material impact on those companies being identified and persisting as leaders in the views of the experts surveyed.

We interviewed David Wheeler, a Body Shop executive who served under founder and CEO Anita Roddick in the 1990s. When reflecting on what led the company to take early positions on issues like fair trade, climate change, renewable energy, sustainability reporting, and more, Wheeler attributes much of the rationale to Roddick.

> No question, it was the personal values of Anita Roddick combined with her trading instincts and public relations flair that both created the mythology and (over time) supported the reality of sustainability oriented action in the 1990s. The international and local franchisees who joined the company from the late 1980s onwards, together with thousands of wonderful shop staff around the world, were the people who carried the commitment in real terms. The genuine enthusiasm for provocative environmental and social campaigns from international franchisees in Australia, Canada, Germany, Ireland, Italy, The Netherlands, Sweden and many other countries was mirrored by the idealism of shop staff in those countries who really did go to work believing they were saving the planet and protecting human and animal rights by selling shampoos and body butters.[5]

Wheeler said this was almost purely driven by instinct, that the company did not have a strategy for this.

> There was no corporate strategy. There was entrepreneurial drive, significant risk-taking (including with the narrative building) and occasional anarchy. The sustainability strategy was simply to clarify policy, try to eliminate contradictions and improve accountability for performance on social, environmental and human issues.[6]

In an interesting twist, one of the highest profile corporate actions of the Body Shop in the mid 1990s was aimed at another company. Looking and sounding every bit the radical NGO, Body Shop ran a campaign against Shell over its alleged complicity in the judicial murder of Ken Saro-Wiwa and other Ogoni activists (See Chapter 5 Culture).

At the same time as Body Shop was honing its Advocacy edge or voice, the company took actions in the business to model behavior that supported its stances, for example:

> the company made some signature moves, including making the first ever corporate offset arrangement to combat climate change when it invested in and co-commissioned a wind farm in Wales in 1994.

While it was ad hoc, The Body Shop demonstrated in the 1990s that corporate Advocacy could help define and build a brand while at the same time changing actual practices from the supply chain right through the retail environment.

Patagonia's Rick Ridgeway also cited personal executive motivations and "the moral obligation to do something" behind the way Patagonia's advocacy and activism emerged in the company's early days and then built to a crescendo with 2011's "Don't Buy This Jacket" and the other anti-consumption campaigns it has used in recent years. "Over time," Ridgeway told us, "we started to realize that, as we grew in size, we had a moral obligation to extend our support into direct actions for social justice.[7]"

In the second edition of his book *Let My People Go Surfing* – part business manifesto, part memoir – Yvon Chouinard describes some of the Advocacy of the company over the years including: running an advertising campaign before the 2004 US elections to persuade people to register to vote and to "Vote Environment" when they did, and holding a "Tools for Grassroots Activists" conference every 18 months to teach the organizational, business, and marketing skills that small groups need – and producing a book of the same name. As to why or motivation, Chouinard said: "These people are often isolated, scared and bravely passionate, and most of them are woefully unprepared to confront big business or big government with their teams of attorneys and 'hired experts.' By giving them the tools to present their position clearly and effectively, we do as much good as by giving them financial support."

Patagonia also decided that rather than financing a river conservation group, they would make a film to support the removal of destructive dams and use Patagonia's retail and marketing teams to broadly distribute it and host events. The film, *Dam Nation*, released in 2014, won awards at film festivals across world.[8]

With work on minimizing the negative environmental and social impacts in its supply chain well established, Patagonia realized there was another critical threshold to cross: consumption. Rick Ridgeway described the situation this way:

> We realized that that consumption was the missing piece and we came up with this ad "Don't Buy This Jacket". We purposefully chose that phrase to shock people so that they would read the copy. That copy said, listen, no matter how much we've tried to make this jacket causing no unnecessary harm, guess what? It took 135 liters of water to make the jacket, and it released 20 pounds of CO2 emissions into the atmosphere, and it left behind two thirds of its own weight in waste . . . it has caused harm. Consequently, the only way we are going to avoid the cliff out on the horizon line is to collectively figure out how we are going to reduce consumption and how we are going to build a global economy, a new form of capitalism that doesn't rely on annual compounded growth. We

at Patagonia don't know what the answer to that one is, but we want
you to think about it and further, as our customer, we want you to only
buy what you need.

When a company finds this kind of voice, making public a message that
simultaneously speaks to its environmental passion and which challenges its
own business model, it has decided the adage *the customer is always right* is
simply not true. With "Don't Buy This Jacket," Patagonia, a consumer goods
company in a consumer goods economy, took a radical step, acknowledging
and identifying their customer as both part of the problem and part of the
solution. Once there, engaging the consumer via Advocacy – alongside delivering great products – was not just an option for Patagonia, but a necessity,
essential to the company's ability to continuously improve its environmental
performance.

Patagonia, like The Body Shop, had its Purpose and values aligned with
its Advocacy at a very early stage. Advocacy is part of delivering Patagonia's
mission statement: *Build the best product, cause no unnecessary harm, use
business to inspire and implement solutions to the environmental crisis*. The
company's clarity and consistency has built a fanatical consumer following,
and they have been a consistent top three performer in the Leaders Survey
(with Unilever and Interface) in the years since the "Don't Buy This Jacket"
campaign. Their Advocacy continues, bolstered in December 2017 when the
company's home page posted the message "The President Stole Your Land"
in response to the Trump administration's decision to radically reduce the
size of the Bears Ears and Grand Staircase-Escalante National Monuments.[9]
In January 2018, that message plus a "Take Action" page[10] educating the
public on how to press the administration on protection of public lands,
were still prominent on patagonia.com, demonstrating their Advocacy is not
fleeting, but persistent over time.

Finally, BP under the leadership of John Browne in the late 1990s and early
2000s defined leading-edge corporate Advocacy. We have already discussed
Browne and BP in our chapter on Culture. While controversial to cite as a
pioneering leader today, given shifting views on fossil fuel use and fossil fuel
companies, as well as the specific operational issues the company has faced,
like the Deepwater Horizon disaster in the Gulf of Mexico, Browne and BP
were in their day exceptional. This was most visible in a few actions that
helped redefine the debate on climate change and the role of business in it.

First, in 1996, BP left the Global Climate Coalition, an industry group
widely viewed as climate denying and lobbying to obstruct climate action.
Next, in a speech at Stanford University in May 1997, Browne took the
then remarkable step for an oil industry leader of acknowledging as fact
that: "The concentration of carbon dioxide in the atmosphere is rising, and
the temperature of the earth's surface is increasing." He also acknowledged
". . . discernable human influence on the climate, and a link between the
concentration of carbon dioxide and the increase in temperature."[11] The

significance was not in Browne the individual's statement, but Browne as CEO of one of the world's biggest energy companies saying what he said.

In 2017, anthropomorphic influence on climate change remains contentious (in political if not in scientific terms). To have the CEO of one of the largest fossil fuel energy companies in the world acknowledge human-related climate change in 1997 was headline news. Browne was not done. In 2000 he rebranded BP as "Beyond Petroleum." While the move invited both acclaim and scorn, and ultimately proved beyond the ability of Browne and the BP of the day to deliver, the signal was clear: the energy future would be low-carbon, and fossil fuel company survival depended on being a productive partner in the rapid transition to a low-carbon economy.

To our minds, while The Body Shop is admirable for the way it built a brand by practicing and trumpeting new business practices, and we are more than impressed by how Patagonia amplified its environmental and social performance by advocating more responsible consumption and inviting consumers to join its efforts, BP's effort was in many ways grander. Browne acted out of step with his own industry and sought to remake the company business model by signaling intent to gradually move BP from petroleum toward renewable energy. New business models, as we can see more clearly today in the Purpose-Driven Era of leadership, are the ultimate challenge. We should regret rather than scorn BP's failure to maintain its commitment.

From soloists to choirs

Not every company embraces Advocacy as individually as The Body Shop, Patagonia, or BP. Such individualism may not even be the best or most effective course, especially when thinking beyond a company's own four walls and through its value chain. During the move from the Harm Reduction Era to the Strategic Integration Era, corporate leaders of the 2000s increasingly formed coalitions with other companies as well as civil society representatives like environmentalists and human rights campaigners to approach issues collectively. This represented in part a tactical shift – a test of the degree to which two heads really are better than one, and how coalitions might be more effective than individual voices – but also an increasing recognition that so many sustainability issues are systemic in their nature and require collective effort to address.

One of the standout efforts of this period was the US Climate Action Partnership (USCAP), which included as a founding member GE. When we interviewed Jeff Immelt, CEO at the time, he suggested that "from . . . 2006 through 2008 . . . USCAP was maybe the most effective advocacy group that existed," precisely because it was not just a multi-company but also a multi-sector coalition, including NGOs and others as well as businesses, with Immelt and Jonathan Lash, then head of environmental NGO the World Resources Institute, its most public faces.[12]

USCAP's approach had peers and imitators both in the US and globally, including broad coalitions and other models. One example is the Ceres BICEP Coalition, which was founded in 2009 by environmental NGO Ceres with businesses including Nike to push for "stronger climate and clean energy policies at the state and federal level in the US."[13] In Europe, The Prince of Wales's Corporate Leaders Group (CLG), was formed to bring together European business leaders to advocate solutions on climate change within the EU and globally and to accelerate progress toward a low-carbon, sustainable economy.[14]

Some companies realized they had the power to drive their own coalitions, most notably Walmart, which founded The Sustainability Consortium (TSC) in 2007 to ". . . [transform] the consumer goods industry to deliver more sustainable consumer products." In partnership with founding university partners Arizona State University and the University of Arkansas, the consortium "translates the science of sustainability into quantifiable metrics and practical tools for buyers and suppliers to address sustainability issues in their supply chains."[15]

Given the scale of Walmart's supply chain and its tremendous leverage with suppliers, TSC membership was essential for many companies from the outset. It has endured by providing information and value, building one of the world's largest research databases ". . . housing scientific evidence on environmental and social hotspots and improvement opportunities within a product's life cycle, covering nearly 90% of the total impacts in all consumer product categories across 8 industry sectors." A (sophisticated) soap box from which Walmart talked transformation at the outset, TSC has evolved over time from an Advocacy effort designed to create a new kind of coalition focused on sustainable supply chain issues to a full-fledged Collaboration, demonstrating our theory that Advocacy sometimes morphs in this way.

Today, if you want to make a consumer product better, TSC participation is one of the best places a company can learn the most efficient way to do so. Kathleen McLaughlin, Walmart's CSO, underscored this in our interview with her, saying the attractiveness of participating in the TSC, which was originally seen by many as a command performance for Walmart suppliers, is rooted in the fact that:

> There is no such thing as just a "Walmart supply chain." These are broad systems that are highly comingled in terms of different actors and issues – social issues, environmental issues, economic issues, and so we are talking about broad systemic change.

This was the Advocacy basis for TSC, i.e., convincing other businesses that a sustainable supply chain is a collective challenge – and an essential one. It became Collaboration when Walmart suppliers were convinced and found their own reasons to participate. McLaughlin continued:

[Now the suppliers] all come. Maybe a dozen years ago it was "Walmart is asking us so I guess we better do this." Now they all have their own customers and investors and their own suppliers and their own communities and their own employees who care about these issues. For their own reasons they are quite excited, and where we can help is providing tools, a platform, something to hook onto to make it easier for them to pursue what most of them want to pursue anyway.

Walmart's determination to become more sustainable, expressed in its Plan and the Purpose it publicly articulated with increasingly force after 2005, led to a realization that Collaboration would be essential to systemic change, and that fostering this would require Advocacy in multiple fora. TSC is emblematic of where they are, but just one of many paths Walmart is on today collaborating and advocating for issues from tropical deforestation to labor practices on deep sea fishing trawlers.

Model modern advocacy

The nature of Advocacy has continued to evolve in near parallel to our leadership eras. Solitary trailblazers owned the Harm Reduction Era, and coalitions the Strategic Integration period. In the current Purpose-Driven Era, there exists a blend – solitary leadership remains essential and sometimes is the only way to stand out and make an impression, but the pursuit of systemic change often requires a chorus as opposed to a soloist. These different approaches were both apparent when, as mentioned earlier, the Trump Administration announced its intention to abandon the Paris Agreement.

The most powerful response to this US government decision was undoubtedly "We Are Still In," a coalition of more than 2,500 businesses and investors, cities and counties, states and tribes, colleges, universities, and faith organizations adamant that "US Action on Climate Change is Irreversible" regardless of the intended and actual actions of the federal government.[16]

According to the We Are Still In website:

> This unprecedented network of networks represents more than 127 million Americans and $6.2 trillion of the US economy. Spanning all 50 states – red and blue – we are demonstrating America's enduring commitment to tackling climate change, ensuring a clean energy future, and upholding the Paris Agreement.

Businesses involved include Leaders Survey companies like Interface, Nike, Patagonia, and Walmart from the US, and companies headquartered outside the US but operating in the American market like Unilever.

We Are Still In's rapid assembly and exponential growth, undoubtedly facilitated by the growth of social media, was a remarkable way to make a statement, but it is interesting to note that one key Leaders Survey company,

GE, did not become a signatory. Instead, then CEO Jeff Immelt wrote a personal letter, telling us in our interview with him that:

> I don't sign petitions because I think actually in something like this . . .
> not that I am against it and I would say Paul [Polman] and I agree on
> almost everything, but I think in some ways a singular voice, the fact that
> you're willing to stick your own neck out, actually works better with
> guys like Trump or any governmental group . . . when he pulled out of
> Paris I singularly issued a press release and said, I disagree and here is
> why. So I have certain well-developed maybe insane points of view that
> I kind of live up to.[17]

Nike is another company (interestingly, another company whose place in the Leaders Survey ranking spans both the Strategic Integration and Purpose-Driven Eras) that undertakes a blend of individual and collective action. Hannah Jones, Nike's CSO, talked us through a 2005 example of Nike acting to disclose information previously considered confidential (identifying the specific factories in its supply chain) as a means of Advocacy designed to encourage and cajole Nike peers and competitors to greater Collaboration on labor standards:

> . . . in 2005, as you will remember, we were the first company to disclose
> our factory locations, and the reason that is an epiphany moment for us
> is it signaled to anyone that was watching – at least what it ought to have
> signaled – was that this was a systems change issue. Only by galvanizing
> the system, and pulling different actors together, and using transparency
> as a tool, would we get the kind of transformative change that we were
> looking for. The factory location disclosure was an effort to push the
> rest of the industry to do the same and to enable greater collaboration
> in enforcing labor standards across the complex supply chain that we
> all participate in.[18]

Like Walmart disclosing its supply chain intentions when it launched TSC, Nike's first-mover Advocacy on this issue was necessary in spurring industry-wide Collaboration.

We expect the toolkit for Advocacy will deepen and diversify further with time, but we recognize that Advocacy will likely be less widely and less frequently practiced than the other *All In* leadership attributes. This will be the case until more companies develop a sufficient track record of sustainability performance and understanding of sustainable development issues. As more companies adopt explicit values which are intended to guide the way in which they do business, however, these value statements create greater internal pressures for business leaders to ensure that they are living up to their own rhetoric and a framework for externally facing Advocacy. Nevertheless, companies also need to confront their innate caution around getting involved

Businesses today use a range of tools and channels for their Advocacy, including:

- CEO speeches, Op-eds, tweets, and public statements
- Private representations to governments
- Advertising and other consumer messaging
- Participation in coalitions – and withdrawing when appropriate from government panels and councils where participation is inconsistent with organizational values
- Becoming signatories to petitions and/or encouraging employees, customers, and others to sign petitions aligned with organizational positions
- Promoting voter registration and civic action
- Threatening to withdraw business from specific regions with discriminatory laws or practices
- Court actions including supporting legal test cases as when technology companies big and small filed an "amicus brief" to fight President Trump's first executive order on immigration, often referred to as his "Muslim Ban"[19]
- Agitating for legislative change as when Procter & Gamble, Walmart, Unilever, General Mills, Target, General Motors, and Nestlé pushed the state of Missouri to pass a bill to make it easier for them to buy renewable energy
- Commissioning and publicizing white papers and/or thought-leadership research on topical issues
- Funding NGO campaigns

Figure 7.1 Critical Success Factors for Advocacy

in public and/or political debate and be confident of their position when they advocate, which can be a slow process. But companies will have to do this, as pressure on business leaders to stand and be counted on sustainability issues will inexorably grow.

While we are certain it will increase, the pressure on business to take Advocacy positions will vary geographically and in relation to the form of government involved. While sustainable development is a global issue, positions and responses need to respect local perspectives and practice. Advocacy, like politics, is after all "the art of the possible," and companies must consider which interventions, when, and where will add value, and use their political capital appropriately.[20]

Finally, some of this of this will be generational. As corporate leaders weaned on maximizing shareholder value pass the baton, we expect the next generation of business leadership will be more comfortable as advocates and as corporate citizens participating alongside civil society and governments in public debates of all kinds.

Conclusion

Going *All In* on Advocacy means advocating for better, more sustainable societal outcomes first. Advocacy needs to be carefully contextualized. It should reflect the Purpose, Plan, and Culture of the business so that employees, customers, shareholders, governments, and publics will have less justification for objecting to it. Such alignment also makes it more likely that the Advocacy will be influential and help create conditions for both sustainability and the business to flourish long term.

Notes

1 Friedman, M., "The Social Responsibility of Business Is to Increase Its Profits," *The New York Times Magazine*, Sept 13, 1970, www.colorado.edu/studentgroups/libertarians/issues/friedman-soc-resp-business. html accessed Feb 8 2018.

2 Chief activist officer – Bosses are under increasing pressure to take stances on social issues. How should they respond? "Rules of Thumb for Navigating the Era of Activism," *The Economist*, Nov 30 2017.

3 Chatterji A. K., Toffel M. W., "The New CEO Activists," *Harvard Business Review*, January–February 2018

4 Chatterji, A.K. and Toffel, M., "The New CEO Activists," *Harvard Business Review*, Jan–Feb 2018.

5 Authors' interview, Aug 11th 2017.

6 Ibid.

7 Authors' interview, Aug 31st 2017.

8 Chouinard, Y., *Let My People Go Surfing: The Education of a Reluctant Businessman*, 2nd edition (2016), Penguin.

9 Patagonia website, www.patagonia.com/protect-public-lands.html

10 Patagona website, http://bearsears.patagonia.com/take-action

11 Browne J., Climate Change Speech, May 19th 1997, Stanford University, www.documentcloud.org/documents/2623268-bp-john-browne-stanford-1997-climate-change-speech.html accessed Jan 3rd 2018.

12 Authors' interview, Oct 13th 2017.

13 Ceres, www.ceres.org/networks/ceres-policy-network accessed Jan 3 2018.

14 Corporate Leaders Group, www.corporateleadersgroup.com/about accessed Jan 8 2018.

15 The Sustainability Consortium, www.sustainabilityconsortium.org/ accessed Jan 4 2018.

16 We are still in, www.wearestillin.com/us-action-climate-change-irreversible accessed Jan 4 2018.

17 Authors' interview, Oct 13th 2017.

18 Authors' interview, Oct 19th 2017.

19 See Winston, A., "Top Ten Sustainability Stories of 2017," *Harvard Business Review*, Dec 2017, https://hbr.org/2017/12/the-top-10-sustainable-business-stories-of-2017

20 We recognize there are questions concerning what are the legitimate boundaries for multinational companies operating outside their home countries to seek to influence the public policy agendas in host countries. Such activities can easily invite allegations of "neo-imperialism." This is a key issue, for example, for many extractive sector companies which, since their businesses are geologically determined, cannot easily pick up their investment dollars and go somewhere else and, therefore, have a particularly strong interest in seeing governance and service delivery (often largely funded by royalties and mining/oil taxes) improved. This is why the extractive sector has seen a cluster of multi-stakeholder initiatives as companies have sought alignment with civil society and reformist elements in host governments around what constitutes good practice; and why they have hoped that such alliances can build greater legitimacy for the use of corporate advocacy/influence.

8 Unilever

Going *All In*

"If you deliver excellence right now, that gives you the best shot at the best future you've got coming."

Robert Forster

Unilever first topped the GlobeScan-SustainAbility Leaders Survey in 2011 and has dominated the top spot since, increasing its margin of leadership each year through 2017. It is instructive, therefore, to examine Unilever's approach in some detail.

Unilever clearly demonstrates all five of our attributes – Purpose, Plan, Culture, Collaboration and Advocacy – and the effective inter-linkages between them. To help us understand the Unilever story, we interviewed CEO Paul Polman in Summer 2017. He began our interview by reflecting on what he had found almost a decade earlier – at the end of 2008 – as he prepared to take the helm:

> The reason that I was brought in, I think, was turnover was in decline. Turnover had decreased from about fifty-five billion to thirty-eight billion USD, and the share price was under-performing. Not surprisingly, activities were focused on the short-term to satisfy market needs, and investment in future growth was neglected. It is hard to build value [this way] in the long-term as you can't save your way to prosperity. Obviously, we needed to address how do we get this company to grow again and how do we get this company to be successful again?
>
> What went through my mind at that time was basically how to move from an internally focused company to an externally focused company. How could we put serving society back in the middle of everything, and that was the first starting point.
>
> The second starting point was obviously the global financial crisis because I joined at the height of the effects of this where many companies were cutting costs and hunkering down and trying to survive. It was a good moment of introspection, if you want, of what really happened there, and what was very clear to me was that businesses had to start playing a different role, and there were some broader macro trends happening

that were important and that needed to be addressed. Then the third thing that we had to do is to go back to Jim Collins's book *Good to Great*, where he talks about nurturing the core before stimulating progress.

I came in from the outside. I had to earn my right to be accepted, and I also had to earn the right to drive the change program. Just to stand on a soapbox and say "Run faster!" was not going to work. One of our first meetings was actually in Port Sunlight to go back to the roots of this company, and why Lord Lever started it, and why he talked about shared prosperity and called one of his first brands Lifebuoy, and how he used his goods to address societal issues. So it was, what I would call, nurturing the core before stimulating progress. So then we had these elements of a force for change: a better contribution to society, and leveraging the core strengths of the company and its values."[1]

A coherent approach

Looking back we can see how Polman's analysis and decisions have shaped the Unilever we see today. A long-term, societal Purpose is at the heart of what drives its empowering Culture. Purpose inspires the comprehensive and ambitious Unilever Sustainable Living Plan (SLP); and an engaged Culture is making implementation of the Plan possible. The ambitiousness of the Plan is forcing Unilever to collaborate at breadth and scale – well beyond what has gone before. As Unilever works to implement its Plan, and extends its Collaboration efforts to do so, the need for Advocacy to create the enabling environment for delivery, and to encourage others to follow suit, becomes ever more obvious. (Please see Figure 8.1 for an overview of how stakeholders describe Unilever's leadership.)

Figure 8.1 Word Cloud Describing Unilever's Leadership

Nevertheless, for all Unilever has done to establish leadership, it still feels market pressure. This peaked recently with a hostile takeover attempt. The company fended this off and remains independent, but outstanding financial returns will be essential to maintaining that over the long term. Being *All In* increases the potential for enduring performance.

Strong heritage, purposeful predecessors

In the 1890s, William Hesketh Lever, founder of Lever Bros, wrote down his ideas for Sunlight Soap – his revolutionary new product that helped popularize cleanliness and hygiene in Victorian England.

Lord Lever sought "to make cleanliness commonplace; to lessen work for women; to foster health and contribute to personal attractiveness, that life may be more enjoyable and rewarding for the people who use our products." Both the English and the Dutch founding companies had social missions to improve health, hygiene, and livelihoods in their communities.

When Paul Polman became Unilever CEO in 2009, coming in as an outsider having spent his prior career at Nestlé and P&G, one of the first things he did was to explore the Unilever archives. It was here that he saw the early power of the company's commitment to Purpose. Polman modernized and updated "making cleanliness commonplace" to "making sustainable living commonplace." The power of being authentic to the company's heritage and taking on an equally pressing challenge of the day – sustainability – helped drive Unilever's leadership.

Today, Unilever's vision is to help people to look good, feel good, and get more out of life; and to grow the business, while decoupling the company's environmental footprint from growth and increasing positive social impact.

Polman stresses:

> The desire to be around for hundreds of years more . . . [means] you have to become a purpose-driven business model where you make your positive contributions and where you don't add to the problems. So you are a giver instead of a taker. We wanted to be very clear that our business was there to serve society and not the shareholders. The shareholder returns would be a result of what we were doing but would not be the purpose for us being there.

He is very clear, however, that Unilever employees understand just how important good financial performance is:

> In our company people feel very strongly about their purpose but also their financial results because they also realize that if the financial results are not there, we will not be able to bring our purpose to life, and others might be circling around you, increasingly so, with all these activist funds and all that other stuff that is out there. So it actually has become a performance thing as well.[2]

To reinforce senior leadership's understanding of and commitment to Unilever's societal Purpose, the top 200 senior leaders have been through two key leadership development experiences. In the first, all senior leaders identified their Purpose as a leader in Unilever and beyond. In the second, they worked on "Purpose Into Impact" projects, drawing on their Purpose to deliver change in the world that realized the SLP and grew Unilever's business. Identifying a personal Purpose is seen as a catalytic aspect of shifting the culture of the leadership team and securing engagement.

Purposeful brands

Unilever is a brands-based business. Even before Paul Polman's arrival, the company had introduced a *Brand Imprint* assessment process – a "simple, intuitively obvious tool to encourage, almost coerce the brands to think more broadly" about their environmental, economic, and social impacts. Effectively, the tool forced brand managers to look beyond their traditional consumer lens and to add a broader stakeholder perspective.

Now, however, under Polman's leadership, the overall organizational Purpose has been extended to Brand Purpose. Starting with the biggest global brands (those with a billion-dollar turnover), there has been a drive to articulate individual brand societal purposes. Unilever reports that by the end of 2016, 18 of their top 40 brands are now sustainable living brands, including the company's six biggest: Knorr, Dove, the Dirt is Good laundry brands (which have different names in different markets), Lipton, Rexona, and Hellmann's. Importantly, these sustainable living brands combined grew 50% faster than the rest of the business and delivered more than 60% of Unilever growth in 2016.

"We have," says Karen Hamilton, Unilever's VP, Global Sustainable Business, "a growing body of evidence in Unilever that a strongly articulated sustainable living purpose brought to life through communications can deliver a powerful emotional response and generate brand fame – the key drivers of memorability."

A powerful example is delivered by Unilever's hand washing campaign across Asia and Africa. Studies have demonstrated that hand washing with soap is one of the most effective and inexpensive ways to prevent diarrheal diseases. This simple habit could help cut deaths from diarrhea by almost half and deaths from acute respiratory infections by a quarter. Over 2010–2016, Unilever reached 379 million people across 29 countries with its hand washing campaign. The goal now is to reach one billion by 2020.[3]

Enduring culture

Think about how complex the adage "culture eats strategy for breakfast" is in Unilever's case. The company has 170,000 employees and more than 400 brands, which it sells in more than 190 countries. Two billion people use Unilever products every day. Creating and projecting a cohesive Culture across so many human, brand, and geographic variables is an enormous challenge. Meeting the challenge depends on a Culture of performance and quality augmented by the right governance, diversity, goals, and transparency. Such a Culture is fueled by employee empowerment and a commitment to diversity, which starts at the top. Half of Unilever's non-executive directors are women. There is clear board oversight through a corporate responsibility committee of the board, currently chaired by non-executive director Strive Masiyiwa, the African mobile phones entrepreneur.

Innovation is the lifeblood of a big-brand company like Unilever and core to its Culture. The ambitious goals of the SLP are creating even more demand for it. In 2012, it established an online platform giving outside experts the opportunity to help the company find the technical solutions it needs. Unilever's commitment to Open Innovation took an extra step, "perhaps unprecedented," suggests sustainability expert, Joel Makower, "by publishing a list of its 'wants' – key areas in which the company is seeking help. That strikes me as a bold move, broadcasting to the world the areas in which it wants to innovate."[4] Today the list includes broad topics (intelligent packaging, "more for less," superior functionality) and some very specific ones (ingredient or technology for prevention of oil oxidation, new and novel freezing and cooling technologies, process for superficial surface modification of non-uniform flat shapes, process for shape transformation of tea leaves[5]).

A well-established tradition of transparency is being extended for the SLP – like innovation, transparency is a foundational element to SLP delivery. Unilever was an early sustainability reporter, producing their first social report in 2001. Now, there is an extensive, online sustainability hub with downloadable summaries of key performance data. In 2015, Unilever produced a report on its human rights performance in line with the UN Guiding Principles for Business and Human Rights (or Ruggie Principles).[6] Unilever also helped pioneer country economic impact assessments, looking at the totality of its impacts first in Indonesia and then in South Africa and Vietnam.

On his first day as CEO, Polman sent a strong signal both internally and externally, reinforcing Unilever's long-term Culture: he abandoned quarterly market guidance and, later, profit forecasts. Simon Zadek, a long-time sustainability expert, likens this ending of quarterly reporting to the 1997 UK Labour government's grant of independence to the Bank of England. It was more than just tinkering or public relations, he says, "This was a new business model."[7]

Subsequently, Polman said that he only wanted investors who shared his view that Unilever needs to shepherd the Earth's future as carefully as it does its own revenues and profits. He had a sharp message for short-term shareholders.

> Unilever has been around for 100-plus years. We want to be around for several hundred more years. So if you buy into this long-term value-creation model, which is equitable, which is shared, which is sustainable, then come and invest with us. If you don't buy into this, I respect you as a human being but don't put your money in our company.[8]

This attempt to change the composition of the Unilever Share Register has paid off. Today, 70 per cent of Unilever's top 50 shareholders have held their shares in the company for more than seven years.[9] This is perhaps positive proof of what Generation Investment Management's Colin le Duc told us in his *All In* interview: "Companies get the investors they deserve – there *are* long-term investors out there."[10]

Unilever has shown itself open to new ideas: its innovation platform, Unilever Foundry, has a global crowdsourcing community to find new ways to tackle global sustainability problems. This enables collaboration between consumers and innovators to look for solutions to sustainability challenges. "Grand challenges" will be regularly uploaded to the platform where community members can submit and comment on other people's ideas. Solutions will then be rewarded with opportunities to pilot ideas and implementations.[11]

An ambitious plan

In 2010, Unilever launched its SLP with a pledge to double the size of the business whilst halving its environmental footprint – subsequently modified to halve the environmental footprint of the making and use of Unilever products by 2030 as it grows its business. This was and remains a ground-breaking commitment and hints at what we believe will be more commonplace in the next era in Corporate Sustainability Leadership: the Regenerative Era – see further in Chapter 12.

The SLP also included bold targets to improve health and well-being for more than one billion people by 2020 through health and hygiene initiatives and by improving the nutritional content of its food products to encourage healthier diets, for example with cuts in salt, saturated fats, sugar, and calories. The company also committed to enhancing the livelihoods of millions of people, including linking more than 500,000 smallholder farmers and small-scale distributors in developing countries to its supply chain.

Like other companies with comprehensive and ambitious sustainability plans, the SLP has forced Unilever into a radical overhaul of relations with suppliers. Unilever's approach has long included "the total value chain" as Section 4 of the company's Social Review 2000 – the company's first social report – makes clear. Still, the SLP raised the bar. The Responsible Sourcing Policy launched in 2014 and revised in 2017 further sets out standards required of suppliers, auditing processes depending on the historic performance of the supplier, and rigorous processes for reporting and remedying violations of the policy. Alongside the "stick" of higher performance standards, has come the "carrot" of extensive capacity-building programs to help suppliers improve their performance and profitability.

In 2016, Unilever announced it was aiming for a zero-waste supply chain through a new collaboration platform. Developed in partnership with the online community 2degrees, the platform will enable Unilever to share lessons and experiences with a network of partners. The new collaboration aims to deliver further reductions both for Unilever and for its thousands of suppliers through a combination of purpose-built technology and expert facilitation.[12]

Figure 8.2 summarizes how Unilever explains SLP and the new business model that it represents.

HOW WE CREATE VALUE

We believe that sustainable and equitable growth is the only way to create long-term value for our stakeholders. That is why we have placed the Unilever Sustainable Living Plan at the heart of our business model.

Unilever

WHAT WE DEPEND ON

PURPOSEFUL PEOPLE	NATURAL RESOURCES	FINANCIAL RESOURCES	INTANGIBLE ASSETS	TANGIBLE ASSETS	STAKEHOLDERS & PARTNERS
161,000 talented people who contribute their skills and purpose to our business	Renewable and non-renewable materials and ingredients for our products	Cash, equity and debt to invest for the long-term	R&D capabilities and intellectual property such as patents, trade marks and know-how	Physical assets such as manufacturing, logistics and office facilities as well as our vehicle fleet and stock	Relationships with governments and other organisations to drive systems change

OUR VALUE CHAIN

CONSUMER INSIGHT → INNOVATION → SOURCING → MANUFACTURING → LOGISTICS → MARKETING → SALES → CONSUMER USE

OUR PURPOSE
To Make Sustainable Living Commonplace

OUR VISION
To grow our business, whilst decoupling our environmental footprint from our growth and increasing our positive social impact delivered through the Unilever Sustainable Living Plan:

IMPROVING HEALTH AND WELL-BEING FOR MORE THAN 1 BILLION

REDUCING ENVIRONMENTAL IMPACT BY 1/2

ENHANCING LIVELIHOODS FOR MILLIONS

OUR STRATEGY
To deliver long-term compounding growth and sustainable value creation by:

Winning with brands and innovation | Winning in the marketplace | Winning through continuous improvement | Winning with people

Supported by Category strategies:

Personal Care: Grow the core, build the premium

Home Care: Margin to industry levels, emerging market-led growth

Foods and Refreshment: Leaner business model, growth in emerging markets

VALUE WE CREATE

CONSUMER BENEFITS	TOP & BOTTOM LINE GROWTH	IMPROVED HEALTH & WELL-BEING	REDUCED ENVIRONMENTAL IMPACT	ENHANCED LIVELIHOODS
We sell products that help people to feel good, look good and get more out of life	We deliver consistent, competitive, profitable and responsible growth	We are helping hundreds of millions of people take action to improve their health & well-being	We are working to halve the environmental footprint of the making and use of our products as we grow our business	We are enhancing the livelihoods of millions of people as we grow our business
		SUSTAINABLE DEVELOPMENT GOALS	SUSTAINABLE DEVELOPMENT GOALS	SUSTAINABLE DEVELOPMENT GOALS

Figure 8.2 How Unilever Creates Value

The SLP provided the goals and programmatic approaches to drive sustainability performance and is foundational to Unilever's strong reputation as a leader.

Collective pursuit: collaboration for sustainable living

Unilever has become increasingly involved in a growing range of collaborations including some well-established corporate responsibility coalitions, a range of issue-specific multi-stakeholder initiatives, ongoing and defined-life partnerships with other businesses such as M&S and Walmart and with NGOs, international institutions, and development agencies such as Oxfam, the World Bank, Germany's GiZ, and the UK's DFID. (Please see Figure 8.3.)

Collaboration for sustainable living is not, however, simply a matter of many more partnerships with a much wider range of partners than in the past. Much more fundamentally, it is that many more of these collaborations relate to core business operations like strengthening the supply chain, finding required new technologies, and developing new ways of marketing, etc.

Part of the thinking behind the SLP was to set such ambitious targets that the company would be forced to work with others if it were to have a hope of meeting them. As Polman told us:

> We said the goals that we are setting are so audacious, we really can't do it alone. So, if you feel strongly about it as well, come join us. There is nothing that we can do in isolation, if you want to attack these bigger challenges. So it made us a little bit more human, [and it gave us] a little bit of humility and humanity at the same time.[13]

The sheer range of the collaborations that Unilever is now involved with is mind-boggling. Unsurprisingly, the company did an internal exercise a few years into the SLP to segment the range of its involvements, with a view to terminating those that were no longer relevant or delivering for them. This meant reviewing and, in some cases, renewing the purpose and form of their involvement with existing organizations, beefing up some collaborations that were strategic to SLP delivery, and, in some cases, joining additional partnerships or creating new initiatives to meet strategic company needs. Polman quoted to us the example of the Consumer Goods Forum:

> We created a body of all the major retailers and manufacturers who together have about $4 trillion of retail sales. It has people in there like Walmart and Tesco but also companies like Coca-Cola and Pepsi. So, it is a very important body and we made a commitment. We got the industry to make a commitment to move out of deforestation for soy, for paper, for pulp, for beef, for palm oil by 2020, and we are really on the right path to get there.[14]

Unilver Collaborations, Early 2000s	Unilever Collaborations, 2017
ABIS: Academy For Business In Society	ABIS: Academy For Business In Society
Business In The Community	Avaaz
CDP	Bop Innovation Center
Gavi, The Vaccine Alliance	B-Team
Global Alliance For Improved Nutrition (GAIN)	Business And Sustainable Development Commission
Kenya Tea Development Agency (KTDA)	Business For Innovative Climate And Energy Policy (BICEP)
Marine Stewardship Council (MSC)	Business In The Community
Oxfam	Carbon Pricing Leadership Coalition
Rainforest Alliance	CDP
Roundtable On Sustainable Palm Oil	Champions 12.3
Sustainable Agriculture Initiative (SAI) Platform	Circular Economy 100 (Ellen Macarthur Foundation)
United Nations Global Compact	Consumer Goods Forum
UNICEF	EU Alliance To Save Energy (EU-ASE)
WASUP: Water & Sanitation For The Urban Poor	Gavi, The Vaccine Alliance
World Business Council For Sustainable Development (WBCSD)	Global Alliance For Improved Nutrition (GAIN)
World Economic Forum (WEF)	Global Canopy Programme
	Global Commission On The Economy And Climate
	Global Task Force For Scaling Up Nutrition
	HRH The Prince Of Waless Corporate Leaders Group
	IDH & Norwegian Government's "Production, Protection And Inclusion" Fund
	International Fund For Agricultural Development (IFAD)
	Kenya Tea Development Agency (KTDA)
	Low Carbon Technology Partnership Initiatives
	Marine Stewardship Council (MSC)
	New Vision For Agriculture
	New York Declaration On Forests
	One Young World
	Oxfam
	PROGRESS, A Foods Sector Industry Partnership On Supplier Standards
	Rainforest Alliance
	RE100
	Reforest Action
	Refrigerants Naturally
	Round Table On Responsible Soy Association
	Roundtable On Sustainable Palm Oil
	Scaling Up Nutrition (SUN)
	Solidaridad And Internet.Org To Boost Opportunities For Young People In Agriculture
	Sustainable Agriculture Initiative (SAI) Platform
	Symrise And GIZ To Source Vanilla In Madagascar
	Transform (Partnership With UK's Department For International Development & Clinton Giustra Enterprise Partnership)
	Tropical Forest Alliance 2020
	United Nations Global Compact
	UNICEF
	Vetiver Together Initiative
	WASH4Work
	WASUP: Water & Sanitation For The Urban Poor
	We Mean Business Coalition Of Coalitions
	World Business Council For Sustainable Development (WBCSD)
	World Economic Forum (WEF)
	World Environment Centre
	World Resources Institute
	World Toilet Day
	Xinjiang (China) Smallholder Farmers Training With Supplier COFCO Thune.

Figure 8.3 Unilever Collaborations Past and Present

One innovative element of the Unilever approach to Collaboration in recent years has been an acceptance that as a leader, there is a responsibility to share learning and knowledge – not just about the processes of embedding sustainability but also on more sustainable technologies. Hence, the decision to share patents for things like smaller deodorant packaging and take leadership roles in a range of collaborative ventures such as Polman's chairmanship of the World Business Council for Sustainable Development from 2015–2017. Unilever also worked to co-found the Business and Sustainable Development Commission to promote business involvement in the fulfillment of the SDGs.

Outspoken

Polman and his leadership team seem to have been almost ubiquitous in recent years in advocating for sustainable business. As the astute corporate sustainability commentator Jo Confino has observed:

> At the heart of Polman's thinking is the desire to show the SLP is not just about doing good but about good business. By providing a concrete example of the business case for sustainability, he hopes it will convince other companies to follow suit and help convince the investment community to move away from their obsession with short-termism.[15]

Because of Polman's intent to demonstrate the value of better sustainability performance, in recent years Unilever has become increasingly vocal in advocating for public policies that will create an enabling environment for sustainable business and sustainable development.

This has included having to persuade competition authorities that creating Collaboration initiatives such as the Roundtable on Sustainable Palm Oil was not a buyers' cartel and, therefore, anti-competitive, but a desirable pre-competitive stage Collaboration.

As Polman shared with us:

> You need leaders that are driven by a stronger purpose than just shareholder primacy or their own company; that want to work extra hours during the week to make things happen; that can handle the setbacks and frustrations of dealing with NGOs or others. The road to change is not that easy otherwise someone would have done it before you, and that is why we are investing more and more in trying to get such leaders. Again, I just want to stress, at the end of the day we know what we need to do but we need it faster and at scale.[16]

Key lieutenants have also taken high-profile advocacy roles. Chief Marketing Officer Keith Weed, for example, has mobilized the "Unstereotype Alliance" to eradicate outdated stereotypes in advertising.[17] Unilever was also the first company in the world to create a specific unit to identify and co-ordinate company Advocacy for pro-sustainable development public policies on climate and other critical issues.

Advocacy is also what you don't do and what you stop doing. In this vein, Unilever has been prepared to withdraw from long-standing corporate memberships of traditional business representative organizations when it believes that the umbrella organization's stances are inconsistent with Unilever's own position on climate and other issues. One example is the company's very public withdrawal from Business Europe in 2014.[18]

Conclusion

Unilever's dominance of the Leaders Survey in recent years has come about from the way that it has embedded all our five leadership attributes and thanks to building on the strong historical foundation stemming from the founder's early commitment to societal wellbeing. This has included:

- A growing commitment to more explicit sustainability practice from Polman's predecessors Niall FitzGerald and Patrick Cescau in the UK and from Morris Tabaksblat and Antony Burgmans in the Netherlands. One of the remarkable things about the company's approach has been the way multiple successive leaders contributed to the steady development and deepening of Unilever's commitment to sustainability from the mid-1990s onwards, which resulted in it being one of six explicit strands of Unilever's corporate business strategy by the time Polman became CEO.
- The integration of sustainability with brands, first through the Brand Imprint Assessment process and now with Brand Purpose, which is crucial for a brands-dominated business like Unilever
- The positive legacy of tools and techniques such as the Oxfam/Unilever Indonesia country impact study
- The processes for identifying Unilever's material impacts as reflected and reinforced in SLP
- Clear board oversight including the dedicated corporate responsibility committee and the external sustainability expert advisory group that exists to advise the board, and
- A commitment to continuous improvement and innovation, including the use of the Better Business Blueprint and benefit corporation-like thinking to keep the business moving forward.

All this suggests Unilever will keep going *All In* even after Paul Polman has stepped down as CEO.

Notes

1 Authors' interview, Aug 11th 2017.
2 Ibid.

3 Unilever website, www.unilever.com/sustainable-living/improving-health-and-well-being/health-and-hygiene/changing-handwashing-habits-for-better-health/

4 Makower, J., "Why Unilever Is Betting on Open Innovation for Sustainability," *GreenBiz*, Mar 29, 2012 accessed Jan 4 2018.

5 Unilever website, www.unilever.com/about/innovation/open-innovation/ accessed Jan 4 2018.

6 "Unilever Releases First-of-Its-Kind Human Rights Report," Press Release, June 20th 2015, www.unilever.co.uk/news/press-releases/2015/unilever-releases-first-of-its-kind-human-rights-report.html The company's second human rights report was published at the end of 2017.

7 Interestingly, however, Unilever had only introduced quarterly profit forecasts in the mid-1990s.

8 Michael Skapinker, M. and Daneshkhu, S., "Can Unilever's Paul Polman Change the Way We Do Business?," *Financial Times*, Sept 29, 2016.

9 Ibid.

10 Authors' interview, Nov 7th 2017.

11 Corporate Citizenship Briefing June 29th 2015.

12 Eco-Business 0808 2017.

13 Ibid.

14 Ibid.

15 Ibid.

16 Ibid.

17 Gwynn S., "Unilever Recruits Industry Giants to Fight Gender Stereotypes in Advertising," Campaign, June 20th 2017, www.campaignlive.co.uk/article/unilever-recruits-industry-giants-fight-gender-stereotypes-advertising/1437041

18 Shankleman J., "Unilever Confirms It Has Quit BusinessEurope Lobby Group," *Business Green*, Aug 22nd 2014, www.businessgreen.com/bg/news/2361524/unilever-confirms-it-has-quit-businesseurope-lobby-group

9 Interface

Scaling Mount Sustainability

"Never doubt that a small group of thoughtful, concerned citizens can change the world; indeed it is the only thing that ever has."

Margaret Mead

Interface is the only company that has been recognized among the top companies on the GlobeScan-SustainAbility Leaders Survey in every year from the Survey's inception through 2017. This is a remarkable example of comprehensive (what Interface calls "holistic") leadership through two decades and three eras of corporate sustainability leadership. As such, we wanted to explore Interface's journey through the voices of the company's leaders.[1]

Our interviews with Interface were unique in that we spoke at length with the Chairman, Dan Hendrix, and the company's Chief Sustainability Officer, Erin Meezan, together in both the summer and autumn of 2017. We quote them extensively in this chapter to bring the Interface approach to life. In this manner, we hope to share the way the company sees the world and how it has anticipated and responded to the challenges and opportunities that come with going *All In* for sustainability.

Like Unilever, the secret to Interface's success has a great deal to do with its ability to drive world-class performance in each of our five leadership attributes – Purpose, Plan, Culture, Collaboration, and Advocacy. Further, it is the blending and reinforcing of its approach and actions in these five areas that have led stakeholders to view the company as a leader for over two decades. (Please see Figure 9.1 for an overview of how stakeholders define Interface's leadership.)

Interface's Purpose, expressed so passionately by the company's founder, Ray Anderson, allowed the company to devise a Plan of great ambition. The Culture of the company encouraged sustainability engagement and innovation and has been reinforced through transparency. The Interface Culture is also one that celebrates risk; Hendrix commented that embracing internal ideas, even before being able to prove their ROI, has been essential to building and maintaining widespread internal support. Collaboration and Advocacy have been hallmarks of the Interface approach and play an increasing role today

Figure 9.1 Word Cloud Describing Interface's Leadership

as the company works with others to influence system change and create the conditions for the transition to a truly sustainable economy and society.

The "little carpet company that could change the world"

Ray Anderson, Interface's founder, was an industrial engineer who graduated from Georgia Tech. He created Interface in 1973. Anderson was an entrepreneur who went into business to make carpet tiles for companies and large institutions. He did not create the business to make a positive difference in the world – he simply wanted to build a successful company.

Dan Hendrix described his original impressions of Interface's founder:

> Ray Anderson was one of the toughest entrepreneurs I ever met. He was a huge capitalist, and he really had a drive – he didn't take no for an answer on anything. His personal transformation became our company's big pivot, and it couldn't have happened if he wasn't driven, courageous, and really a true visionary.[2]

The transformation Hendrix references Anderson experiencing in 1994 was the beginning of a journey that led Interface to become a standard bearer for corporate sustainability leadership. By this time, Interface was a nearly billion-dollar company, one of the largest interior furnishing businesses in the world. However, customers, architects, and interior designers, all critical stakeholders for Interface, were beginning to ask about the company's environmental performance. At the heart of these inquiries was the fact that carpets at that time were almost all petroleum based and manufactured with a "take-make-use-dispose" approach, which meant significant environmental impacts.

Hendrix explained the lead-up to Anderson's transformation:

> Take yourself back to 1994 at Interface. We'd just come off the biggest recession that Interface had faced, which wreaked havoc within the company from 1991 to 1994. We had made a lot of acquisitions. We had eighty-five hundred employees and we had a lot of different businesses. The architect and design community were really talking about "What are we going to do about the environment?" Ray came into my office one day frustrated, and, if you knew Ray, when he got frustrated, he got red-faced. He said, "Dan when we are talking about the environment, isn't it just complying with law, there is nothing else to it?" He sat down and had a conversation with me asking if I knew anything else we should be doing around the environment. I'm a CFO and I'm like, "Hell no, we're not spending another dime on this."[3]

Customers, however, continued to ask about Interface's environmental impacts. Because of this, and due to his innate customer focus, Anderson brought a group of internal people together to come up with a company manifesto on the environment. The team asked Anderson to give a kick-off speech about his vision – and he realized that he didn't have one. That's when Anderson began to study sustainability.

Hendrix told us:

> Ray was an engineer by education and so he had to have a formula, a roadmap of where he was trying to go and what he was trying to do. So he started reaching out to all these experts . . . we eventually called them the Dream Team, people like Paul Hawken, John Picard, Amory Lovins, Bill Browning and Janine Benyus. Ray was just asking questions and meeting with them, saying "Would you meet with me and talk about sustainability?" Ray was trying to formulate the business case for sustainability – one that he could get the company galvanized around. He spent a lot of time doing that and trying to figure that out.

Here is how Ray Anderson himself described this journey in 2004:

> For 21 years, I never gave a thought to what we were taking from the earth or doing to the earth in the making of our products. And then in the summer of 1994, we began to hear questions from our customers we had never heard before: "What's your company doing for the environment?" And we didn't have answers. The real answer was, "not very much."

And at sort of the propitious moment, this book landed on my desk. It was Paul Hawken's book, *The Ecology of Commerce*. And I began to read it, really desperate for inspiration, and very quickly into that book I found the phrase "the death of birth." It was E.O. Wilson's expression for species extinction, "the death of birth," and it was a point of a spear into my chest, and I read on, and the spear went deeper, and it became an epiphanal experience, a total change of mindset for myself and a change of paradigm.

. . . One day early in this journey, it dawned on me that the way I'd been running Interface is the way of the plunderer. Plundering something that's not mine, something that belongs to every creature on earth, and I said to myself "My goodness, the day must come when this is illegal, when plundering is not allowed." I mean, it must come. So, I said to myself "My goodness, some day people like me will end up in jail."

And when I think of what could be, I visualize an organization of people committed to a purpose and the purpose is doing no harm. I see a company that has severed the umbilical cord to earth for its raw materials. Taking raw materials that have already been extracted and using them over and over again. Driving that process with renewable energy. It is our plan, it remains our plan, to climb Mount Sustainability. That mountain is higher than Everest, infinitely higher than Everest, far more difficult to scale.[4]

Purpose then and now

Ray Anderson's spear through the chest marked the beginning of Interface's commitment to sustainable business. It led to a clear articulation of the company's Purpose: *Be the first company that, by its deeds, shows the entire world what sustainability is in all its dimensions: people, process, product, place and profits – and in doing so, become restorative through the power of influence.*[5]

Interface's Purpose was (especially when crafted) and remains remarkable for its comprehensive and holistic quality. The Purpose captures the essential elements of leadership from all three eras of corporate sustainability leadership from 1997–present identified in this book and foreshadows the coming Regenerative Era we predict, especially with the phrase "become restorative through the power of influence." This powerfully emphasizes the importance of Advocacy to drive systemic change and the impact that moving from a harm reduction to a regenerative approach could have.

A fundamental turning point for the company came at a global sales team meeting in 1997. Anderson was able to find a way to rally the full team and share his vision that being sustainable made good business sense too. Dan Hendrix explained:

Ray didn't just recruit our leadership team around his vision, he was able to energize 8,000 people at our company to buy in. One mind at a time, he used to say, as one by one we had our own epiphanies. We all believed we could really change the world if we could do this. And the capitalist in Ray was still in there, because he always ended his pitch by saying, "And you know what else? We are going to sell a hell of a lot of carpet tile if we do this." It's a better business model and one that will be hard for our competitors to follow. And so you got a lot of people, including the CFO, who rallied around this as the right thing to do. If you talk about what was the transformation point, the pivot point that really launched Interface on its sustainability journey, it was that sales meeting where people said, "You know what, we are getting on board."[6]

But the journey ahead was challenging. Hendrix shared with us an anecdote about how the company's Purpose helped drive decisions internally, even when it went against short-term financial realities:

There was a point in the journey in 2002 when we were really struggling financially. The economy was in recession. I was the CEO, we were spending millions more on sustainability than our competitors, and we were in the huge downturn after the dotcom bust. I was sitting in a meeting and we're debating a new technology, Cool Blue, which would be our takeback and recycling system. It was a fifteen-million-dollar investment. We were having a debate in the room: David Oakey was our head of design, still is today. John Wells ran our biggest business, the Americas business. I had pushed the initiative back about three times. First of all, I didn't think it could work, and second of all, we didn't have the money. That is when John Wells said to me, "You realize you got our people more energized around this idea than they have been about anything before. They are all getting creative and thinking outside of the box. If we turn down an innovative idea because it doesn't have an ROI that makes sense right up front, they are going to quit caring, and they are going to quit trying. We are going to lose some of them and we are going to lose this whole momentum around sustainability. So are we going to walk this talk or not?" I am like, "Well, hell, if you made that speech I guess we're going to walk the talk."

And walking the talk matters, as Hendrix noted in saying "If you don't have a higher purpose that includes the environment and society, you are not going to get or keep the best people."[7]

What has made Interface such a strong leader in sustainability is its capacity to evolve over time. Climbing Mount Sustainability has been an ambitious North Star for the company for two decades. Just as the company began to see that it would meet its goals for 2020, it began to look for the next frontier. In today's Purpose-Driven Era, it is fitting that Interface has updated its own Purpose. For 24 years, it stuck to Ray Anderson's original North Star for the company, but in 2016 it began looking beyond its 2020 Mission Zero strategy and exploring what might be next. The company

Figure 9.2 Interface Strategic Purpose

asked what a revised Purpose might look like, one that would be true to Anderson's vision, but also simpler and ready for future sustainability challenges. The result was a new Purpose that will take the company into the next decade: "Lead Industry to Love the World."

With this new Purpose, Interface has a new mission. In 2016, the company launched its Climate Take Back mission, with a focus on running the business, and inspiring change across society, in a way that reverses global warming (see Figure 9.2 on how this aligns with the company's strategy). Climate Take Back is optimistic because the company is ". . . convinced fundamental change needs to happen in our global response to climate change. We need to stop just thinking about how to limit the damage caused by climate change and start thinking about how to create a climate fit for life."[8]

This Purpose will need a new Plan to deliver on its ambitions to take the climate back. Let us now go back to the beginning and see how Interface has aligned Purpose and Plan over time.

A Plan to climb "Mount Sustainability"

Interface operationalized its original Purpose with a Plan in 1995 when the company committed to a 25-year journey to the top of "Mount Sustainability," Ray Anderson's metaphor for creating a sustainable business.

In the early years of the journey, there were fits and starts in learning and the development of management tools and variability in terms of the degree to which different parts of the business embraced sustainability. Dan Hendrix told us this story outlining some of the early experience at Interface:

> I was then CFO, and Ray asked me to develop zero waste standards, saying "We are not going to throw away anything – we are eliminating the idea of a waste allowance in manufacturing altogether." He started

getting a lot of traction with the manufacturing folks – the shop floor was engaged in thinking outside the box about waste elimination, but sales and marketing and admin folks not so much. We measured our carbon footprint years before anyone really understood what a carbon footprint meant. We measured how much water and energy we were using, started talking about benign emissions. We started asking, how do we minimize our footprint? This was all new, so all of a sudden the company was getting a lot of visibility and a lot of energy. Then Ray got into recycling, and we got into all this dialogue around what today we call the circular economy. But it all started with eliminating waste, [and that] is the idea that became transformational in manufacturing.

Hendrix further noted that: "When Ray envisioned sustainability it was holistic. It wasn't a hero product. It was: you transform your whole company."[9] Erin Meezan added that, "The plan has to be not just a vision but it has to be the business strategy to get there. How you're going to make that work across your multi-stakeholder model and how you're going to actually measure and frankly disclose progress."[10]

Together with several external advisors, Interface worked through the question of "If Nature designed a company, what would it look like?" This became the basis for what Interface called the "seven fronts" of the climb to "Mount Sustainability," each of which sought to have operations and business models emulate natural systems as much as possible:

Front 1 – Eliminate Waste: Eliminate all forms of waste in every area of business.

Front 2 – Benign Emissions: Eliminate toxic substances from products, vehicles and facilities.

Front 3 – Renewable Energy: Operate facilities with 100% renewable energy.

Front 4 – Close the Loop: Redesign processes and products to close the technical loop using recovered and bio-based materials.

Front 5 – Resource Efficient Transportation: Transport people and products efficiently to eliminate waste and emissions.

Front 6 – Sensitize Stakeholders: Create a culture that uses sustainability principles to improve the lives and livelihoods of all of our stakeholders – employees, partners, suppliers, customers, investors, and communities.

Front 7 – Redesign Commerce: Create a new business model that demonstrates and supports the value of sustainability-based commerce.[11]

Together, progress on these fronts would allow the company to convert from a traditional, linear, twentieth century business into a modern, circular, twenty-first century business. This conversion required significant redesign of

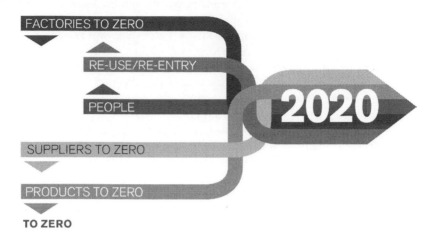

Figure 9.3 Interface Mission Zero Focus Areas

the industrial process and the products it produced, and for Interface to be driven by innovation and technology and fueled by renewable energy. (Please see Figure 9.3 for the key focus areas for Mission Zero.)

One of the most tangible outcomes of this transformation was a reinvention of the company's business model. The traditional approach to carpeting was to sell enough flooring to cover the entire room. As parts became worn, the entire carpet would be replaced – even those parts that were virtually untouched and remained pristine. This wasteful process was at the core of Interface's negative environmental impacts. The company turned this model on its head and created a service approach, whereby carpeting was broken down into tiles, allowing for replacement of only the parts that needed replacing (high traffic areas, etc.). Interface also began recycling used tiles back, literally putting them back into the manufacturing process to generate new carpet tiles. This innovation changed not only Interface but also the entire carpet industry.

Erin Meezan described her sense of why Interface's strategy has been so successful:

> As a sustainability person coming into the business I think what is really interesting about Interface's approach, and why it has taken hold, and why it was as successful as it was in transforming the business, is that it started out really from a transformational place. It was led from the top by a really strong leader and it was not about incremental goals or how do we transform a little part of the business. It was fundamentally at its heart about how do we transform our business to be something different. So it acknowledged that we were going to create a new business framework and a model and it was going to be comprehensive.[12]

In 2004, when Interface named its sustainability strategy, "Mission Zero," to convey its commitment to getting to zero environmental impact by 2020, Ray Anderson described the vision of Mission Zero this way:

> If we're successful, we'll spend the rest of our days harvesting yester-year's carpets and other petro-chemically derived products, and recy-cling them into new materials; and converting sunlight into energy; with zero scrap going to the landfill and zero emissions into the ecosystem. And we'll be doing well . . . very well . . . by doing good.[13]

Interface's commitment has not wavered despite Ray Anderson's death in 2011, leadership changes, competition, and recessions. On the latter point, it has been argued that the savings the company made from its waste elimina-tion strategy enabled them to survive economic downturns and prosper while competitors with shallower sustainability programs struggled.

As we approach 2020, Interface is close to achieving its Mission Zero goals. It has accomplished remarkable progress, reducing its impacts sig-nificantly across its operations. The company transparently reports on its progress annually. Figure 9.4 outlines its "Mission Progress" at the end of the year in 2017.

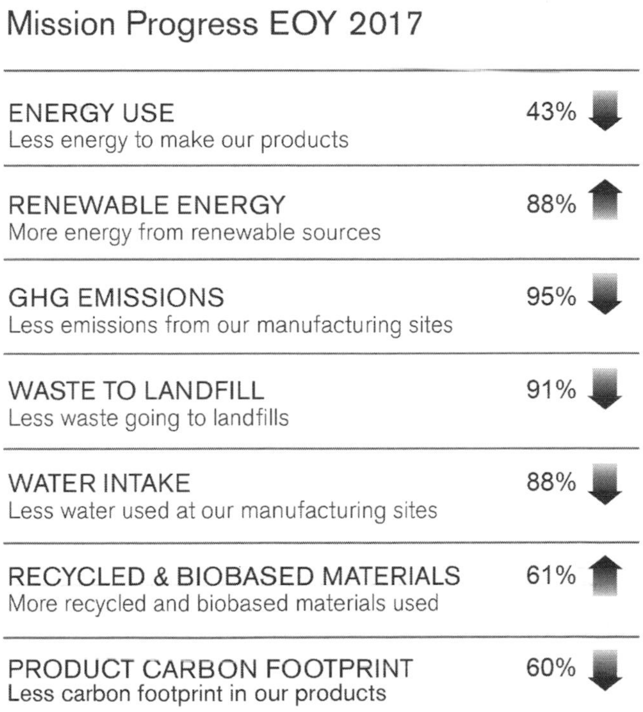

Mission Progress EOY 2017

ENERGY USE
Less energy to make our products
43% ⬇

RENEWABLE ENERGY
More energy from renewable sources
88% ⬆

GHG EMISSIONS
Less emissions from our manufacturing sites
95% ⬇

WASTE TO LANDFILL
Less waste going to landfills
91% ⬇

WATER INTAKE
Less water used at our manufacturing sites
88% ⬇

RECYCLED & BIOBASED MATERIALS
More recycled and biobased materials used
61% ⬆

PRODUCT CARBON FOOTPRINT
Less carbon footprint in our products
60% ⬇

Figure 9.4 Interface Sustainability Progress

The Plan that Interface put in place to transform itself into a zero-impact enterprise has been difficult to deliver, but rewarding for the company and a catalyst in the broader societal debate on the role and future of business. If a petro-chemical intense industrial company like Interface can achieve Mission Zero, and do it in a way that mobilizes its people, supply chain, and wider stakeholders, while delivering strong financial returns, why can't all companies?

Let us now turn to look at how Interface's Culture helped it scale Mount Sustainability.

A culture of sustainability

The drive of the entrepreneurial Culture that made the company the largest commercial carpet company in the world, along with a willingness to innovate while being transparent and engaging along the way has created a unique alchemy inside Interface that facilitates it success today.

As Dan Hendrix told us, feeding the Culture was a fundamental success factor in becoming a sustainability leader:

> We really had a great culture going in 1994 when Ray had the epiphany, but it was more of a family culture . . . an entrepreneurial culture. Then Ray had the epiphany and later we had that sales meeting in 1997, where 1,200 of our people from around the world heard from Ray and his Dream Team for the first time. They were all in. Sustainability created a challenge within our culture to become more innovative; it challenged the culture to figure out how to create a roadmap when there wasn't a roadmap; and it empowered the heck out of them to actually get there. It reinforced how important this purpose and mission was around sustainability. We fed that culture by empowering and empowering and innovating . . . the innovation pipeline that came out of sustainability was what fueled the whole culture: "Hey we can do this, let's go." That was all driven from the top with Ray and then with me and now with Jay [Gould, the current CEO].[14] Then you have people like Erin [Meezan, the current CSO] who are the purpose-driven zealots about how we get the sustainability out there, talking to our people and teaching our people, so I mean it came from the ground up and it came from the top down, and it came with innovation and empowerment.[15]

Culture was recognized as a fundamental component required to convert a "brown" industrial company to a "green" one. In fact, at one point, the company invited in a PhD student[16] to study the company's Culture and how it was a factor in the transformation. Erin Meezan shared the key learning from this research:

> It has been a really good roadmap for how we did it at Interface. A couple of the things that she pulled out were things like giving people

permission to engage. One of the things Interface did was have Ray and the other senior leaders in the business, like Dan and our business presidents, explicitly say to people: "We want your ideas, you have an opportunity to experiment, we expect you to engage in this."

Second, by not presenting it as a finished strategy, but saying we have this broad mission, and it is ambitious enough that you can kind of make it your own, and so you can help us define that. As we've gone back and interviewed employees and said: "Why did you feel connected to this?" It is because it was broad enough in the beginning that they could help make it their own. You knew you could become a waste champion; you could be someone who was really interested in doing volunteering in your community, and there was a way for you to personalize this and to bring your own kind of take on sustainability that fit into our framework.

A third was consistency. I mean, you know, Ray had the vision, but Dan was actually the guy who funded all this stuff and who took the crazy risk to invest in a recycled backing line or a program that would bring back carpet from customers or a big renewable energy purchase. So that consistency, the teams consistently knowing that they would get things funded, and that Interface was behind this even when we had financial challenges, even when we really struggled with some of our core customer markets, that was huge. We consistently funded stuff. We never really took it off the table and I think that was a huge message to our people.

Finally, another thing that we did is even though the zero footprint vision is huge, we really broke it down into very specific bites. In the early days, we focused on something really tangible which was waste. We made that very real. I mean down to the level of teams in the local businesses scooping yarn up off the floor, pasting that ball of yarn onto a poster and saying to people: "this is not sustainable and by the way, this is $75 worth of yarn or $300 worth of yarn." They really got focused on making it tangible and translatable at the factory associate level.[17]

Innovation has been a critical thread throughout Interface's journey and has pushed the organization into different directions. One example is how it moved into the residential carpet business. FLOR, a carpet tile business for residential consumers, launched in 2005, brought to the public a sustainable residential carpet tile option. With sustainability at the product's core, FLOR was a breakthrough product for residential consumers and a good example of the type of innovation that has become commonplace at Interface.

Going forward, the company remains committed to engaging its employees and cultivating the culture to foster more innovation and progress on its sustainability agenda. Part of this has to do with ongoing efforts to be transparent both inside and outside the organization. Measuring its impacts, progress on its goals, and overall performance has become a fixture of the company's Culture. Dan Hendrix explains his thinking on the importance of transparency:

> There is so much transparency out there today that companies really can't run and hide. We're really focused on the next generation of millennials and really do believe they will dedicate their careers to the people and the companies that are transparent, that are trying to do the right thing. They'll vote with their careers and they will vote their wallets.[18]

Erin Meezan told us that after Ray Anderson's passing Dan Hendrix asked her to:

> figure out how we keep people connected and engaged in Mission Zero after Ray's death. What are the things we should do? We actually went around the world to our global factories and just asked people, what is it that we are doing well now to keep you connected to this? What makes you passionate about coming to Interface and working on sustainability? We identified in the European business that they had created a learning program that was three levels of sustainability learning. Once you completed those three levels you were allowed to be an Interface Sustainability Ambassador. That had a huge impact on really motivating people to stay connected; to learn what we were doing; to become an advocate for it not just externally but internally. One of the lessons we took from that is building out a program that will launch in 2018 that every associate of Interface will go through will be modeled on that [European] program.[19]

The corporate Culture at Interface has been molded to facilitate sustainable business progress, with deep roots, according to Dan Hendrix: "There is no turning back when it comes to our culture. It's part of our DNA."[20] That same culture has a huge influence on Collaboration and Advocacy, which are the aspects of Interface's efforts that we explore next.

Scaling together

Ray Anderson understood early on that he needed the knowledge and experience of others who had been thinking about sustainability for a long time. He sought out people like Amory Lovins,[21] Paul Hawken,[22] Janine Benyus,[23] and Jonathan Porrit,[24] and many others including the organization The Natural Step.[25] Interface now saw Collaboration as a critical part of its journey.

This early Collaboration around the science and potential solutions to sustainability challenges, and the openness to listening and allowing others to influence the direction of the company was near unprecedented. The "Dream Team" of advisors that Anderson pulled together agreed to support the effort because the invitation included the opportunity to influence Interface's strategic direction. Erin Meezan suggested that: "Some of the original reasons why Paul Hawken and Amory Lovins and Janine Benyus engaged with us is because they had a vote in some of those early decisions about where we were going. They truly had the leverage to make some big decisions with us, and that to me goes beyond collaboration."[26]

Hendrix confirmed the centrality of Collaboration in Interface's approach to its sustainability strategy: "Collaboration is at the heart of everything we have done – we couldn't have done it without suppliers, vendor partners, customers, field experts and industry peers. We had to innovate our way, every step of the way."[27]

An example of how Interface collaborated with its supply chain to drive its sustainability performance forward related to its yarn suppliers. At one of its Supplier Summits, Interface shared with suppliers its business case for switching to sustainable raw materials and the vision the company had for a closed-loop system which would require recycled content for its carpets. When some of its main suppliers refused to innovate around recycled content, two lesser known manufacturers of yarn, Universal, and Aquafil, "got inspired by the vision and said: 'We'll follow Interface,'" says Hendrix.[28] Interface offered an incentive of secure and significant business if suppliers could innovate at the pace required. They did, and to this day they enjoy a substantial business relationship with Interface.

This mindset of Collaboration has also included engagement with investors. Hendrix told us of his recent engagements with Interface's top institutional investors and the changes he is seeing in how they approach sustainability:

> I talked to ten of our largest shareholders and I asked them, how does sustainability rank in terms of your investment decision? Nine of them said it is a risk factor filter and one of the key investment decisions today. It is not just about profits. They understand climate change is a business risk, and they believe that social inequity is a problem for business. So investors like companies like Interface because they understand that a social mission can drive innovation, goodwill in the marketplace and employee engagement. So I think the investors are on board now.[29]

Interface is keen to engage the investment community further in future years, going beyond its own shareholders and working with other companies to challenge some assumptions around sustainability and financial performance. As Meezan explained: "I feel like there is a voice that some of the sustainable business community has around challenging the dominant narrative that sustainable companies don't perform as well that we need to challenge collectively."[30]

Perhaps the most radical collaboration that Interface has engaged in is with nature itself. Early on, the company worked with Janine Benyus and her Biomimcry Institute. Biomimicry uses nature as an inspiration for human innovation. The thinking is based on the idea that, after billions of years of evolution, nature is replete with solutions to many of the world's challenges.

Interface has applied biomimicry to its product design. One example is its Entropy collection which became the first in a new line of carpet tiles that use patterns found in nature to improve the aesthetics of flooring while also reducing waste. Another is its "factory as a forest" initiative through which Interface envisions future factories that provide the same ecosystem services – clean air and water, carbon sequestration, cycling nutrients, etc. – as a natural forest.

Advocating for the planet

The final sustainability leadership attribute, Advocacy, has also had an important role to play in Interface's journey. Right from the beginning, Ray Anderson saw the importance of demonstrating to the wider world that reaching "Mount Sustainability" was possible and that by doing so it would give courage to others to follow.

After his 1994 epiphany, Anderson spoke wherever he could – conferences, colleges, TV, documentaries, etc. He was an indefatigable advocate for sustainability and told his personal and corporate story with great humility and passion. He inspired thousands of people across the world to think differently about business and how it could be an agent for positive change.[31]

Interface's Chairman, Dan Hendrix, described Anderson's belief that Interface could be influential well beyond its operations: "If you looked at all his workings and writings and speeches, Ray always believed in this restorative concept of Interface, and that by influencing a lot of people along the way, that this little carpet company could actually change the world."[32]

This belief persists today. There is a commitment to engage externally and build a case for sustainable business based on Interface's experience. Dan Hendrix told us that:

> One of the things that we did was our people got engaged with the outside world and became big advocates for sustainability. I think one reason that we get mentioned in the Leaders Survey is because we're out there talking about sustainability and trying to convince other companies to get on this bandwagon and go. From day one we've had speaker bureaus, Erin is on planes all the time going out and speaking; Ray Anderson spoke a hundred times a year; I speak. We all feel like we need to pay it forward.[33]

Today, as the company embarks on its Climate Take Back journey, it still has a great deal of work to do across the board when it comes to Advocacy. Erin Meezan acknowledged this firstly requires greater engagement with the financial community:

> We need to be more active in the broader conversation in the investment community. Maybe the angle is not around whether we perform

better, but if we're much better positioned as the world finally wakes up to the reality of climate change or the reality of the deep challenges we face around sustainable development. These companies who've already internalized it and created a business model to not just deal with it but to actually benefit from it are much better positioned. We have failed to make that argument and I do think it is because a lot of the sustainable pioneers are family owned and they don't have to deal with the market. I think we've suffered by not making the case but we need to.[34]

Meezan also feels that Interface needs to have more missionary zeal regarding its radical approach to climate change, saying it must be about:

trying to convince more companies and to really frame the conversation around shifting your corporate strategy from a low carbon strategy to a strategy that goes beyond that. Climate Take Back, if we are able to do that at Interface, we are quite aware that it will have a very small impact. But if we are able to build a roadmap and change a conversation and get a bunch of corporates who are ready to have this conversation about what a new corporate climate strategy looks like, if we can shift that and frame that much like we did with Mission Zero, I think we can have a really big impact on helping other companies advance.[35]

Conclusion

Looking ahead to 2030, it will be fascinating to see how Interface develops not only with its new Climate Take Back as the Purpose-Driven Era continues, but also how it might lead the transition to the predicted Regenerative Era. Will it play a meaningful role in delivery of the Sustainable Development Goals? Will it be involved in addressing global inequality? How might Interface become more of a leader on Collaboration and Advocacy, attributes vital to achieve its stated objectives?

In many ways, Interface possesses leadership characteristics of the coming Regenerative Era already. Ray Anderson was a keen supporter of Industrial Ecology and drove his company to embrace a closed-loop business model, an early precursor to the circular economy business models being trialed by others today. The company's initial Purpose specifically referenced "becoming restorative" – a pioneering idea in the 1990s, and one that we believe will really take hold in the coming decade.

The environment and society both need regenerative business models to become the norm. Interface has been a champion for approaches to industry that align with nature for longer than almost any other business. The latest leg of its journey, Climate Take Back, will require regeneration or regenerative practices at scale. While the pathway to achieve this is unknown, Ray Anderson's legacy and the company's experience to date make it likely it will successfully go *All In* and achieve its Climate Take Back ambitions, providing a regenerative business model for others to learn from along the way.

Notes

1 There is a more personal reason for our connection to Interface, as one of us (Chris) had the pleasure of meeting Ray Anderson on a few occasions and in one of those, he shared how much he valued the GlobeScan-SustainAbility Leaders Survey as a pure and simple approach to measuring progress for his company. Mark and Chris also led the Regeneration Roadmap project in the lead-up to Rio+20 UN summit, where we interviewed pioneers in sustainable development and named them the
   Ray Anderson Memorial Videos, www.theregenerationroadmap.com/videos. html
2 Authors' interview, Aug 21st 2017.
3 Ibid.
4 The Corporation, 2004.
5 Interface website, www.interfaceglobal.com/sustainability.aspx
6 Authors' interview, Aug 21st 2017.
7 Authors' interview, Nov 27th 2017.
8 Interface website, www.interface.com/US/en-US/campaign/climate-take-back/ Climate-Take-Back
9 Authors' interview, Aug 21st 2017.
10 Authors' interview, Nov 27th 2017.
11 Interface website, www.interfaceglobal.com/sustainability/interface-story.aspx
12 Ibid.
13 Interface website, www.interface.com/US/en-US/about/mission/Our-Mission
14 Jay Gould was promoted to the CEO position in March 2017.
15 Authors' interview, Nov 27th 2017.
16 Amodeo, R.A., "Becoming Sustainable at Interface: A Study of Identity Dynamics within Transformational Culture Change," unpublished doctoral dissertation, Benedictine University, Florida, 2005.
17 Authors' interview, Nov 27th 2017.
18 Authors' interview, Aug 21st 2017.
19 Authors' interview, Nov 27th 2017.
20 Authors' interview, Aug 21st 2017.
21 Co-founder and Chief Scientist for the Rocky Mountain Institute.
22 Environmentalist, entrepreneur, and author. His most recent book is *Drawdown*.
23 Co-founder of the Biomimicry Institute.
24 Founder of Forum for the Future.
25 A non-profit organization founded in Sweden.
26 Authors' interview, Nov 27th 2017.
27 Ibid.
28 Authors' interview, Aug 21st 2017.
29 Authors' interview, Nov 27th 2017.
30 Ibid.
31 In 2004, for example, Anderson was invited to a Walmart retreat with senior leaders where he helped plot a course for Walmart toward a more sustainable enterprise.
32 Authors' interview, Aug 21st 2017.
33 Authors' interview, Nov 27th 2017.
34 Ibid.
35 Ibid.

10 What businesses should do now to go *All In*

"Have a bias toward action – let's see something happen now. You can break that big plan into small steps and take the first step right away."
Indira Gandhi

Purpose

1 Create an authentic and clear company Purpose that drives both business and sustainability impact in line with all five leadership attributes.
2 Build credibility by using Purpose to ensure consistency and excellence in company Culture and Plan at a macro level, and by using Purpose as a litmus test for company performance metrics, measurement, and reporting.
3 Empower people across the organization to apply the Purpose as a decision framework to make quicker, better, and more aligned decisions consistent with company Purpose and Plan and which reinforce company Culture.
4 Ensure the Purpose inspires and mobilizes people inside and outside the organization to drive sustainability impact.
5 Evolve company products and services in line with Purpose, taking Purpose into consideration during all aspects of every product and service life cycle.
6 Align company Purpose with the SDGs; use Purpose to prioritize pursuit of the most relevant SDGs in Plan.

Plan

1 Develop a comprehensive Plan for the full value chain including time-bound goals, metrics, and science-based targets plus rigorous measurement and reporting systems; ensure Plan aligns with and enriches company Purpose and Culture and enables company Collaboration and Advocacy

2   Undertake a detailed and regular process to identify social, environmental, and economic impacts; cross-reference these to stakeholder wants and needs and feed results into business planning and execution.
3   Design, test, and evolve a circular or regenerative business model.
4   Anticipate and proactively address societal issues of growing importance such as plastic reduction, tax, lobbying, executive compensation, gender pay equity, artificial intelligence, and hyper global inequalities.
5   Assign roles and responsibilities across key functions, business lines, and geographies to ensure a joined up and integrated Plan execution.

Culture

1   Nurture a Culture aligned with and supportive of company Purpose and Plan and which enables company Collaboration and Advocacy.
2   Develop and apply clear and complete metrics; measure and report publicly on performance against Plan and hold people accountable for results.
3   Ensure company personnel have the required leadership competencies to deliver Plan and that top leadership especially is committed and credible: *committed* to Purpose and Plan and *credible* in their pursuit of it as well as in Collaboration and Advocacy efforts, i.e., consistent, authentic, walking the talk, and modeling the right behavior.
4   Develop and nurture board members so that they are simultaneously mentors, monitors, stewards, and auditors of management's commitment to corporate sustainability.
5   Empower employees to advance sustainability initiatives by giving them the permission and capacity to do so.
6   Put stakeholder engagement mechanisms in place; encourage board and senior management access to internal and external sustainability experts and advisors.
7   Put sustainability at the core of company innovation and R&D; use the SDGs to frame a broad view of desired outcomes for both the company and society.
8   Push change in the composition of the Share Register to increase the percentage of long-term shareholders.

Collaboration

1   Make Collaboration an essential organizational competency aligned with company Purpose, Culture, and Advocacy, which helps deliver the company Plan.
2   Equip all personnel involved with Collaboration with the skills required to optimize results for both the company and its partners.
3   Engage, empower, and share sustainability performance knowledge with and among suppliers.

4   Review external Collaboration efforts and prioritize those best match-
    ing company Plan, most closely aligned with company Purpose and
    consistent with company Culture.
5   Embrace diverse and complex Collaboration initiatives to understand
    and address systemic challenges and to bring about the adoption of
    pro-sustainable development public policy more quickly with businesses
    inside and outside your own industry and with government and civil
    society.
6   Ensure Collaboration and Advocacy efforts mutually support; convert
    Advocacy programs into Collaboration initiatives when appropriate.

Advocacy

1   Use Advocacy to clarify organizational values and intentions in line
    with company Purpose, Culture, Plan, and Collaboration and to build
    support to address systemic sustainability challenges.
2   Ensure company leadership at every level understands and is equipped
    to explain how the company's sustainability commitment is reflected
    in Purpose, Culture, Plan, and Collaboration, and how it helps create
    and maintain long-term value and provides benefit to society.
3   Align board, executive, and staff Advocacy positions to support pro-
    sustainable development public policy regionally, nationally, and
    internationally.
4   Share sustainability knowledge and experience to inspire and encourage
    other companies and to deliver greater scale and impact as fast as
    possible.
5   Foster the permission and skills to effectively advocate, which includes
    understanding the context, driving change, and having the courage to
    be a torchbearer.

Part three

Now for the future

11 Individual leadership

"If your actions inspire others to dream more, learn more, do more and become more, you are a leader."

John Quincy Adams

The management guru and social philosopher Charles Handy reminds us that businesses are communities of people. Ultimately, it is these communities that drive sustainability.

Now that we have defined Purpose, Culture, Plan, Collaboration, and Advocacy as the key organizational sustainability leadership attributes, we want to explore what individual leadership characteristics are required of the people leading such organizations. There is a wealth of work on this topic, which we explore in brief later and complement with insights from our interviews with leaders from the top ranked companies in the Leaders Survey.

We start with a landscape review, after which we try to distill some of the common individual leadership characteristics that link to each attribute. We then look at the current leadership development offerings available from business schools as well as some of the more experiential learning providers and ask how well they provide the competencies required. Finally, we speculate how sustainability leaders might influence the world's 13,000 business schools to become more proactive in developing leadership for sustainability directly and through Collaboration initiatives.

Individual sustainability leadership

A decade ago, Chris Tuppen – then BT's Chief Sustainability Officer – produced what he described as "a first shot at defining what excellent performance in sustainability leadership should look like, in behavioral terms." Tuppen drew on a number of sources including Peter Senge's work on leadership and initiating and sustaining profound change; Jonathon Porritt and the think-tank Forum for the Future; the Centre for Excellence in Learning; and Interface. Tuppen's seven top-level behaviors were:

1   *Thinking the big picture*
    Having a good understanding of the interactions between natural, political, social, and economic systems – nationally, regionally, and globally – that create the environment in which we do business today and which will be fundamental in defining how we will do business in the future.
2   *Anticipating radical change*
    Appreciating that sustainability-related failures may cause radical dis-continuities, and that the solutions to many of today's problems will require redefined political and economic structures that will destroy some old markets and create some entirely new ones.
3   *Creating the future*
    The ability to envision and articulate a compelling future which is both positive and mutually reinforcing to the benefit of your organization, your customers, employees, individuals, society, the natural world, and the economy.
4   *Inspiring change*
    Based on a foundation of appropriate knowledge, to inspire a can-do culture that delivers innovation in new ways of doing business and profitable commercial solutions with positive sustainability impacts.
5   *Connecting actions*
    Responsible and sustainable leadership is about integrating it in the way we do business, not reserved for special occasions.
6   *Collaborating across boundaries*
    Engaging with stakeholders, listening to their views, working across internal and external boundaries, and taking an inclusive, open, and transparent approach to decision-making.
7   *Walking the talk*
    Demonstrating support for responsible and sustainable business through personal behavior at work and voluntary action in the community.[1]

Tuppen's summary has found resonance in numerous studies. One we find particularly complimentary to his work, which was also backed up by what we learned in the *All In* interviews, is "Sustainability Leadership – Linking Theory and Practice," (2011) by Wayne Visser and Polly Courtice, from the Cambridge Institute for Sustainable Leadership. Visser and Courtice offer a Sustainability Leadership Model with a mix of traits, styles, skills, and knowledge for individual leaders (see Figure 11.1).[2]

Another valuable piece of work was led by Cranfield School of Man-agement visiting fellow Anita Hoffmann – an experienced board-level/C-suite executive coach and search specialist. Hoffman surveyed CEOs, Chief Human Resources Officers, Chief Sustainability Officers, Board Chairs,

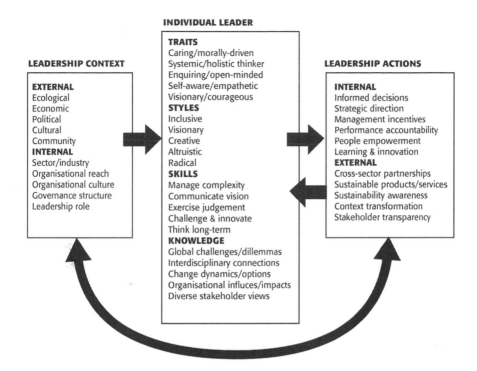

INDIVIDUAL LEADER

TRAITS
Caring/morally-driven
Systemic/holistic thinker
Enquiring/open-minded
Self-aware/empathetic
Visionary/courageous
STYLES
Inclusive
Visionary
Creative
Altruistic
Radical
SKILLS
Manage complexity
Communicate vision
Exercise judgement
Challenge & innovate
Think long-term
KNOWLEDGE
Global challenges/dillemmas
Interdisciplinary connections
Change dynamics/options
Organisational influces/impacts
Diverse stakeholder views

LEADERSHIP CONTEXT

EXTERNAL
Ecological
Economic
Political
Cultural
Community
INTERNAL
Sector/industry
Organisational reach
Organisational culture
Governance structure
Leadership role

LEADERSHIP ACTIONS

INTERNAL
Informed decisions
Strategic direction
Management incentives
Performance accountability
People empowerment
Learning & innovation
EXTERNAL
Cross-sector partnerships
Sustainable products/services
Sustainability awareness
Context transformation
Stakeholder transparency

"Sustainability Leadership - Linking Theory and Practice, (2011) by Wayne Visser & Polly Courtice, from the Cambridge Institute for Sustainable Leadership.

Figure 11.1 Cambridge Sustainability Leadership Model[3]

industry observers, Pension Fund Advisors, and NGOs across the world for a study of sustainability leadership competencies on behalf of the corporate responsibility coalition Business for Social Responsibility (BSR). Hoffmann and BSR concluded that six competencies were key for the future: Ethics and Integrity; External Awareness and Appreciation of Trends; Visioning and Strategy Formulation; Risk Awareness, Assessment, and Management; Stakeholder Engagement; and Flexibility and Adaptability to Change.[4]

From these and other studies and sources,[5] we distilled some key personal elements of leading for sustainability which relate to the organizational attributes we have previously discussed in this book. These include:

> *Purpose: having a personal purpose and authentic values*
> Paul Polman described to us the kind of leadership that is needed now: "People that are more purpose driven; People that have a long-term focus; People that are more systemic thinkers." He

added: "And a different level of partnership and courage that is needed to succeed." Perhaps unsurprisingly, Unilever has now developed four key leadership competencies for its managers: adaptability, systems thinking, empowerment, and purpose and authenticity.[6]

Plan: understanding the context of sustainable development trends and how/where your organization and its Plan fit into the wider system

According to Dr. Mukund Rajan, Chairman, Tata Global Sustainability Council:

> "Having identified the critical relevant and material issues around sustainability that impact your organization, you should be able to translate your determination to deal with these into coherent and deliverable strategies. This includes identifying goals, targets, and mitigation actions to tackle climate change and environmental issues, and getting those approved through the governance structure and embedded across the organization."[7]

Culture: the humility to be an active listener, and the ability to inspire and empower both innovation and engagement

As Steve Howard, IKEA's former Chief Sustainability Officer, told us:

> "Leadership involves taking a stand for the future you want. It is driving change. It is reminding people about what good looks like and going after all of the material areas with a relentless campaigning approach. You need authenticity, honesty, and talking to people in a straightforward way. . . . You have to understand in these functions success has many parents and you deliver through everybody else."[8]

Collaboration: the capacity to conceive, create, continuously improve, and, where appropriate, end collaborations with other businesses and with other parts of society including governments, NGOs, academia, and international development agencies);

Sir Mark Moody-Stuart, ex-CEO, Royal Dutch Shell and former Chairman: Anglo-American told us: "I think the key characteristic most important in a sustainability leader is the ability to switch from your corporate hat to your societal hat – because as the World Business Council for Sustainable Development says, 'you can't do good business in a broken society' and there is a lot of truth in that."[9]

Advocacy: being politically aware and social media savvy, knowing how to navigate complex systems, having the courage to speak out

beyond narrow self-interest, and possessing the networking/convening skills to build a movement for system change

Rick Ridgeway from Patagonia stated:

> "I hold up in high regard the way [Walmart's] Doug McMillan publicly challenged Trump's announcement following the disaster in Virginia.[10] I really admire what Paul Polman is doing at Unilever. Taking that company just as far as he can. Paul and Doug have to handle that so carefully. I really admire the job that they've done. They all are super aware what happens when you cross the line too far."[11]

Personal – and feminine

As three male authors, we have observed – and many of our interviewees have affirmed – that many of the leadership elements essential to sustainability are traditionally identified as feminine. These include: empathy, vulnerability, humility, effective communication, more active listening, more consensual/more democratic or team-styled work, greater disposition toward collaboration, patience, and more of a stewardship mindset.

We share the views of those writers who emphasize that these feminine qualities produce results for leaders of both genders,[12] and we reflect that it is likely no coincidence that so many Chief Sustainability Officers (CSOs) are women.

Who are the Chief Sustainability Officers?

The role of Chief Sustainability Officer, or CSO, was formally defined in the early 2000s.[13] It was created to integrate business objectives with corporate social and environmental responsibility. It reflected an underlying need to improve performance, instead of or in addition to monitoring and reporting (a shortcoming of the short-lived Head of Sustainability model which was generally less action oriented). Typically, a new CSO role reflected a company's ambition to fully integrate sustainability into core business, in a transformational way and to maximize long-term profitability. Hence in many cases a new dimension and role of the CSO was to drive change, rather than to be bogged down in execution. Besides the ability to influence and implement behavioral and operational change, CSOs needed a strong understanding of the company Culture.

CSOs often have influence without operating in a traditional corporate power structure. Typically, they run extremely lean functions, where teams may be spread across departments and geographies. Hence a crucial skill is resourcefulness, which must be coupled with knowing how to work the organizational matrix (vertically and horizontally) to get results and get things implemented.

As the example of Nike's Hannah Jones has made clear throughout this book, CSOs need commercial understanding and the ability to leverage

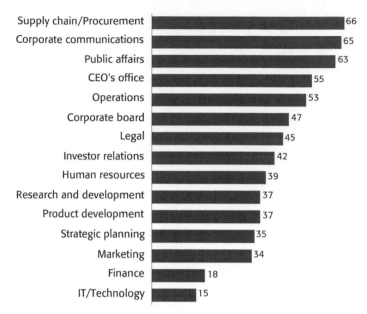

*Percentage of respondents who selected a 4 or 5 on a 5-point scale where 1 is "Not engaged at all with sustainability" and 5 is "Very engaged with sustainability."
**$n = 287$

Figure 11.2 Sustainability Engagement with Business Functions*
BSR-GlobeScan Survey of BSR Member in 2016 State of Sustainable Business Survey**

external opportunities into internal innovation and the capacity to recognize an external market challenge and convert it into internal progress.

Without guaranteed C-suite status and authority, in-company sustainability professionals often find it hard to build essential cross-company relationships which are essential, as GlobeScan surveys of attendees at the annual conference of Business for Social Responsibility (BSR) have revealed (see Figure 11.2). Sustainability professionals generally report far lower levels of working with other key functions like Innovation, New Business Development, IT, and Finance than we consider essential for going *All In*.

Leadership skills for all types of business

While this analysis has been based principally on sustainability leaders in multinational businesses, we believe these individual leadership skills are universal. Even entrepreneurs who are consciously building a business with the intent to sell it want to build to last in order to realize the best sale price.

Those running multi-generational family-owned businesses and large publicly quoted companies are stewards, managing for future generations. Again, these businesses aspire to continue into the indefinite future. To do so, they need leaders at all levels of the business that are empowered to lead sustainably. True empowerment means having both the skills and the authority to lead.

Building individual leadership skills

"The last thing that is obviously the most important thing – we are short of leaders. We are short of the right leaders because at the end of the day it really boils down to people and the courage of people to make these changes and go beyond their own comfort zone."

Paul Polman[14]

We have now identified the skills, but knowing what's needed and getting it are completely different things, so we now explore how individual leaders can acquire these skills.

Organizations typically rely on a mix of internal leadership development programs, MBAs and other Management Masters programs, open and customized executive education programs from Business Schools, and a range of more experiential and immersive programs such as Leaders Quest, Aspen Institute for Business & Society's First Movers, Forward Institute, Common Purpose, and IDEAS, whose offerings are summarized in Figure 11.3.

As is evident given the earlier examples, there are myriad development pathways for nascent sustainability leaders. Various options are often applied in concert to provide the right skills for specific people in different organizations. Ursula Mathar from BMW explained that the company sends young high-flyers to the One Young World summit, and then gives them specific, follow-up projects to consolidate the learning gained. Subsequently, there are opportunities to join the leadership program run by the WBCSD. For middle and senior management teams at BMW, sustainability is woven into their specific, personalized training programs. This might, for example, include working with social entrepreneurs.[15]

Several of the top ranked companies in the Leaders Survey run sustainability-related competitions for young people. Shell's LiveWire Young Enterprise program started in the UK in 1982 and quickly spread internationally. In recent years, it has increasingly emphasized sustainability. Unilever's Young Entrepreneurs Awards, delivered by Unilever and The Cambridge Institute for Sustainability Leadership, supports and celebrates inspirational young people aged between 18–35 from all over the world who have developed initiatives, products, or services that are tackling some of the planet's biggest sustainability challenges. Nestlé operating unit Nespresso runs a sustainability challenge for MBA students across the globe. These and other initiatives are helping to build the pipeline of sustainability-orientated future leaders.

Leaders Quest

We develop wise, compassionate, and adept leaders – people who are capable of leading in fast-changing, disrupted environments with competing priorities and inter-connected challenges.

As a social enterprise, with a charitable foundation, our mission is to work with leaders from business, government, and civil society to catalyze change across three levels: Individuals, Companies, and Systems.

www.leadersquest.org

First Movers Fellowship Program

The Aspen Institute First Movers Fellowship Program is an innovation lab and leader-ship development program for corporate social intrapreneurs – accomplished innova-tors inside companies – who are creating new products, services, and management practices. It equips Fellows with the tools, skills, and network they need to deliver financial value to their company and positive social and environmental outcomes for the world.

www.aspeninstitute.org/programs/first-movers-fellowship-program/

The Forward Institute

The Forward Institute was set up by a coalition of major organizations to help our next generation of leaders meet the demands facing business and society in the twenty-first century. We have a particular focus on exploring the challenges and practices of responsible leadership. To engage, equip, empower.

www.forward.institute/

Common Purpose

"We develop leaders who can cross boundaries"

There are over 70,000 Common Purpose Alumni, from students to senior leaders. http://commonpurpose.org/

IDEAS (Innovative Dynamic Education and Action for Sustainability) Indonesia

The IDEAS program convened small cohorts of leaders from different sectors and diverse ethnic and cultural backgrounds. Through a combination of leadership training and spiritual transformation, the program was designed to help the Fellows put aside differences and work toward a common goal of building a better future for Indonesia.

Figure 11.3 Experiential Learning Programs for Sustainability Leaders

Klaus Schwab, the founder of the World Economic Forum, has also created The Global Shapers Community as a network of young people driving dia-logue, action, and change, in 156 countries across the world.

Nudging providers of leadership education

Top ranked companies in the Leaders Survey are also actively seeking to influ-ence business schools to provide more sustainability-focused curricula both through direct partnerships and through supporting the work of groups such as the UN Principles for Responsible Management Education (PRME), the

50+20 group of management educators, the Global Responsible Leadership Initiative, and the Academy of Business in Society (ABIS). Businesses can:

1   **Open their doors to business schools, schools of engineering, public policy, etc.,** to facilitate research and teach cases about their challenges in embedding corporate responsibility and sustainability.
2   **Collaborate with other companies** to offer mentoring and privileged access to faculty members wanting to make their academic names with relevant and rigorous research around corporate responsibility and sustainability.
3   **Communicate expectations** to business school career services offices and MBA/MSc course directors that graduate recruits must have a good understanding of sustainable development and how sustainability factors affect business (both as risk mitigation and opportunity maximization). All too often, the signals corporate recruiters are sending to business schools are just the opposite.
4   **Unite business school alumni** in the company who are interested in corporate responsibility and sustainability in becoming activists who press their schools to take these issues much more seriously in the future.
5   **Plan top talent development and executive learning programs** to achieve learning outcomes in sustainability and corporate responsibility. Specify that this is part of what the business is commissioning.
6   **Create new dialogue.** Provide senior leaders from the company to speak on business school campuses and make ideas about sustainability performance integral to their narrative. And make it clear to the schools that if a CEO or other senior executive director is speaking on campus, it is expected that faculty members as well as students will attend.

Conclusion

The bottom line is that businesses need to ensure that they have the desired leadership competencies for going *All In*. Businesses need to be proactive in specifying these competencies to business schools and other providers of management and leadership education.

We hope that leading companies in some of the corporate responsibility and sustainability coalitions will be more proactive in pushing the world's business schools to integrate sustainability fully into the core curriculum for key subjects such as finance, innovation, marketing, strategy, and HR. We are delighted that at the time of writing at least one of the leading global coalitions is canvassing a new work program about sustainability leadership with business schools.

Notes

1   Tuppen, C., "Leadership Capabilities for Responsible and Sustainable Business," unpublished, Provided to Authors by Chris Tuppen, 2008.

2 For latest CIS: thinking on Sustainability Leadership, see: The future we want, the leadership we need, CISL, Feb 2018, www.cisl.cam.ac.uk

3 Reproduced with permission of Cambridge Institute for Sustainability Leadership.

4 BSR-Executiva 2012.

5 See for example, Gitsham, M., *Developing the Global Leader of Tomorrow* (2008), Ashridge School of Management and ABIS; *Leadership Skills for a Sustainable Economy* (2010), Business in the Community; Strandberg, C., *Sustainability Talent Management: The New Business Imperative* (2015); and Lovegrove, N., *The Mosaic Principle* (2016) Public Affairs.

6 Hull, P., Unilever Global Leadership Development director, Conversation with author, Oct 2016.

7 Authors' interview, Nov 3rd 2017.

8 Authors' interview, Aug 10th 2017.

9 Authors' interview, Sept 19th 2017.

10 Referring to the civil unrest in Charlottesville, Virginia and President Trump's subsequent remarks – August 207: Trump says both sides to blame amid Charlottesville backlash, https://edition.cnn.com/2017/08/15/politics/trump-charlottesville-delay/index.html accessed Feb 8 2018.

11 Authors' interview, Aug 31st 2017.

12 See, for example, Buchanan, L., "What a Leader Needs Now: 7 'Feminine' Qualities These Traits, Typically Associated with Women, Make for Great Leaders – Whether Women or Men," *From the June 2013 Issue of Inc. Magazine*; Schwab, N., "Why Feminine Leadership Is Not about Women," *Huffington Post*, Jul 19, 2017; Hwang, V., "Are Feminine Leadership Traits the Future of Business?," *Forbes*, Aug 30, 2014 accessed Dec 24 2017.

13 We believe the first CSO was Linda Fisher at DuPont, appointed in 2004.

14 Authors' interview, Aug 2017.

15 Authors' interview, Nov 17th 2017.

12 2030 leadership horizon

"One never notices what has been done; one can only see what remains to be done."

Marie Curie

Today's leaders on 2030

In writing *All In*, we asked representatives of businesses ranked highly in the Leaders Survey today which companies they expect to top the list in 2030. While this is usually a question we would put to an individual, we posed this question to Mike Barry of M&S, Joanna Yarrow of IKEA, and Sue Garrard of Unilever when they were together to participate in a Leaders Survey webinar. Their collective replies are interesting and illuminating.

Mike Barry, M&S:

> Reflecting on this study about the leaders a decade ago, some of them remain very good companies and some are a lot less relevant, and I think that exactly the same will happen by 2030. You are going to see new models like Tesla, and there are many more Tesla's to emerge than we have seen yet. . . . Complacency kills, and I think that by 2030, unless you have totally re-engineered your business model from being less bad to a fundamentally more sustainable model that is genuinely low carbon, circular, restorative, and committed to a quality of fairness and well-being which is vastly different from what any scaled business model in this world is now, you will simply not register on that leader board – and probably frankly not register as existing as a business.

Joanna Yarrow, IKEA:

> Any company that doesn't have a circular business model and that isn't actively contributing to well-being I think is going to struggle to be a leader in the future. I think any company that doesn't have a clear purpose above and beyond making money, a purpose defined by contributing to better living, is similarly going to struggle to be viewed as a leader in 2030. And I think companies that can't demonstrate that they are

relevant, and that their business model is about providing solutions to challenges that we all face, is also going to seem pretty irrelevant by 2030.

Sue Garrard, Unilever:

> For me one of the big potential breakthroughs is how you turn consumer concern and interest into action and make consumers into a real army for change. Massive! Untapped! So, can that power of retailing really go from "do no harm" to "do good" and codify that in a way that consumers trust and can understand? That's a massive challenge but they've got until 2030. The other thing I think is that it will be completely breakthrough businesses. It will be people who are genuinely led by inspired leaders. I am thinking about Elon Musk at Tesla, and I am thinking about people who are prepared to lead for huge change in the face of risk because they believe passionately and deeply in driving change; because I think that is part of what recognized leadership encapsulates.[1]

On the horizon

All In has discussed how sustainability leadership has evolved over the 20 years of the Leaders Survey and explained the five essential and interlocking attributes of sustainability leadership today. We are now going to look ahead and explore what leadership might require through 2030 – the end of the implementation period for the UN's Sustainable Development Goals.

We consider first how the five essential attributes: Purpose, Culture, Plan, Collaboration, and Advocacy might develop further. Then we pause to look at how several of today's leadership companies are already honing the characteristics we expect to define the coming Regenerative Era of leadership. Following this look at incumbents on the leading edge, we discuss how new types of business such as the benefit corporation model might influence where we are heading more generally, as well as the future role of SMEs, entrepreneurs, and disrupters of all sizes. Next, we consider some of the major business sectors that have been conspicuous by their absence from the Leaders Survey and what might be required of them if this is to change. Finally, we examine the likely growth in sectoral and geographic diversity of those topping the Leaders Survey in the years ahead and some of the reasons why this appears to be inevitable.

Evolving attributes

We are very clear that the five attributes of leadership will become even more deeply ingrained and interlinked in the sustainability leaders of 2030. We also expect considerable stretching of each attribute to occur. We note that, as Purpose, Plan, and Culture are more familiar and well-established in companies today, Collaboration and Advocacy likely will be – and will need to be – the attributes that evolve farthest and fastest, which means we will see stretching not only of the attributes, but also of the capacity and comfort zone of business as this happens. (Please see Figure 12.1.)

ATTRIBUTE	STRETCH
PURPOSE	**Mobilizing investors:** BlackRock's Larry Fink, in his annual letters to the CEOs of major companies in which BlackRock is invested, has made very clear his expectations that boards and senior management teams must better manage the risks and opportunities associated with their environmental, social, and governance (ESG) impacts and be able to articulate their long-term strategy for doing this. Our reading is that fewer and fewer investors see a dichotomy between optimizing shareholder value over the medium- to long-term and managing sustainability or ESG impacts. Indeed, they recognize the two go together. Corporate sustainability leaders of 2030 will engage investors in more effective discussion of long-term strategy, actively change the composition of their Share Register toward long-term owners, focus capital on the long-term, and have a Purpose defined not only to suit internal, but also external needs, i.e., a Purpose shared with society.
PLAN	**Mobilizing suppliers more systemically and becoming more regenerative:** Today's leadership companies emphasize the crucial need to engage their supply chains. This will intensify with more use of big data to improve traceability and transparency; greater capacity-building of suppliers' key staff; more use of "Challenge" and "Capex Innovation Funds" to help suppliers to transition faster; and greater burden sharing around capacity-building of Tier 2 and 3 suppliers. Plans of the future will also increasingly emphasize the development and delivery of circular and net positive or regenerative business models, which will be underpinned by transparent goals and metrics informed by societal context and the best available science.
CULTURE	**Mobilizing employees and other stakeholders more fully:** Sustainability leaders will actively confront the challenges of automation and job losses from the Fourth Industrial Revolution by sharing responsibility with employees for ensuring continuing employability through lifetime learning accounts and platforms. As Lord Browne has argued, leading businesses of the future will need to "engage radically" with both internal and external stakeholders, which will require that they embrace new levels of transparency, openness, and responsiveness. Additionally, diversity in all forms will be increasingly recognized and valued, with corporate cultures adapting to ensure their equitable treatment of all people keeps them attractive to present and future employees in the war for talent.
COLLABORATION	**Mobilizing consumers:** We expect the next frontier in Collaboration for sustainability to be greater consumer engagement. Some companies might follow Patagonia's lead and blend consumer Advocacy and education on topics like sustainable consumption in ways that inform and empower consumers to collaborate with brands. Such Collaboration will accelerate the process by which business models become regenerative. Benefit corporations will proliferate in part by broadcasting their societal Purpose to consumers and inviting them to collaborate for change. Technology will play an increasing role, for example, through smart phone apps that use gamification to make sustainability fun and rewarding by encouraging consumer competition on energy use, food waste, and other aspects of sustainable lifestyles. The fastest adapting incumbents will form breakthrough partnerships with entrepreneurs and disrupters. Finally, we expect more – and more exacting – multi-sector and multi-stakeholder Collaboration where corporate sustainability leaders play both catalytic and key supporting roles.

Figure 12.1 Stretching to the Future

ATTRIBUTE	STRETCH
ADVOCACY	**Tackling hyper global inequality:** The UN Global Compact/Accenture CEOs' Survey in 2013 reported that sustainability efforts had plateaued and that companies needed governments to intervene with hard measures (e.g., new taxes and laws) to create a more enabling environment for corporate sustainability. Today, it feels like business itself has decided it must be more proactive in Advocacy for pro-sustainable development public policies and norms. This will continue to include Advocacy on established sustainability issues like climate change, water, and waste, but also increasingly integral will be tackling hyper global inequality, including in-work poverty. Inequality will be a frontline issue because of increasing acceptance that it threatens commerce generally and individual business models specifically. There will also be more joint corporate-consumer Advocacy to promote pro-sustainable development approaches to policy-makers, the media, and others. Finally, 2030 Advocacy will reflect an amplified version of the kind of CEO Activism discussed in Chapter 7, with corporates ever-more increasingly expected to take positions and advocate change when the rules of the game, as they relate to fundamental freedoms like freedom of the press, freedom of speech, etc., are imbalanced, unfair, or out of date.

Figure 12.1 (Continued)

Regenerative stirrings

Our confidence in predicting that the five essential leadership attributes will stretch as described previously is bolstered by evidence that some companies are already testing the ability of Purpose, Culture, Plan, Collaboration, and Advocacy to carry business from the current Purpose-Driven Era of leadership to the Regenerative Era we anticipate will come next.

We expect the hallmark of the Regenerative Era of leadership that will take hold between now and 2030 will be the widespread adoption of circular, regenerative, or net positive business models – systems of commerce that take complete accountability for products and services at every stage from sourcing through to end of life, and which contribute more to the environment and society than they take.

There have been experiments with such business models already, some of which we learned more about during the interviews conducted for *All In*. Ian Cheshire, the former Kingfisher Chief Executive, talked about how and why Kingfisher's Net Positive[2] was designed to commit the company to "transforming our business to have a restorative impact on the environment" through aspirations like creating "more forest than we use."[3] Cheshire told us the company's effort to become Net Positive under his leadership required a whole new way of thinking:

> We came from a different angle which was a bit more of a future scan effort about how things might change. I think what we tied it into was whether we could think about different business models and different

ways of working that would generate new opportunities for the business and our customers. That is what led us into experimenting on ideas around the sharing economy; trying to redesign products so they could be maybe sold as a service rather than one-off.[4]

Cheshire suggested urgency and a competitive rationale for regenerative approaches as well:

I think the key is being able to model a twenty-year out view of the world and say: "Will my business still be around in this shape or form? If it looks under threat, what can I do now to get ahead of it – because undoubtedly the leaders in these sectors will do better."[5]

Similarly, Erik Fyrwald of Syngenta discussed how that company's Good Growth Plan aims to preserve and improve farmer livelihoods and agricultural yields via six commitments that include: "Rescue more farmland" and "Help biodiversity flourish."[6] Like Kingfisher's Net Positive ambitions, Syngenta's Plan provides an example of the kind of regenerative approach that we believe must become the future business norm.

What is the regenerative difference, the new thing inherent to the approaches of both Kingfisher and Syngenta? The maxim attributed in various forms to world scouting movement founder Robert Baden-Powell captures the intent of regenerative and net positive approaches: "Leave this world a little better than you found it."[7] While simple to say, this is hellishly difficult in practice – the kind of difficulty described by Rick Ridgeway of Patagonia when he framed the challenge his company faces in trying to build a regenerative business model while producing consumer goods in a consumer economy. But difficult is not impossible, and making regenerative ambitions public (a form of Advocacy for such business models) helps make them tangible enough to pursue. This sentiment was captured by Cheshire when he described Kingfisher Net Positive as essential to communicate to the company's employees ". . . next generation leaders . . . what would make them proud to work at Kingfisher . . . something that would fulfil our purpose and give them a real challenge, and that increasingly crystalized into the idea of don't just be less evil or have less impacts, but go one step beyond."[8] Fyrwald similarly attributed Syngenta's Good Growth Plan with making "a real difference in delivering sustainable growth, revenue, and profits that are also having a sustainable impact on the environment and people."[9]

The Regenerative Era will be enabled by organizations like the Ellen MacArthur Foundation and its thought leadership on the circular economy, and Forum for the Future and the tremendous effort it is applying to defining and developing net positive as a practical concept. Who will the pathfinders be? In addition to examples like Kingfisher and Syngenta, which are already in the marketplace, we expect to see the top three companies in The

Leaders Survey over the last few years – Unilever, Patagonia, and especially Interface – define themselves as leaders in this area.

At its foundation, the Unilever Sustainable Living Plan (SLP), which we explored in Chapter 8, is regenerative. The SLP serves as the company's "blueprint for achieving our vision to grow our business, whilst decoupling our environmental footprint from our growth and increasing our positive social impact."[10] Such ambition is becoming more common. In 2016, Nike's CEO and President Mark Parker announced a "moon shot" challenge for the company to "double our business and halve our impact." As Hannah Jones commented:

> It's a bold ambition that's going to take much more than incremental efficiency – it's going to take innovation on a scale we've never seen before. . . . It's a challenge we are setting for ourselves, our collaborators and our partners as we move toward a circular economy future.[11]

Similar commitments will need to become the norm between now and 2030 for the Regenerative Era to fully take hold.

Rick Ridgeway told us that Patagonia ". . . started its food division, Patagonia Provisions, because we believe food can and should be part of the solution to the environmental crisis. Through Provisions, we've found that regenerative organic agricultural practices – which don't require chemical fertilizers or pesticides, rebuild soil health, use less water, and hold more carbon in the ground than conventional agriculture – can be a powerful part of that solution."

Ridgeway also described the tremendous excitement in the company at how climate change might be addressed through "regenerative farming and grazing protocols . . . [that] can begin to pull the carbon back out of the air and put it back into the ground."[12]

Patagonia Provisions is committed to food manufacturing rooted in regenerative practices, and, in typical Patagonia fashion, it displays Advocacy on the topic. The Patagonia Provisions website[13] is headlined with this quote from founder Yvon Chouinard: "Instead of waiting for some miraculous, high-tech solution to bail us out of our climate-change disaster, the real miracle turns out to be simply working with nature instead of against it. Our grasslands, and the soil beneath them, might just save the world." This is coupled with a short video from Patagonia's "What if" series providing visitors an opportunity to watch and learn more about regenerative agriculture, a sketch of how Patagonia supported the creation of a Regenerative Organic Certification standard, descriptions of the Patagonia Provisions products available, and recipes to help people prepare and enjoy food that is better for the planet.[14]

Finally, the trademarked Interface Climate Take Back[15] program, described in Chapter 9, represents the kind of "model modern advocacy" we believe will be typical in the Regenerative Era – you can even argue Interface is establishing itself as regenerative already. The Climate Take Back headline on the Interface website poses the question: "If humanity has changed the climate by mistake, can we change it with intent?" This question is followed by detail on how – and why – Climate Take Back was created to "start the path to reversing global warming by changing how we think" and outlining Interface's belief that we can "reverse global warming if we focus on four key areas:"

1   Live Zero – Do business in ways that gives back whatever is taken from the Earth.
2   Love Carbon – Stop seeing carbon as the enemy, and start using it as a resource.
3   Let Nature Cool – Support our biosphere's ability to regulate the climate.
4   Lead Industrial Re-Revolution – Transform industry into a force for climate progress.

These four areas – ambitions if you will – are regenerative through and through.

Climate Take Back uses Advocacy as a platform to support the emergence of a new and regenerative business model. This is designed to draw attention to the climate issue and to enthuse others to join the challenge in partnership. In the same way that there will have to be exponential growth in Plans such as Unilever's and Nike's that commit to delink growth and environmental impact, the Regenerative Era will be defined by programs like Climate Take Back that take as a central tenet the need to Advocate and recruit others into system-level Collaboration.

For public benefit

We share the view of Marcello Palazzi of the Progressio Foundation, who has written:

> Just like different assets classes constitute the investment universe, we see the business universe being greatly enriched by the emergence of the B Corps as a new class of corporations leading the quest to grow a true well-being economy.[16]

This new class of companies is trying to redefine the purpose of business by including "public benefit and positive impact on society, workers, the community and the environment in addition to profit as . . . legally defined goals."[17]

While the number of benefit corporations – often referred to as B Corporations or B Corps thanks to the success of the B Corp certification[18] – existing today is relatively small (estimated variously at a few thousand, mostly in the US), and B Corps themselves tend to be predominantly entrepreneurial start-ups and smaller firms, we are intrigued by their potential and by what they represent – the notion that corporate charters (a means of expressing Purpose) can be written or re-written to better balance shareholder and societal interest.

In explicitly recognizing a range of stakeholders' interests and committing to external verification of performance, B Corps are trailblazers in doing business more inclusively and sustainably. They are proving successful in conventional financial and broader market terms too – so much so that a number of them have proven attractive acquisition targets for several Leaders Survey ranked businesses like Unilever, as discussed in Chapter 8. Such acquisitions are happening in the wider Leaders Survey universe as well, for example, SC Johnson's acquisition of Ecover and Method, and Procter & Gamble's purchase of supplements brand New Chapter.

Jonathan Trimble, CEO of advertising agency and B Corp 18 Feet & Rising, and Katie Hill of B Lab UK suggest such acquisitions are happening because:

> New metrics of deal measurement are in play and organizations are making investments with one eye on consumer trends, one eye on innovation and talent, and both eyes on living out the tenets of their oft-stated corporate social responsibility pledges.[19]

We believe companies from the Leaders Survey see B Corp acquisitions as laboratories for new ways of doing business as well as strong cultural additions. Perhaps as a sign of things to come, Unilever has bought Sundial Brands, a $240 million portfolio of personal care brands serving the growing new majority multicultural and Millennial market. The deal included the establishment of a New Voices Fund with an initial investment of $50 million to empower women of color entrepreneurs. This has been described as an inspiring example of putting the B Corp Declaration of Interdependence (which states that leaders of a global economy who use business as a force for good must act with the understanding that: "We are responsible for each other and future generations") into practice. It may equally be a smart extension of corporate venturing with an eye on long-term value creation. Perhaps in the future we will see sustainability leadership companies rotating staff between B Corp subsidiaries and other business units to spread B Corp culture and ideals and broaden employee horizons. They may also decide to test new collaborative approaches with civil society organizations and public sector agencies through B Corp subsidiaries.

Whilst attaining and retaining B Corp status is just one route to becoming a purposeful business (which only a handful of large companies like Natura, Danone, and Patagonia have yet pursued[20]), we expect that the mindset, values, and some of the innovative practices of B Corps will become more widespread amongst corporate sustainability leaders. We also see similar commitment to balance financial and social performance in other societal-orientated businesses that are not formal B Corps, such as many multi-generational family-owned businesses, which often possess a strong spirit of stewardship.

Finally, whether a B Corp or otherwise, we would be remiss to not to mention the boundless potential of the many kinds of disrupters now emerging. Here, we generally mean start-ups and small and medium-sized enterprises (companies that many studies show enjoy higher societal trust than multinational corporations). We note and admire companies created with entirely new and more sustainable business models with the intent of upending what has gone before them (most notably, Tesla, with its vow to remake mobility and transport, but also, for example, the "buy one, give one" models behind retailers like TOMS for shoes and Warby Parker for eyewear). There are even what we might call "disruption collaborations," as typified by the January 2018 announcement by Amazon, Berkshire Hathaway, and JP Morgan Chase that, out of sheer frustration at the high cost and uncertain efficacy of the US health care system, they will "form an independent health care company for their employees in the United States," which will be "free from profit-making incentives and constraints" in order to test whether their collective acumen and size can produce different and better health outcomes.[21] As we can see, while B Corps are a uniquely identifiable type of disrupter, lightning shifts are happening economy wide. This will continue to be a major influence on the journey to 2030.

Conspicuous by their absence

When we asked interviewees for *All In* who they thought would be the sustainability leaders of 2030, some mentioned today's best performers – Unilever, Patagonia, Interface, and their ilk – and suggested those companies still have room to run. Others pointed to historic leaders and predicted resurgence. As we noted in the Plan chapter, Chad Holliday argued that oil and gas companies have the Capex power to make wholesale business model shifts as new energy sources and technologies come to scale and suggested that this might put companies like Shell back on top of the rankings again someday. As Shell's CFO Jessica Uhl told us:

> We're expecting a much more significant shift in the energy system over the next ten/twenty/thirty years, a shift that I expect will be more challenging to the current status quo of business models. We need to, as the Dutch say, get our skates on and we need to be ahead of that shift as a company.[22]

Others mentioned the B Corps discussed previously and their unique potential to be different because they are designed differently from the outset. But the one common concern from across nearly all interviewees was that technology and financial services companies have been so conspicuously absent from the Leaders Survey and other responsible business rankings. Interestingly, interviewees also cited genuine hope and earnest expectations that these sectors will exert greater leadership soon.

The reasons behind this yearning for tech and finance leadership are numerous. Both sectors wield enormous power over consumers and the economic system, and both will be critical to the fulfillment of the SDGs, providing the necessary innovation and investment to enable other sectors to reach the targets set. Unfortunately, technology companies are perceived to be insular – even immature – by many other business leaders. We find this view not so much a condemnation as a statement of fact; most technology companies are genuinely young, and they don't always have rounded and/ or deep views of what comprehensive sustainability leadership entails; and, in the wake of the role of social media in the US and other recent elections, there is evidence they don't fully realize how their platforms can be used just as easily for ill as for good.

Just tech

Technology businesses face growing public and political criticism over a range of topics including failure to differentiate fake news, insufficient efforts to stop dissemination of extremist and even terrorist content, lax oversight of interference by foreign powers in domestic election campaigns, mental health impacts, child pornography, tax avoidance, e-waste, supply chain issues, protection of customers' data, privacy, and more. They are also at the forefront of wider debates about both the protection and ownership of individuals' data. Corporate Citizenship's Mike Tuffrey says:

> The big tech companies have rapidly built businesses worth billions, with valuations based on the market potential of the data they hold and the customer access they control. However, data and the controls around it are major issues for all companies, not just tech. Concern about data privacy is growing fast in parallel. . . . [It's] only been discussed in geek circles so far, [but] I'll hazard a prediction that in 2018 the question of whose data it is – and who can profit from it – will go mainstream.[23]

Such concerns are likely to grow as the implications of rapid advances in artificial intelligence become more apparent. Outstanding performance in, say, the environmental sphere will not and should not shield technology companies from popular and regulatory scrutiny of the totality of their impacts.

Some interviewees compared the technology sector to angsty, self-absorbed teenagers. CNBC used this analogy in an article entitled "Dear Tech: A letter to the deadbeat teenage son at the end of a tough year" at the close of 2017.

In the article, writer Matt Rosoff tells his metaphorical teenage son "We don't feel like we can trust you anymore," adding that it's time the son ". . . grew up and took some responsibility for yourself. Connect to the outside world a little bit. Find a larger purpose."[24]

Tongue in cheek, Rosoff's piece packs a tough-love message, but more seriously, these companies will have to earn our trust by thinking about their businesses and their impacts more holistically. Anathema to those who believe tech builds neutral platforms that others exploit for good and ill, the shift underway recognizes that these companies also have accountability for how the tools they create are used. We believe this shift in thinking is behind Facebook founder and CEO Mark Zuckerberg declaring his personal 2018 challenge to be: fixing Facebook.[25]

We will watch closely to see if and how the technology sector develops more rounded, comprehensive, and integrated sustainability Plans; develops its models of Collaboration with other businesses and other parts of society; and particularly, how it uses its privileged global voice in Advocacy in coming years. Still, we must note that there has been some progress in terms of sustainability leadership already.

Google, and especially Tesla, have figured strongly in the Leaders Survey in recent years. As discussed in Chapter 4, people are captivated by Tesla founder Elon Musk's vision and his company's determination to deliver electric vehicles to the masses. Google, for its part, is taking at least a more careful approach to artificial intelligence (AI) than some. An interesting example of this is the decision of DeepMind (a British AI company owned by Google) to create a new research unit, "DeepMind Ethics & Society," to "help technologists put ethics into practice, and to help society anticipate and direct the impact of A.I. so that it works for the benefit of all."[26] The new unit will include researchers with backgrounds in areas such as philosophy, ethics, and law and will be overseen by six distinguished independent researchers who will function as a kind of academic peer review board. Such transparency is not an optional extra – it is a vital prerequisite for a license to operate. Stakeholder advisory panels, Chief Ethics Officers, ethical screening processes, social impacts research units, regular thought-leadership white papers, and round-tables with critical friends and even hostile critics will be important tools for big tech going forward.

Finally, there are areas like renewable energy – as borne out by the leadership of companies like Facebook within the Renewable Energy Buyers Alliance and RE100 – where technology companies are literally re-writing the rule book with regulators and utilities to make it possible and cost effective to access renewable energy for data centers and the rest of their operations. Convincing regulators and utilities to alter regional power production and supply benefits others too, as once tech companies pioneer renewables in a specific geographic region, it becomes exponentially easier for other companies to do the same in that region in their wake.

Bank on it

Few financial services firms have appeared even in regional rankings for the Leaders Survey over the last twenty years, and none have made it into the top global leader set. Australian bank Westpac, which has topped the Dow Jones Sustainability Index sectoral list for years, and Triodos Bank, headquartered in the Netherlands, which brands itself "The World's Leading Sustainable Bank," are rare examples appearing in regional results.

Beyond the Leaders Survey, financial services companies are sometimes more prominently noted as sustainability leaders. The group of financial institutions who are signatories to the UN Principles for Responsible Investment are undertaking serious work in support of sustainability.[27] There is certainly sustainability-related product innovation in the industry, for example the rapid proliferation of green and social impact bonds.[28] Financial services also influence the sustainability performance of other companies, with Larry Fink of BlackRock the most prominent, but far from the only, investor demanding better ESG performance from the companies whose shares BlackRock owns.[29] JPMorgan Chase topped the *Fortune* Change the World list 2017 in good part due to its urban revitalization and job creation efforts in places like Detroit – not to mention the personal leadership and vision of CEO Jamie Dimon who, as noted previously, has partnered with Amazon and Berkshire Hathaway to remake US health care. Ant Financial, the most valuable Fintech company in the world[30] also features in the *Fortune* Change the World top ten,[31] so maybe serious change is afoot in financial services.

As an enabler sector, finance may have its greatest impact through others. Colin le Duc, Co-Founder and Partner with Al Gore and David Blood at Generation Investment Management, told us:

> We are increasingly concerned that incrementalism isn't sufficient: With the twin challenges of climate and hyper inequality you've essentially got an imperative that is forcing companies to evolve in a way that they have never done before . . . our assessment is obviously multifaceted in the sense of looking at how the company is run, what their product suite looks like and their readiness for non-linear change driven by sustainability.[32]

Pressed on how widespread he thinks this perspective is amongst institutional investors, le Duc told us:

> The train has left the station on sustainable business. . . . My view is that ESG/sustainability is widely accepted now within the best global public equity investors. You can just see that when you look at BlackRock, Fidelity, Capital Group or any of those very large asset managers. They are doing very integrated ESG investment.[33]

Le Duc also highlighted two important developments that he believes are accelerating changing attitudes amongst investors:

> The Taskforce on Climate-related Disclosure. That is a major initiative because it is going to force climate disclosure onto corporates . . . if you want an indicator of the mainstreaming of sustainability into capital markets, the fact that the regulators, the SEC, the Bank of England and the FCA in the UK are all taking it on tells you that this is very much mainstream. We still have an implementation lag, but on the intellectual understanding of the need for us to embrace sustainability, it is night and day to where it was a decade ago, and we are now more in the implementation phase rather than the advocacy phase.[34]

BlackRock's Michelle Edkins amplified some of Le Duc's thinking and deepened our perspective on financial services by talking through her view of the "proper" role of investors:

> There tends to be a misunderstanding about the role of investors. For example, investors are not meant to be co-managing the companies in which they invest or act as shadow directors. Fundamentally, investors are meant to allocate capital to companies and monitor how that capital is used, which means ensuring sound corporate governance at these companies. As a starting point, investors should set out a framework that clearly articulates their policies and expectations of companies. The framework should also outline their commitment to engagement and voting, and for monitoring how companies are performing against policies and expectations.
>
> Good governance is an indicator of a company's ability to achieve long-term growth, so it's important that investors engage companies around ESG. Good governance includes companies with qualified, engaged and informed directors on the board who appoint, monitor and counsel executive leadership. Directors must also make sure there are proper controls and policies in place, and that they are implemented throughout the organization. Where investors don't believe companies are performing in line with expectations, it is their responsibility to engage and provide guidance on their position and outline concerns. Where they do not feel that companies are responsive to engagement, they may use the sanction of their vote against them.[35]

Not missing much longer

Politicians, regulators, and consumers across the world are reinforcing similar messages, demanding that the technology and finance sectors be more transparent and trustworthy as well as better partners and bigger contributors. We think that the 3 P's discussed in Chapter 2 – Pressure, Perspective, and People – will conspire to force both industries to change radically and quickly.

The financial sector has already has gone through significant Pressure in the aftermath of the global financial crisis; Perspective appears to be what is changing rapidly there now, and there is a new generation of employees and leaders reshaping the People element.

In technology, all the 3 Ps are also fully in play. While this might be uncomfortable for these sectors, their development as sustainability leaders is essential to other industries and society more broadly, and we believe will result in them being more resilient in the long run. We also believe that tech and finance companies will be commended in the Leaders Survey very soon.

Where next?

As discussed in Chapter 1, the companies topping the Leaders Survey both now and over the last twenty years are concentrated in Europe and North America – frankly, far too much so.

While we believe that the Leaders Survey top cohort have more than earned their positions, we wish more and more global competition on them – in fact, we believe that without outstanding corporate sustainability leadership from every major global economy, sustainable development efforts like the SDGs will fall short, with disastrous consequences for humankind and the planet.

The sheer size and rapid growth of the Global South makes it likely that more top companies in future Leaders Surveys will come from Africa, Asia and Southeast Asia, and Latin America. The *Better Business, Better World: Asia* report produced by the Business and Sustainable Development Commission in mid-2017 claims the private sector could unlock $5 trillion in business opportunities and create 230 million new jobs in Asia by 2030 by implementing the SDGs. The report identified, for example, that affordable housing in the developing world, especially in China, is the highest potential market opportunity, with an estimated future valuation of $505 billion. Renewable energy was found to be the second largest, followed by reducing food waste in the supply chain, and moving the automotive industry toward more circular practices. The SDGs represent, as Paul Bulcke, Nestlé's Chair told us, "a fantastic framing" for corporate strategies[36] – and also an exceptional economic opportunity.

One of the strengths of the SDGs is that, unlike the earlier Millennium Development Goals (MDGs) that only covered the poorest counties in the world, they apply to all countries. They also represent an opportunity to reconcile different world views. As Cherie Nursalim, Vice Chairman of GITI Group,[37] told us:

> We have put ourselves in a mess today, because we have put aside the spiritual aspect, the mindfulness, peace and partnership at the top of the SDG Pyramid. In business we almost think it is not right to talk about

these issues. I realize that our ancestors have appreciated spiritual values much better than us. We often replace the spiritual with economics. In the SDG Pyramid, the economics is there but it is the base of the Pyramid, the people portion (goals 1–10), followed by ecology (goals 11–15), we shouldn't take away spiritual values (goals 16–17).[38]

Undoubtedly, if companies are to create shared value for themselves and for society, this will require bold leadership. Victor Zhang, President of Global Government Affairs, Huawei Technologies Co., Ltd., told us:

> Corporate sustainability leadership needs to move from individual action to collective empowerment. The SDGs agenda is very ambitious and the sum of individual initiatives will not be enough to achieve the Goals. The leadership needs to be even stronger, crossing industries and geographies, to truly embrace the Goals, the challenges they entail and the collective thinking and resources they require. Sustainability Leadership needs to be out of the box, borderless and bold enough to make the changes needed to achieve the 2030 agenda.[39]

China first

As stated, we expect that a new generation of sustainability leaders will emerge from Africa, Asia and Southeast Asia, and Latin America. This will be in good part because of acute pressures stemming from issues including inequality, human rights, environmental degradation, and insufficient economic development. But regardless of the specific drivers, of all these regions, China will lead.

China was the world's largest economy for eighteen of the last twenty centuries. What we are seeing today, therefore, is not the emergence of China but its renaissance.[40] The nation's sheer size and scale, its torrid economy, and its massive population are now inevitably producing more and more powerful corporations. And in sustainability terms, the country and its leading companies are just getting started.

Johnny Kwan, the recently retired Chairman of BASF's Greater China Country Board, told us that serious consideration of corporate sustainability in China is only a decade old:

> In China, 2008 was year zero for sustainability and corporate social responsibility. . . . First it was the Beijing Olympics with the theme of being the Green Olympics; this was certainly one of the trigger points. Then at the same time there was a major earthquake in a small city in Sichuan province. Many companies were publically making donations and rebuilding schools and so on. It turned out to be a little bit of . . . I would not say competition but a little bit of "if you are [a responsible company] you have to donate."[41]

Huawei, the Chinese multinational networking and telecommunications equipment and services company, for example, published its sustainability strategy in 2008, after having joined the UN Global Compact in 2004. The strategy was enhanced in 2010 to include: bridging the digital divide, ensuring stable and secure network operations, promoting environmental protection and win-win development. Huawei strengthened its sustainability management system based on ISO 26000 and has a sustainability committee to monitor and assess its initiatives.

Also in 2008, SASAC – the State-owned Assets Supervision and Administration Commission of the State Council, the official agency that manages the Chinese government's holding in the 118 largest state-owned enterprises (SOE) – published the SASAC CSR Guidelines. These specified that SOEs should "enhance their CSR awareness, actively fulfill social responsibility and become model companies with legal compliance, integrity, energy efficiency, environmental protection and harmony." These guidelines positioned CSR and sustainability as a key component of the transformation of SOEs into modern corporate institutions and as a means of enhancing competitiveness. The SASAC Guidelines included requirements to report on performance. In 2007, there were fewer than 100 reporters. Today, there are more than 3,000, and crucially, as Johnny Kwan notes:

> This includes all the central state-owned companies, some multinational companies that operate in China, and some local companies. Initially, there was a learning curve but now it is not just reporting what you have done perceptually, but it is essentially a trend line of your development, and it has to be integrated with your business strategy.[42]

Chinese influence will be greater due to its technological prowess. Kwan told us: "China has been pursuing electric vehicles development very aggressively: Wan Gang, the Minister of Science and Technology, said already in the last decade that China can only compete with the west in the automotive industry by going beyond internal combustion engine technology. We call this disruptive innovation while in China they call this 'overtaking at the bend.' Aligning sustainability solutions to a bigger picture of business competitiveness is a clear path forward."[43]

Furthermore, behind the so-called "Great Firewall of China" are some of the most innovative and sophisticated technology apps and digital marketing tools on the planet, produced by companies like Alibaba, Sina Corp (with Weibo), and Tencent (We-chat). This is already producing innovative sustainability solutions such as China Mobile's M-Health service to improve health care and access to health care. We also anticipate rapid innovation in the use of digitalization in, for example, the traceability of food, thereby improving transparency and accountability.

It's notable too that escalating Chinese Foreign Direct Investment means Chinese growth in economic and influence terms will have impact well beyond China's own borders. After three decades of massive inward investment into China, China's outward direct investment (ODI) now exceeds Foreign Direct Investment into China.[44] This shift has included the acquisition of significant or controlling stakes in a number of major Western companies like Syngenta, the global Swiss agribusiness, that produces agrochemicals and seeds, and which is helping to improve food security by enabling millions of farmers to make better use of available resources through world class science and innovative crop solutions. In 2017, the SOE ChemChina acquired Syngenta in what was then the largest takeover of a foreign company in Chinese history.[45] Given Syngenta's new ownership and its role in global food security, our interview with Syngenta CEO Erik Fyrwald provided important perspectives. How, for example, do Syngenta's new owners see sustainability. Fyrwald was very clear:

> There are a couple of dynamics here that I think net out very positively. One is China itself is getting very focused on the environment. I have been there at least once, usually three/four/five times a year ever since 1990, so for twenty-seven years. There is no place that has progressed economically like China, it's just unbelievable. I would say until five years or so ago it was at the expense of the environment. In recent years there has been much greater attention put on the environment and sustainability, and so as we talk about sustainability and what we are doing here, we get full support from the two members of our board from ChemChina, and by the way they are obviously very influential because they're the financial owners. They are anxious for us to do more in China and drive sustainability and agriculture in China and are opening the doors for us to do that.
>
> Another [thing] is the Chinese do take a long-term view. Yes, they want us to perform this year and they care about this year, but a lot of the conversation we have in board meetings is about what are the long-term programs, the research programs, the sustainability programs. By the way, we talk about our research programs, our coming products, in financial but also sustainability terms. What is the product going to do for the customer? What is the impact on the environment? What is the safety profile of the product? Is it improving based on the standard of use today? So that long-term view allows you not only to invest in the long term – including R&D, which in our industry takes on average about ten years from discovery until you start selling a product – but also making sure that we've got that sustainability angle on what we're thinking and how we are investing.[46]

Johnny Kwan also highlighted The Belt and Road Initiative (BRI) – the development strategy championed by China's president Xi Jinping that focuses on connectivity and cooperation between Eurasian countries,[47] and how this will likely stimulate more integration of sustainability and responsibility within

Chinese companies. Kwan also argued that: "Corporate Sustainability Leadership helps Chinese companies to achieve much more than a linear projection of the triple bottom line, it is a transformation and a quantum leap."[48] Other experts have pointed to the advantages being generated by China's Green Credit Policy, described by some as the most advanced in the world.

Africa next

Consider this remarkable fact: there are 1.2 billion Africans today, and this population is predicted to double to 2.4 billion by mid-century.[49] Intertwining our learning on China and Africa, we were fortunate to access a fascinating perspective on what this population growth could mean when we interviewed Chinese international development expert and entrepreneur Helen Hai, United Nations Industrial Development Organization (UNIDO) Goodwill Ambassador for Industrialization in Africa; CEO of the Made in Africa Initiative (which advises African governments on industrialization, investment promotion for job creation, and FDI promotion); and the owner of a successful clothing manufacturing business in Ethiopia.[50] Hai was passionate about the potential for Africa to quickly leapfrog to a more sustainable version of industrialization.

> In the industrial zones we are now creating . . . we have the concept of an SDGs Industrial Zone. We are learning the success lessons from Asia on job creation and economic transformation. At the same time we are also learning [from] the pitfalls from Asia to make sure we don't sacrifice the environment and that we take care of the workers' issues, human rights and gender equality. So, we are trying to move, I would say, to the 4.0 or the 5.0 version of industrialization in Africa.[51]
>
> There is this golden opportunity for Africa if they can take it. Why is this? Because when China becomes a high-income country by 2025, that means 85 million labor intensive jobs have to be relocated out of China. It happens every 20–30 years globally to reshape the global value chain. Southeast Asia doesn't have enough population to absorb all of those 85 million jobs. That is why for the global value chain there is this golden opportunity for African countries. If they can capture this relocation of 85 million jobs that means they can share the same prosperity as China and Asia [and] jump-start their economic transformation.[52]

Helen Hai's own African entrepreneurship example is telling. Her Ethiopian footwear and apparel company needed just three months from the initial investment in her factory in 2011 to begin actual production for the US market. Hai was subsequently able to attract other inward investors to fill industrial zones, first in Ethiopia, and then in other countries such as Rwanda and Senegal. All this shows the huge latent potential that exists if African governments can create the enabling environment for Asian entrepreneurs to manufacture in Africa for Western consumers open to "Made in Africa" products. Hai argues the situation requires Collaboration between the public and private sectors. She is now working for eight African heads of state on their industrialization strategies, helping them to link up to the private sector. "The industrialization movement has already started in the African continent and I believe this is with a new model. We are talking about shared prosperity."[53]

We also talked to Dr. Amy Jadesimi[54] of LADOL, an oil and gas logistics support company based in Lagos, Nigeria.

Like Helen Hai, her fellow Business and Sustainable Development Commissioner, Jadesimi sees how crises sometimes create platforms for new approaches to sustainable development. In Jadesimi's case, she believes the current European refugee and migration crisis signals an opportunity to reduce the pattern of displacement of young Africans crossing continents in search of a better life by providing more and better jobs at home:

> There is hope if you launch a sustainable business in a place like Nigeria because we adopt things very quickly . . . we need to find responsible private companies, private organizations – small, medium and large – in these local low income, high growth markets, and we need to engage with them and we need to find ways to finance them because they are the ones that are actually going to solve problems.[55]

As Hai and Jadesimi's experiences indicate, despite myriad challenges, Africa is showing increasing entrepreneurial energy. Another sector where this is evident is power generation. Today 600 million Africans lack access to electricity. Thankfully, businesses like M-KOPA Solar, a Kenyan company selling solar power systems to the poor, are beginning to fill the gap. M-KOPA Solar's type of incubation and innovation, directly targeting massive market opportunities rooted in real and growing human needs, is likely to spur the creation, scaling, and replication of many interesting and innovative business models between now and 2030 across China, Africa, and the rest of the Global South. As Generation Investment Management's Colin le Duc told us "It is likely that the Paul Polmans of the next twenty years will come from entrepreneurial start-ups in the developing world."[56]

Time limits

There remain only twelve years to 2030 – enough time to witness three cycles of Summer and Winter Olympic Games and to endure the next three American presidential elections.

When we look back twelve years from today, less than a third of the top-ranked companies in the Leaders Survey remained in the top echelon in 2017. Without exception, *All In* interviewees believe that the performance bar is only going to rise.

We are confident, therefore, in predicting that the corporate sustainability leaders of 2030 will have progressed on all five key attributes of Purpose, Plan, Culture, Collaboration, and Advocacy. Some of them – perhaps even most – do not currently feature in the Leaders Survey. It is possible that some don't even yet exist. Leading companies in 2030 will have integrated the SDGs into their core offerings as one of many means of appealing to the 99% and not just the 1%. Some, at least, will be based on technology platforms providing services like remote access to education and learning, health and well-being, and shared experiences rather than simply more sophisticated options for consumption. Undoubtedly, at least some of the leaders in 2030 will be businesses from or dominantly servicing the Global South. Overall, regardless of their founding date, place of origin, or sector, we are confident that they will be the best companies we have seen, and critical to delivering on the promise of sustainable development.

Notes

1 GlobeScan-SustainAbility Webinar on 2017 Leaders Survey results: June 28th 2017.
2 www.kingfisher.com/sustainability/index.asp?pageid=173 accessed Jan 9 2018.
3 www.kingfisher.com/sustainability/index.asp?pageid=185 accessed Jan 9 2018.
4 Authors' interview, Oct 30th 2017.
5 Ibid.
6 Syngenta website, www.syngenta.com/what-we-do/the-good-growth-plan accessed Jan 9 2018.
7 Letters of Note, www.lettersofnote.com/2010/11/to-boy-scouts.html accessed Jan 14 2018.
8 Authors' interview, Oct 30th 2017.
9 Authors' interview, Oct 10th 2017.
10 Unilever website, www.unilever.com/sustainable-living/ accessed Jan 13 2018.
11 Butler-Young S., "How Nike Plans To Double Its Business with Half the Environmental Impact," *Footwear News*, May 11th 2016, http://footwearnews.com/2016/business/retail/nike-plans-double-business-environmental-impact-2015-sustainability-report-220481/ accessed Feb 9 2018.
12 Authors' interview, Aug 31st 2017.
13 Patagonia Provisions, www.patagoniaprovisions.com/ accessed Jan 9 2018.
14 Patagonia Provisions, www.patagoniaprovisions.com/pages/what-if-series accessed Jan 9 2018.
15 Interface website, www.interface.com/US/en-US/campaign/climate-take-back/Climate-Take-Back#copy accessed Jan 9 2018.
16 Palazzi, M., "Global Ambassador," *Towards a New Business Civilization B Corporations*, Jan 2018.
17 BCorp website, http://benefitcorp.net/faq accessed Jan 14 2018.
18 BCorp website, www.bcorporation.net/ accessed Jan 13 2018.
19 Ibid.
20 Major multinationals such as Campbell's Soup, Danone, Unilever and several global accounting firms have joined the B Corp Multinational and Public Markets Advisory Council, www.bcorporation.net/what-are-b-corps/the-non-profit-behind-b-corps/standards-advisory-council accessed Jan 5 2018.

21 Wingfield N., et al., "Amazon, Berkshire Hathaway and JPMorgan Team Up to Try to Disrupt Health Care," *New York Times*, Jan 30th 2018, www.nytimes.com/2018/01/30/technology/amazon-berkshire-hathaway-jpmorgan-health-care.html accessed Feb 4 2018.

22 Authors' interview, Oct 3rd 2018.

23 Tuffrey, M., Corporate Citizenship Briefing, Dec 14, 2017, https://ccbriefing.corporate-citizenship.com/2017/12/14/tis-season-much-consumption-year-end-predictions/ accessed Jan 5 2018.

24 Rosff, M., "Dear Tech: A Letter to the Deadbeat Teenage Son at the End of a Tough Year," *CNBC*, Dec 27, 2017.

25 Mark Zuckerberg Facebook post Jan 2018, www.facebook.com/zuck/posts/10104380170714571 accessed Jan 5 2018.

26 Why We Launched Deep Mind Ethics & Society, https://deepmind.com/blog/why-we-launched-deepmind-ethics-society/

27 UN Principles of Responsible Investment, www.unpri.org/directory/ accessed Jan 11 2018.

28 See, for example, the new loan facility for Danone, led by BNP Paribas, which links Danone's ESG performance to the pricing, offering a discount when outperforming on their two sustainable goals, or even a premium when underperforming: Gérardin Y., "The Next Frontier in Sustainable Finance: Linking Loan Pricing to ESG Performance." *LinkedIn*, Feb 16th 2018, www.linkedin.com/pulse/next-frontier-sustainable-finance-linking-loan-pricing-yann-g%C3%A9rardin/

29 See, for example, Fink's annual letters to CEOs of companies in which BlackRock is invested.

30 Ant Financial Services Group, formerly known as Alipay, is an affiliate company of the Chinese Alibaba Group.

31 Fortune, "Change the World," http://fortune.com/change-the-world/ accessed Jan 11 2018.

32 Authors' interview, Nov 7th 2017.

33 Ibid.

34 Ibid.

35 Authors' interview, Sept 27th 2017.

36 Authors' interview, Oct 10th 2017.

37 Sustainable Development Solutions Network, A Global Initiative of the UN, "About Cherie Nursalim," http://unsdsn.org/about-us/people/cherie-nursalim/

38 Authors' interview, Dec 15th 2017.

39 Authors' email interview, Jan 2018.

40 Gosset, D., China Europe International Business School (CEIBS), Shanghai conversations with author – various: 2008–2014.

41 Authors' interview, Dec 7th 2018.

42 Authors' interview, Dec 7th 2017.

43 Follow-up email exchange Jan 2018.

44 China's Outward Investment Tops $161 Billion in 2016: Minister, Reuters, Dec 26, 2016, www.reuters.com/article/us-china-economy-investment/chinas-outward-investment-tops-161-billion-in-2016-minister-idUSKBN14F07R accessed Dec 24 2017.

45 Tsang, A., "Deal's Approval Buoys China in Its Quest for Food Security," *The New York Times*, April 6, 2017, p. A1 accessed Dec 24 2017.

46 Authors' interview, Oct 10th 2017.

47 The Silk Road Economic Belt and the 21st-century Maritime Silk Road, better known as The Belt and Road Initiative (BRI)-THE STATE COUNCIL, THE

PEOPLE'S REPUBLIC OF CHINA, http://english.gov.cn/beltAndRoad/ accessed Dec 24 2017.
48 Follow-up email exchange Jan 2018.
49 Potentially, there will be 4.1 billion Africans by 2100 – more than 1:3 of the total world population. Some predict Nigeria will have 1 billion people in 2100 and Tanzania 276 million: "Population Growth in Africa: Grasping the Scale of the Challenge," *The Guardian*, Jan 11, 2016, www.worldpopulationreview.com accessed Dec 23 2017.
50 Ambassador Hai is Co-Founder of C&H Garments, which is a pioneer Pan-Africa export-oriented garments manufacturer. She is a member of the Global Commission on Business and Sustainable Development.
51 Authors' interview, Nov 20th 2017.
52 Ibid.
53 Ibid.
54 Dr. Amy Jadesimi is a Nigerian physician, businesswoman, entrepreneur, and chief executive officer of the Lagos Deep Offshore Logistics Base (LADOL), a privately-owned state-of-the-art logistics and engineering facility in an industrial Free Zone, located within the Port of Lagos, Nigeria. She is a commissioner of the Business and Sustainable Development Commission.
55 Ibid.
56 Authors' interview, Nov 7th 2017.

Conclusion

"To succeed, jump as quickly at opportunities as you do at conclusions."
Benjamin Franklin

From elite cadre to mass movement

As much as *All In* reflects their experience, learning, and excellence, this book is not written primarily for the companies ranked highest in the GlobeScan-SustainAbility Leaders Survey.

Its focus is on what needs to happen by 2030 to enable the attainment of the UN's Sustainable Development Goals through the laying of a foundation for an economy in which systemic sustainable development challenges are addressed. *All In* hopes to influence and motivate the leaders of many more companies to make sustainability central to their strategy and performance.

The importance of this came through in many *All In* interviews.

Mike Barry of M&S, declared:

> The Interface's of this world have done an amazing job, but I am always interested in replicability. How repeatable is the model that we are developing? Because it doesn't matter if we create a few dozen "Gold" or "Platinum" performers but the myriad of companies doing nothing remain. I am a great believer in "Silver Sustainability" – I would rather have 100,000 companies do a pretty good job than just 10 doing brilliant jobs. So I would urge us as a community to celebrate the good guys, but then to turn our attention to the 100,000 sitting on the sidelines and say: "How do we get them involved?"

Lise Kingo, formerly Executive Vice President and Chief of Staff, Novo Nordisk, now CEO and Executive Director, United Nations Global Compact, agrees with Barry, stating:

> We consulted the UN Global Compact (UNGC) signatory companies and received responses from more than two thousand. This gives us a

pretty good picture of how companies are faring. Some of what we have learned is good news, and some of it gives a signal that we really need to speed up – especially because the companies that took part in our survey represent just a fraction of private sector enterprises globally. So we have a huge challenge to get out there and engage many, many more companies.

While the challenge for corporate sustainability activity to scale dramatically and immediately is starkly evident, Kingo also cited reason for optimism:

Fortunately, we see many companies working to understand the thinking and the spirit behind the SDGs and using the Goals as inspiration for developing their future business strategy. They see the Goals as a lighthouse indicating where investment and development priorities will be over the next twelve years. Seeing increasing numbers of companies doing business according to the UNGC Principles while using the SDGs as a North Star to guide strategy and innovation is amazing. Two years ago, when the Goals were adopted and the Paris Agreement was reached, I really felt that this was one of the moments in all my years working on sustainable development where the planets were most aligned. It was just incredible that all countries unanimously signed up to the 2030 agenda. Today I think the planets have drifted a little out of this nice alignment and that the world is looking a bit chaotic, but I still feel that the UNGC Principles and the Goals have never been more relevant.

Kingo went on to speak about a key aspect of the required scaling of corporate sustainability: increasing internationalization. Kingo told us about recent trips to countries like Japan and Korea, where the SDGs are taking off thanks especially to local networks, saying:

We have made it our vision to mobilize a global movement of sustainable and responsible companies and organizations capable of creating the world that we all want and meeting the SDGs. I think we can only do that in partnership, and that what we need to do is to mobilize a movement where we all have the same compass, the same North Star, which are the SDGs. . . . I hope that this common agenda can be the tipping point that makes the sustainability agenda mainstream for business and for all the people who work in business.

Considering the perspectives of Barry, Kingo, and nearly every other of our interviewees on the need to rapidly scale corporate sustainability efforts, we were encouraged to see factors external to companies conspiring to make this more possible and more likely as we brought *All In* to completion.

Quickening trust

One important enabling factor shifting in favor of business leadership at present is trust. While trust in business remains relatively low compared to other institutions (as shown in Leaders Survey results and elsewhere), there are emerging signals of a potential upswing. As corporate sustainability experts and practitioners, all three of us are watching this closely because we see a close relationship between trust and corporate success. In fact, the very purpose of Chris's organization, Globescan, is *Building trusted leadership to create a better future*. Mark's organization, SustainAbility, has trust in its theory of change, holding that *transparency* is critical to building *trust*, that *trust* is essential to accessing the partners and expertise found in *collaboration*, and that *collaboration* plus *innovation* are the key means by which business models can adapt and address the systemic challenges inherent to sustainable development.

For these reasons, we were struck by the headlines from the Edelman Trust Barometer 2018. The 2018 iteration "reveals a world of seemingly stagnant distrust," where overall results show "trust in business, government, NGOs and media remained largely unchanged from 2017."[1] Further analysis reveals deep polarization, however, with Edelman reporting:

> The world is moving apart in trust. In previous years, country-level trust has moved largely in lockstep, but for the first time ever there is now a distinct split between extreme trust gainers and losers. No country saw steeper declines than the United States, with a 37-point aggregate drop in trust across all institutions. At the opposite end of the spectrum, China experienced a 27-point gain, more than any other country.[2]

This is fascinating, but it is what Edelman's 2018 Barometer summary then said about companies that transfixed us. Amidst the staggering drops in trust in US institutions, and record growth of trust in China, respondents reported growing faith in the private sector:

> Business is now expected to be an agent of change. The employer is the new safe house in global governance, with 72 percent of respondents saying that they trust their own company. And 64 percent believe a company can take actions that both increase profits and improve economic and social conditions in the community where it operates.[3]

Beyond business in general, CEO credibility jumped for reasons echoing some of what we discussed about the role of the "CEO Activist" or the notion of the CEO as "Chief Advocacy Officer" in Chapter 7 on Advocacy:

> This past year saw CEO credibility rise sharply by seven points to 44 percent after a number of high-profile business leaders voiced their

positions on the issues of the day. Nearly two-thirds of respondents say they want CEOs to take the lead on policy change instead of waiting for government, which now ranks significantly below business in trust in 20 markets. This show of faith comes with new expectations; building trust (69 percent) is now the No. 1 job for CEOs, surpassing producing high-quality products and services (68 percent).

Keen investors

While the Edelman Trust Barometer reflects broad societal views suggesting companies and CEOs are building greater reservoirs of goodwill, investor pressure is shifting, encouraging companies to spend relationship capital and act to improve sustainability communication and performance.

Notable in this arena, and reflective of a deepening sustainability or environmental, social, and governance (ESG) focus in the investment community broadly, was the release of BlackRock CEO Larry Fink's "Annual Letter to CEOs" in January 2018.[4] Written as an open letter to the CEOs of all the companies in which BlackRock – the world's largest asset manager – holds equity positions, the missive underscores the reality that mainstream investors care increasingly about ESG performance. These investors are bringing their influence as owners to bear, demanding companies improve performance in this area because they believe it will generate better and more lasting returns on investment.

Reflecting tenets of the Purpose-Driven Era of Leadership that *All In* argues is ongoing, Fink's 2018 letter is entitled "A Sense of Purpose." In the opening paragraph Fink states that: "As a fiduciary, BlackRock engages with companies to drive the sustainable, long-term growth that our clients need to meet their goals."

What this means and why it is currently seen as critical is elaborated on as the letter progresses, with Fink writing:

> We are seeing a paradox of high returns and high anxiety. Since the financial crisis, those with capital have reaped enormous benefits. At the same time, many individuals across the world are facing a combination of low rates, low wage growth, and inadequate retirement systems. . . . For millions, the prospect of a secure retirement is slipping further and further away – especially among workers with less education, whose job security is increasingly tenuous. I believe these trends are a major source of the anxiety and polarization that we see across the world today.

The BlackRock CEO continues, emphasizing what he believes companies must do:

> Society is demanding that companies, both public and private, serve a social purpose. To prosper over time, every company must not only

deliver financial performance, but also show how it makes a positive contribution to society. Companies must benefit all of their stakeholders, including shareholders, employees, customers, and the communities in which they operate.

Without a sense of purpose, no company, either public or private, can achieve its full potential. It will ultimately lose the license to operate from key stakeholders. . . . And ultimately, that company will provide subpar returns to the investors who depend on it to finance their retirement, home purchases, or higher education.

Fink's letter goes on to explain that the need for BlackRock to engage with the companies in which it invests is even more important given the current popularity of index investing, which restricts divestment as an option. As a result, Fink says shareholder-company ". . . engagement needs to be a year-round conversation about improving long-term value" and that ". . . to make engagement with shareholders as productive as possible, companies must be able to describe their strategy for long-term growth." He then reiterates a past request, that CEOs ". . . publicly articulate your company's strategic framework for long-term value creation and explicitly affirm that it has been reviewed by your board of directors," and affirms his belief that companies' financial performance depends on understanding the ". . . societal impact of your business as well as the ways that broad, structural trends – from slow wage growth to rising automation to climate change – affect your potential for growth."

Fink's letter is a remarkable call to arms that in the recent past may have come from an academic, an NGO, or the socially responsible investment (SRI) community. That today it comes from the world's largest asset manager brings full circle the classic Milton Friedman position we referred to earlier – that the only social responsibility of business is to maximize profit within the confines of the law – by effectively stating that good financial results depend on a clear and well-articulated social purpose and outstanding ESG performance.

The time is right

We believe *All In* makes a compelling case that the future of business leadership is synonymous with continuously improving sustainability performance, and that the leadership attributes we have described – Purpose, Plan, Culture, Collaboration, and Advocacy – present the framework business needs to meet the challenge inherent to current circumstance.

We believe deeply that the dramatic and immediate scaling of corporate sustainability efforts – taking it from being the focus of a few thousand companies to the remit of every private sector enterprise – is essential and urgent. And we see the UN Sustainable Development Goals and the Paris Agreement on climate change combined as the best North Star to guide this journey, better than has ever existed.

There's profit on this path too. We have referred to the $12 trillion commercial opportunity the Business and Sustainable Development Commission estimates is available to the businesses that lead implementation of the UN Sustainable Development Goals. We also cited the deepening evidence that ESG investing outperforms traditional approaches. Increasingly, market rewards are built on the back of sustainability performance.

Gail Klintworth, Business Transformation Director at the Business and Sustainable Development Commission, suggests there's something natural about the now unfolding convergence of profit potential and sustainable development. Taking diversity and inclusion as one example, she argues that a more equitable and sustainable society will be inherently good for business, saying:

> The simple economic truth behind advocating for gender and other diversity is that a more inclusive future will be better for everyone. Greater inclusivity will mean that there are more engaged citizens, more empowered consumers and more stable markets, all of which create conditions good for markets and sustained growth.[5]

Klintworth also points to the business possibilities latent in new forms of Collaboration, declaring:

> So far we have seen mostly competition between incumbents and disruptors. What the future needs is more collaboration between radical incumbents and disruptive insurgents to demonstrate new models that can advantage both of these types of organizations, ultimately to help us scale new approaches and opportunities.[6]

All In's five leadership attributes – Purpose, Plan, Culture, Collaboration, and Advocacy – provide a roadmap for companies ready to pursue sustainability excellence and the market benefits that will come with it. They comprise a clear route to superior business performance and resilience. They do not – and cannot – guarantee success, but offer the best platform for business growth and continuity into the future.

What you can do

We said at the start of this Conclusion that this book was not primarily written for today's sustainability leaders. It was written for all the businesses that aspire to such leadership and have set out on the journey. Even more, we hope that it enthuses the leaders of companies that have not yet begun this work – but which feel that they must engage between now and 2030 to ensure their own long-term business viability and improve the odds that the world achieves the Sustainable Development Goals. Finally, it was written for everyone who might partner with business on this journey: government officials, NGOs, academics, students, employees, and consumers.

Regardless of who you are, there are actions you can take. If you work for a company, demand that it has clarity of Purpose and a comprehensive Plan referencing the Sustainable Development Goals and science-based targets. Help build the kind of transparent, open, and responsive Culture inherent to attracting and retaining employees and the kind of partners you need for Collaboration. And push your company's leadership to model and enable in others, Advocacy for system changes that support a sustainable future. As a member of government, civil society, academia, and, above all, as a citizen, please support and encourage the businesses you see pursuing this roadmap with integrity and push for others to join them in going *All In*.

Notes

1 2018 Edelman Trust Barometer, www.edelman.com/trust-barometer accessed Feb 2 2018.
2 Ibid.
3 www.edelman.com/news-awards/2018-edelman-trust-barometer-reveals-record-breaking-drop-trust-in-the-us accessed Feb 2 2018.
4 BlackRock, "LARRY FINK'S ANNUAL LETTER TO CEOS: A Sense of Purpose," www.blackrock.com/corporate/en-us/investor-relations/larry-fink-ceo-letter?cid= twitter:larryslettertoceos::blackrock
5 Authors' interview, Feb 1st 2018.
6 Ibid.

Afterword

All In: **what business needs to do over the next decade
to achieve enduring sustainability leadership**

The first thing that I think business needs to do is to be sure to **develop the
right leaders** to manage the environment of tomorrow. It is difficult to predict
everything, so you need the right people that can operate in a more volatile and uncertain environment. You take for example the Fourth Industrial
Revolution: artificial intelligence; robotics; the Internet of Things. What is
it going to do to the workforce? We already have 11% of the world's youth
unemployed right now. We need to create 1.2 billion more jobs in the next
few years. And we are not going to do that – we are actually in a phase of job
destruction. Climate change and increasing inequality will also be challenges
of importance and magnitude. Consequently, you need leaders able to think
more systemically about some of these global challenges and then internalize
them for action. That requires a different type of leadership. I think that is
one of the reasons why the tenure of CEOs is so short and has fallen to less
than five years on average. Some leaders clearly aren't equipped to deal with
today's challenges. So, my first investment would be in leadership: in people
that are more purpose-driven; in people with a long-term perspective; in
people that are better systemic thinkers; and in people who feel comfortable
with a different level and type of partnership and collaboration, and who
possess the courage that is needed to succeed.

The second thing that companies then need to work on is to **become more
purpose-driven**. Companies need to understand what that means, and that
starts at the top. You cannot just lead with the head; you have to lead with both
the head and the heart. In the UK, several of us worked together to create the
Blueprint for Better Business to bring more purpose to companies. It is purpose that provides the necessary beacon in uncertain times. It rallies employees
and gives you permission to operate and lead. After all, if a company cannot
communicate its purpose beyond shareholder value, why should society give
it permission to exist? A strong, purpose-driven business model also implies a
longer-term business perspective focused on environmental, social, and economic impact – that is, focused well beyond the needs of only shareholders.
Such a multi-stakeholder, longer-term approach requires companies and boards

to focus not only on the pressure of next quarter's profits, but to operate with the livelihoods of future generations in mind. Driving multi-stakeholder, longer-term models is hard – especially so in a market environment that seems to be increasingly short-term in its thinking – but this is crucial to the long-term survival of any company. Many believe that shareholder primacy and short-term thinking are why the average lifetime of an American publicly listed company has fallen below 17 years. Is that what we want?

A third area that I believe is going to increase enormously in importance is **social compliance**. It is very clear that we cannot delegate responsibilities only to governments, especially as so many sustainability challenges are global in nature. In fact, businesses must increasingly understand that they have to help **de-risk the political process**. To sit here and laugh or shout or scream or belittle our politicians is not productive. We must find a way for business to become much more active in de-risking the entire policy environment. You saw that happening recently in the US with the LGBTQ issue, where states and governors were taking debatable positions on the human rights of individuals based on sexual orientation and reproductive rights. Business stood up and said, "Well, we are not going to invest in those states anymore because employees wouldn't want to work for our company if we would support these types of things." The business position was clear and unequivocal and made different political outcomes possible.

The fourth topic that comes to mind is **the value chain**. Many companies think that by outsourcing their supply chain they can also outsource their responsibilities. That does not work anymore, as we have seen in the case of Rana Plaza and as related to child labor practices in cocoa and coffee supply chains. We really need to take a much more holistic approach on fair wages, anti-slavery, migration, child labor, and so on, and we need to consider what to do about the astonishingly high levels of people disengaged from the workforce by long-term systemic unemployment like we have seen in Southern Europe over the last decade.

Finally, **social cohesion** is going to be one of the bigger issues that companies will have to deal with – people will reject companies and reject CEOs if they don't participate in finding solutions. This is one of the reasons why research like the Edelman Trust Barometer finds trust in institutions is so low. Unfortunately, trust is declining. And one thing we know is that we cannot build trust without transparency, nor long-term prosperity without trust.

The good thing, despite all the challenges, is that **young people** want to make this a better world. Most millennials, especially in the developing world, believe that business is central to finding solutions – they expect business to fill the leadership void. Many millennials in the developing world have much lower trust in their governments than even what we see in Europe or the US, and those same developing world millennials have higher trust in business. If we can make responsible business a force for good, I think we can address many of the issues that we all face. My final advice would be to fully include the young in this exciting journey.

Paul Polman

Appendix
The GlobeScan-SustainAbility Leaders Survey methodology & historical ranking of leaders

In 1997, through an international survey of opinion leaders, GlobeScan began tracking the extent to which specific companies are recognized as sustainability leaders in its annual Leaders Survey.

The objectives and applications of this research program have remained consistent from origin. Another constant has been the ongoing reliance upon the collegial common interest and goodwill of the panel of expert survey respondents. While the objective has remained steadfast, the methodology has subtly evolved over the decades.

During the 1990s, GlobeScan created a database of hundreds of sustainability experts concentrated in Europe and North America where the profession traditionally has been most established. Panelists were selected based on their expertise, reputation, and sector representation. Members spanned the voluntary, corporate, governmental, institutional, and service sectors.[1] No weighting factors have ever been applied to the survey data because the panel is not purported to represent a definable universe beyond expertise in sustainability.

The early surveys were conducted using paper copies of questionnaires and fax- or mail-back answer sheets, which were mailed to panelists along with personal letters of request. Between 20% and 25% of these panelists typically completed the questionnaire. They received exclusive reports of highlight findings in recognition of their time.

As email gradually became commonplace during the later 1990s, the GlobeScan Survey transitioned to an online methodology using personal email invitations and survey programming software.

The year 2009 marked a significant milestone in the research program's timeline. GlobeScan and SustainAbility joined forces that year to scale the study to a new level, leveraging each other's organizational networks and databases of sustainability practitioners to extend the survey's reach and increase the number of participants in each study. Thenceforth, the GlobeScan-SustainAbility Leaders Surveys have been conducted in equal partnership. Today, the core panel consists of thousands of experts from around the world. On each survey, contributions are received from 60 to 90 countries with a response rate of circa 15–20%.

Across the survey's history, the panel of expert respondents has grown and been refreshed constantly as new experts have been added to it and out-of-date ones removed. At all times, survey participants have been required to have three or more years of professional experience in sustainability. Typically, at least 60% of expert survey respondents have ten or more years' sustainability experience.

As Figure A.1 illustrates in detail, the wording of the survey question used to identify sustainability leaders was updated in 2012 in the interests of simplicity and clarity. On two other occasions during the 2000s, essentially the same question was asked in the context of social responsibility. In none of these cases was any noticeable impact on response patterns detected.

The sample size of the survey evolved over time, as well. In the early days, fewer than 200 stakeholders completed the survey, while in the past few years most surveys have had samples sizes close to 1,000 (see Figure A.2).

Question Wording	Years
Some large companies are committed to sustainable development, seeing it as being in their strategic advantage to pursue aggressive policies and actions, often going beyond what they are required to do under environmental legislation. What individual companies can you name that are leading in this area?	1997–2002, 2004–2007, 2009–2011
Please name any specific large companies that come to mind as fulfilling their responsibilities to society better than others.	2003, 2008
What specific companies do you think are leaders in integrating sustainability into their business strategy?	2012–2017

Figure A.1 Leaders Survey Question Wording

Year	n =	Year	n =
1997	154	2008	331
1998	114	2009	1691
1999	199	2010	1261
2000	225	2011	559
2001	283	2012	825
2002	210	2013	1170
2003	201	2014	887
2004	361	2015	816
2005	322	2016	907
2006	240	2017	1035
2007	319		

Figure A.2 Leaders Survey Sample Sizes (1997–2017)

COMPANY	# of years on top 15 ranking	Top ranking achieved	Year first mentioned in top 15	Sector	Home country
Interface	21	1	1997	Industrial	US
Novo Nordisk	19	4	1998	Pharma	Denmark
Unilever	19	1	1998	Consumer goods	UK
Shell	16	1	1997	Oil & gas	Netherlands
DuPont	15	3	1997	Chemical	US
BP	14	1	1997	Oil & gas	UK
Toyota	14	3	1999	Auto	Japan
Patagonia	13	2	2001	Apparel	US
GE	13	2	2005	Industrial	US
Nike	12	7	2001	Apparel	US
Walmart	11	1	2006	Retail	US
IKEA	10	4	2001	Home furnishings	Sweden
M&S	10	4	2008	Retail	UK
Natura	9	5	2009	Cosmetics	Brazil
Dow	9	1	1997	Chemical	US
Coca-Cola	7	9	2010	Food & beverage	US
Suncor	7	8	1999	Oil & gas	Canada
The Body Shop	7	5	1997	Cosmetics	UK
Nestlé	6	5	2012	Food & beverage	Switzerland
3M	6	3	1997	Industrial	US
Procter & Gamble	6	9	1997	Consumer goods	US
Google	5	10	2010	Tech	US
BT	5	10	1998	Telecomms	UK
Cooperative Group	4	10	2004	Retail	UK
Electrolux	4	12	1997	Electronics	Sweden
Ford	4	8	2000	Auto	US

Figure A.3 Ranking Summary of Sustainability Leaders, Part 1

Figure A.3 provides an overview of all 51 companies that have been mentioned as a top 15 ranked company each year over the two decades. The companies are ranked by the number of years each company has been mentioned as a leader, along with the highest ranking achieved, the year the company was first mentioned, the company's sector, and home country.

COMPANY	# of years on top 15 ranking	Top ranking achieved	Year first mentioned in top 15	Sector	Home country
Johnson & Johnson	4	10	2002	Healthcare	US
Tesla	3	5	2015	Auto	US
BASF	3	9	2015	Chemical	Germany
IBM	3	11	2011	Tech	US
SC Johnson	3	12	1998	Consumer goods	US
Alcan	3	8	2005	Mining	Canada
Philips	3	12	2004	Electronics	Netherlands
TransAlta	3	11	1997	Energy	Canada
Monsanto	3	2	1997	Chemical	US
Siemens	2	11	2012	Industrial	Germany
Puma	2	10	2013	Apparel	Germany
Starbucks	2	11	2005	Food & beverage	US
HP	2	14	2005	Tech	US
Noranda	2	13	1997	Mining	Canada
Microsoft	1	15	2008	Tech	US
Rio Tinto	1	11	2007	Mining	UK
Whole Foods	1	15	2006	Retail	US
BHP Billiton	1	12	2006	Mining	Australia
Novartis	1	14	2002	Pharma	Switzerland
Baxter	1	15	2002	Healthcare	US
Volkswagen	1	12	2000	Auto	Germany
Volvo	1	9	1999	Auto	Sweden
ABB	1	7	1997	Engineering	Switzerland
Northern Telecom	1	13	1997	Telecomms	Canada
Xerox	1	15	1997	Tech	US

Figure A.3 Ranking Summary of Sustainability Leaders, Part 2
Based on % of Experts, Total Mentions, Unprompted, 1997–2017

Note

1 Sustainability experts responding to the Leaders Survey are now classified as: Government, Corporate, Service & Media, Academic & Research, NGO, and Others.

Disclosures

In the period since January 2013, GlobeScan has worked with the following organizations quoted in *All In:*

3M
BASF
BP
BT
Coca-Cola
Danone
Dow
FairTrade
GSK
Hewlett-Packard
Huawei
IKEA
Interface
Johnson & Johnson
Marine Stewardship Council
Marks & Spencer
Natura
Nestlé
Nike
Oxfam
Philips
Procter & Gamble
SC Johnson
Siemens
Starbucks
Syngenta
Toyota
Unilever
Vodafone

Volkswagen
We Mean Business

SustainAbility has worked for the following:

BASF
Baxter
BMW
Dow
DuPont
Ford
General Electric
GRI
GSK
Hewlett-Packard
Huawei
Interface
Johnson & Johnson
Leaders Quest
Microsoft
Nestle
Nike
Novo Nordisk
SC Johnson
Shell
Siemens
Starbucks
Syngenta
Unilever
Vodaphone
Volkswagen
Walmart

Index